GENDER REBELS

GENDER REBELS

50 INFLUENTIAL CROSS-DRESSERS, IMPERSONATORS, NAME-CHANGERS, & GAME-CHANGERS

ANNEKA HARRY

Little
a

Published by Little A, New York

www.apub.com

Amazon, the Amazon logo, and Little A are trademarks of Amazon.com, Inc., or its affiliates.

ISBN-13: 9781542044691
ISBN-10: 1542044693

Cover design by Lisa Horton

Interior illustrations by Tegan Price

Printed in the United States of America

In memory of Theodora Arrowsmith Burgoyne
(who always wore the trousers).

Contents

INTRODUCTION

Throughout history, women have had to make all sorts of compromises to be considered seriously (if at all) alongside their male counterparts. The sheroes who succeeded before us are never suitably storied or shouted about because they are the victims of a system that undervalues, ignores and abuses women and girls. *Gender Rebels: 50 Influential Cross-Dressers, Impersonators, Name-Changers and Game-Changers* is a celebration of those who fought back. Women who have stuck their skulls above that parapet everyone's always banging on about, women who have taken matters into their own hands and made quite the point about the cursed patriarchy while doing so. The fifty women you are about to non-stop party with (and maybe even mosh with) were and are diverse, defiant and daring. They are superbly spirited females who made the world shake and will still get us shook to this day. Those I've selected are by no means the only ones who had to pretend to be – or presented as – men at some point in their lives or careers, but they have gained enough fame or notoriety in their time to go down in history. That said, I needed to delve so deep into the vaults of the British Library to discover some, I was trawling eBay to try and get my hands on a *Ghostbusters* proton pack.

My life as a female creative isn't exactly a laugh a minute, believe it or not . . . And I say *female* there because it's an industry-preferred prefix. A constant reminder that we are battling to be allowed to exist in the b*llock-heavy bubble, never mind all the tedious, archaic 'debates' they are having about whether we are relevant/funny/talented/worthy/intelligent enough or not. The first time a TV commissioner told me (in no uncertain terms) that *he* wouldn't be making my (obviously hilarious and Emmy-worthy) show idea because I was the wrong gender was understandably a right smack in the face. For the #*GenderRebels* who faced similar sexism (and as a consequence went on to change their name or their dress), their stories are not a case of '*if you can't beat 'em, join 'em*', rather '*pretend to be them to seemingly get anywhere*'. It's not as if they opted to do so because of a big, over-elaborate plan to avoid manspreaders or mansplaining that got out of hand, they chose to do so because they had NO OTHER CHOICE. Every time I think the world is slowly changing on these issues, I continue to be smacked in the face. My belief has always been that if you want something enough you will find a relentlessness that smacks back – but we should be a million miles away from having to put up, shut up, or feel like we constantly have to have our fists up in self-defence by now.

For me, it wasn't important that this book hit the shelves, it was *imperative*. Hashtags and handmade 'Instagrammable' placards may have kick-started a new (new) wave of feminism but they are, equally, ignored and easily forgotten. Books aren't going anywhere; they are ensuring we celebrate women's histories, give voice to those who were silenced, and tell these untold tales. It doesn't change what went down but it certainly helps us to look around the corner. Sorry to be a Debbie Downer, but rose-tinted reading glasses are not enough – we need to change the language so we reclaim these women from age-old and blatantly biased accounts by male historians. We need inclusive narratives that encourage us to rethink feminist action. And we need the books, we ain't waiting for the movies (don't get me started on the hot mess that is Hollywood . . .). The glass ceilings won't be smashed, the pay gaps bridged or the patriarchy busted if we just sit around in unicorn onesies talking about it. Words inspire deeds, and researching these women alone has fired me up to not only write a book about them but to fight back harder myself. Whoever we are, whatever we do for a living and wherever we live, we are still having to compromise and use disguises to survive.

Women and girls have forever been judged on how they look while men have mainly been judged on what they say. Sorry to break it to you if this has blown your mind, although I very much doubt it has as it's a fact that is impossible to avoid. A pernicious, pervasive truth that is having a negative effect on every level of society and holding us back from that equality finishing line at every turn. And, sadly, it also happens *among* women. When I *had to* come out (because anyone that is not entirely straight as a line supposedly needs to do a press release on the matter) I had a barrage of 'jokes' from other females, running their mouths, pondering if I'd be favouring Dr Martens, Birkenstocks or Crocs with socks now. *Crocs with socks?* I know I'm waxing lyrical about equality, personal choice and not judging appearances here but, seriously, CROCS WITH SOCKS? First of all, how dare you; second of all, I said I was in love with a woman, not that I'd had a frontal lobotomy. Imagine a world in which women could go about their day looking however they liked and for their appearance not to be a constant conversation topic or erection agitator! Imagine a world where we could dress to make a statement if we so pleased and for that decision to be applauded and respected! *Dreamy.* Clothes do not maketh the person (though you should *totally* bump your own fists together if you leave the house feeling like you're dressing so fly you should change your name to Vinaigrette). Oh, and for the record/to be perfectly queer on the matter, Dr Martens are hella cosy and I AM about that life. Thank you very much.

As discussions around gender evolve, we are (FINALLY) challenging sex, sexuality and identity stereotypes. We may be at an ellipses bubble and WIP stage of proceedings but at least we are bubbling and progressing. There are women among the fifty who certainly would have had a different experience today being able to describe themselves as intersex, agender, multigender, genderqueer, gender-fluid, non-binary (please insert identification term of choice here). Neither the aforementioned nor those who were posing temporarily for personal gain were treated kindly, and accusations about them being 'sexual deviants', 'perverts', 'lewd lesbians', 'inverts' and/or 'troublemakers' were never far away. The systemic delusions around LGBTQ+ and identification issues run deep and have, on many levels, produced a hellscape of 'otherness' politics through which I've had to mine-hop. As such, homophobic history would have us think that the majority of #GenderRebels still saw themselves as women while masquerading as men but there will, of course, be some trans pioneers among the undecided, unlabellable and unboxable, who fought the cis-tem. The mixture of motivations throws up all sorts of complex intersections, swings, roundabouts and even a couple of see-saws. Perhaps a pinch (or truck load) of salt might be required upon occasion. Perhaps this paragraph will be an even more bonkers read in the not too distant future? *Fingers and flaps crossed!* We can draw parallels between contemporary and historical identities, but appropriation should be reserved for profits and property, not people. If you believe and strive for oneness and kindness, I know you'll join me in reading between the lines of some of the premodern history book gobbledygook and assumption.

For anyone who has even a speck of knowledge or insight into how women who speak up, achieve or try to are treated today, the experiences of some of these #GenderRebels might set off *FFS* alarm bells loud enough to make your ears bleed. But, as a fervent, forward-thinking, full-throttle (alliteration-loving) feminist, I believe in the power of history to help us feel comfortable with and inspirit the present. I think you do too. I love you already for being here and long may we stay unitedly hydrated on solidarity juice. Keep supporting women and the world will see itself right. Big up yourself because we are the people that can and will change the ending. Women across the globe are still having to masquerade as men to advance. Let's kill that. Let's redefine the power structure itself rather than the idea of powerful women. Let's dial up the feminism. Let's take up space. Let's wear whatever the heck we desire while doing so. Let's scream and ruddy shout. Let's grab 'em by the patriarchy. LET'S GET STUFF DONE!

HATSHEPSUT (1507–1458 BC)

THE ANCIENT EGYPTIAN POWERHOUSE QUEEN (FORWARD SLASH KING)

Hatshepsut, meaning 'Foremost of Noble *Women*' (how's about THAT for an opener to a book about powerful wimmin!), was the fifth pharaoh of the eighteenth dynasty in Ancient Egypt, only the second woman to reign and the first female to do so as a male. She is largely considered one of Egypt's most successful pharaohs, and if that wasn't enough (wo) man power for you, you may have picked up the wrong book (I'm sure I told the designers not to make the cover too similar to *The Idiot's Guide to Equality*). If later on you feel like these early chapters are iddy-biddy in comparison to the rest of the book, please remember we are bringing women out of the shadows from all the moons ago where the history and stories are as jumbled as a tin of Alphabetti spaghetti (and in Hatshepsut's case, we're going back as far as an age when society accepted crocodile dung and fermented dough as an effective form of birth control – these were very nuanced times indeed). Some of the history books are as helpful as the Christmas cracker 'miracle' fish when it reads your fortune as 'Dead One' but I'm collecting all the dropped hints and slam-dunking them for you because, as the author, *I sort of have one job*.

Hatshepsut enjoyed an on the whole peaceful and prosperous reign and left behind more monuments and works of art than any other ruler. *Of course she did* – she was a *she!* She's even got 'SHE' slap bang in the middle of her own name! So why is she depicted as a beardy bloke in most of the surviving artefacts and why was that name omitted from the Egyptian kings list for thousands of years? *Spoiler alert of a common theme that you may come across once or twice during this book*＊ SHE HAD A VAGINA and therefore she was maltreated and erased. (Please join me in a '*Boo! Hiss!*' and may I let it be known that there is due to be a glut of injustice assaults on your heart.) But we're not here to wallow and weep under the crushing weight of female oppression that has plagued society since day dot, are we? We're here to celebrate rebellious revolutionaries – and what better way to kick off than with *a queen so mighty*, she got the other royals sweating like a menimist attempting a four-piece jigsaw puzzle? *A queen so formidable*, Egypt panicked and decided the only thing for it was to make her a *king* . . .

Hatshepsut took the throne in 1478 BC, by which point the institution of Egyptian leaders was already well over a millennium old. It was pretty stuck in its ways and (sorry to bring genitalia into proceedings again so soon into our relationship) if you didn't have a penis, you did not fit that regal bill. Our poor Hatshepsut was up against it from the get-go and her family life wasn't exactly easy breezy either. The only child born to the Egyptian king Thutmose I and his *principal* wife Ahmose, Hatshepsut was expected to be queen. (I use italics for *principal* as old Thutmose-boy kept a harem of side chicks and wives – Ahmose was simply his main squeeze.) Not only did her dad have more wives than I've had catcalls while out jogging, at the mere age of twelve Hatshepsut was made to marry her half-brother when her father passed away – so as to preserve the royal bloodline. Now, apart from the whole 'child bride' and 'inbred marriage' thing, the half-brother, Thutmose II, might not exactly have been Hatshepsut's first choice for *many* reasons. Not least the rumours of a grizzly skin condition that would sicken a trypophobic to death on the spot, and having to put up with a lifetime of him going AWOL on benders and being dragged half-drowned from the Nile. Luckily for Hatshie,[1] that lifetime was short-lived and she was a widow by the age of thirty.

What happens next may read like an episode of *Keeping Up with the Thutmoses*, but hang on in there – we're nearly at the bit where she claims all power over the country, empire, throne and invisible kingdom of gods and spirits. As Hatshepsut had no sons and the pre-mentioned willy-waving royal rule makers would NEVER consider a woman, they found a son of Thutmose II's by one of his sideline baby mommas to take the reins and, *ahem*, reign. But Thutmose III was too young to assume the throne unaided and so Hatshepsut took control of all the affairs of state until he came of age. In the seventh year of acting as his regent, she changed the rules and crowned herself pharaoh of Egypt. JUST. LIKE. THAT. How she got away with this isn't exactly clear but she had some influential supporters and she was leaning in and asserting her authority left, right and centre. Perhaps there was a flash blip in the matrix in 1478 BC and all the men saw sense for a sublime, sacred nanosecond? Perhaps her pledge to save the country from fighting and killing and her offer to be king of peace and wealth (not war) was too good to miss? Perhaps she chanted '*MAKE EGYPT GREAT AGAIN!*' Perhaps not . . .

The problem was (and here comes the whole having to dress as a man *to get stuff done* bit), rather than change the ideology, she ended up having to adapt herself to trad male forms to be taken seriously. She donned the kilts and crowns, and her pharaoh image was captured forever in artwork showing her with a strange, snubby hipster beard, in all sorts of lunge stances – reaching out and leaning forward. Women could only ever stand passively in the shadows with their head bowed

---

1   Casual nickname usage for one of the most celebrated and controversial women of the ancient world there. Hope you enjoyed it as much as I did.

and arms by their sides (presumably staring down the men, wishing they would burst into flames). This strong 'male' iconography was vital to the concept of pharaoh and, apparently, the easiest way for Hatshepsut to royally represent. And REPRESENT she did. Hatshepsut went on to remain king for twenty years and flourish for them all, despite Thutmose III still being on the scene. She was Egypt's longest-reigning ruler (before Cleopatra's indomitable twenty-one-year reign beginning in 51 BC) and her beard endurance most likely lit the way for Cleo to dress freely in frocks and become everyone's favourite costume-party crush. Some believe Thutmose III murdered Hatshepsut in the end, but whatever happened, he definitely tried to wipe all mention of her – backdating his reign to the death of his father and blotting out her presence entirely. A bitter man erasing a powerful gurl from history? Who'd have thunk it! (Forewarning: an abundance of tools are left in this book overnight – this certainly won't be the only one you meet.) However, the Egyptian belief that a person lives on as long as their name is remembered has been exemplified by Hatshepsut since her memory was saved by Egyptologists, and her temple at Deir el-Bahri remains one of the most impressive and visited in Egypt to this day.

So, there you have Hatshepsut. She served up real 'King of the Humans' with a side order of absolutely owning her virtue and feeling the fantasy. Let's make sure she is never forgotten again: say her name, sing her name, chant it, express it through the medium of Krump, tattoo it across your knuckles, name your firstborn after her – it's, like, *totally* gender neutral (get in there before the next some-couple-or-other from the latest structured-reality series crack on to it and ruin it for us all).

HUA MULAN (NORTHERN AND SOUTHERN DYNASTIES PERIOD 420–589 AD)

THE LEGENDARY WOMAN WARRIOR AND CAMEL RIDING KWEEN

All cards on the table from the take-off here, there's no *actual* archaeological proof that Mulan ever existed . . . but if Disney said she did in their 1998 animated comedy-drama-action-musical-box-office-smash-that-went-down-a-total-treat then she *must* have been real. (Can I get a *whup whup!*) Walt and chums even went on to make *Mulan II*, further proof of her existence *surely* as everybody usually hates Disney sequels. (Name me ONE THING that happened in *Lady and the Tramp II: Scamp's Adventure*? In fact, name me one person who even knows who 'Scamp' *is*?) We should just be rejoicing in the fact that Mulan is a genuine(ish) wonder woman who is still being championed all these thousands of years later. But enough about Disney for now; we all know what really happens when Disney princesses meet feminism and it's way less pretty than any of their pookie ball gowns. I'm pretty certain '*Feminisney*' won't be taking the 'Oxford Dictionaries Word of the Year' title any time soon, but if it does I'll eat my Disney hat – Mickey ears and all.

The real Hua Mulan didn't have a cocky little red dragon side-kick because she didn't need to rely on anybody but herself. Often thought of as a grandmother to all later historical female warriors, she first appeared in Chinese folklore sometime between the fourth and sixth century AD. Although Mulan has gone on to be the star of films, operas, TV series, books and even video games, she originally popped up in the form of a type of singing ballad known as 'Yuefu' by an anonymous author in the Northern Wei Dynasty. The story elements of the original, *The Ballad of Mulan*, remain *mostly* consistent through-out all retellings but just so nobody gets their undies in a bundle over the details (if indeed you wear any), let's stick with the Yuefu version of events. The poem is actually very short, considering how deeply ingrained it has become in Chinese (and later global) folklore and classic literature. There may only be thirty-one couplets to dissect, but you'll soon understand that Mulan's exquisite life choices were all there to be seen, broad as daylight, beans and the gender pay gaps.

For Mulan, life was pretty snore at first. It was described as a domestic one; the robustly defined gender roles in Chinese culture had her sitting at a weaving loom most days and you couldn't even hear the sound of the shuttle over her sighs. (We know *those* sighs, that's for sure.) Back in Mulan's China, outlying tribes had invaded the central plains and the government declared that every household must send a man to the front line without excuse or sick note – this was *war*, not double gym class . . . Mulan's Pops was old and unwell, she had no older brothers and so, without hesitation, she decided to take her dad's place in the Khan army. Women were absolutely *not* allowed to fight but our girl was a jumpy-jack and she wasn't about to let a tiny thing like the ancient law of the land stand in her way (my forevermood). Mulan could only serve by impersonating a man and so she set about obtaining armour, weaponry and whatever other 'man paraphernalia' she saw fit.

The ballad describes how 'In the East market she buys a spirited horse, in the West market she buys a saddle, in the South market she buys a bridle, in the North market she buys a long whip . . .' Now, call me spoilt by malls and the like but I do wonder if she could have organised that shopping spree with a tad more geographical consideration. All that gallivanting about seems an awful faff.

Mulan travelled thousands of miles and fought for her family and country for the next twelve years. She remained in disguise for the entirety. Although later story adaptations go on to fill in some of the gaps, the ballad leaves gaping wide holes for imaginations to fill, and the fact that Mulan cross-dresses remains a focus because there are still gender taboos ruining this shindig we call society and this soiree we call life. Similarly, modern-day versions fixate on her *somehow*-surviving-her-life-among-the-men bit, the clickbait qualities of the tale. The dangers of women experiencing war and the constant threat of rape, sexual exploitation or, indeed, death, are all high up on the suspense agenda. But Mulan was tearing down those notions long before the Netflix-and-chillers were demanding and box-setting strong, diverse, female leads. Her efforts in battle were so top-notch that the top-dog Khan offered her a top-job as a top-kick minister in his top-tier cabinet. But Mulan's plan was only ever to stick to her own. She dared turn down the Khan's promotion and instead asked for a camel so she could ride home to her family. I love this part of the story for two reasons: 1) imagine the Khan's face when somebody said 'no' to him. That ego bruise must have smarted hard. And 2) A CAMEL WAS NEVER PART OF THE DEAL!

Upon returning to her village, history loves to have us think that Mulan put on her 'old-time clothes', changed her hair and in a J.Lo-montage-type sequence (artistic licence in force re J.Lo) made a big fuss about putting her make-up back on and re-emerging as a woman: *Don't be fooled by the rapier that she's got, she's still Mulan from the block . . . no matter where she goes she knows where she came from, from NORTHERN*

WEI! Mulan presented herself to her male companions who all flipped out like the locals from downtown-wherever after a Dynamo trick. In the midst of war, the soldiers clearly weren't distinguishing between sexes; everyone was simply trying to stay alive. Take from the ballad's conclusion what you will but I think it's pretty crystalline: 'The buck bounds here and there, while the doe has narrow eyes. But when the two rabbits run side by side, how can you tell the female from the male?' I have no explanation for the decision to use rabbits to make a gender equality point but if this was an English exam paper, you wouldn't need a double-digit IQ to score high. You'd only have to join the dots and write something along the lines of *STOP UNDERESTIMATING THE FEMALE RABBITS! FEMALE RABBITS ARE DOPE!* to get an A*.

These days Mulan's story is taught in Chinese schools, she has shrines across China and several localities in the country claim to be the hometown of our hero – she ain't going *nowhere*. Way more than just a time-honoured classic, she has transcultural, universal appeal because she is ultimate life goals. Word on the *Strasse* is that modern-day adaptations have turned Mulan into a feminist but she *clearly* always has been. Mulan escaped the humdrum domestic sphere, cross-dressed to get ahead, worked tirelessly for her family and country and kicked some serious badunkadunk during proceedings. Female empowerment at its finest, *surely?* Mulan is still an evolving tale, with brand-new meanings and messages every time, but I think we can all sleep soundly knowing that they will continue to cross boundaries and get more and more 'drop the mic' with every year.

SAINT MARINA (715–750 AD)

THE DEVIL BEATING MONK AND BABY 'FATHER'

Saint Marina aka Marina the Monk aka Marina the Ascetic aka *Marinus* the Monk, was a real fan of a moniker. It's sort of like when you try to give yourself a nickname at school and you realise you are the only one referring to yourself as 'Prophet YOLO the Great' so you have to float a plan B, C, D, E . . . anything to stop them calling you 'Cock-block o'clock'! And talking of cock-blocking, it's a miracle that Marina has been canonised and celebrated at all because she is venerated in the Maronite Catholic, Eastern and Coptic Orthodox churches – none of whom are *particularly fond* of feminism or any messing about with gender 'roles'. Cross-dressing is, in fact, seen by them as a 'moral disorder', and yet Marina and her fellow female cross-dressers of the time now have churches named after them. These were women who then lived as or disguised themselves as men, and did so to survive or become monks. But it wouldn't be fair of me to yak on about the hypocrisies of certain religious establishments still living in the times they were founded. Therefore, I won't mention how DUH NUGGET, POXY ASS, MOUTH BREATHER, STOOPID UPON STOOPID centuries-old sexism is. And vent we mustn't, because, huzzah and woot, Marina shines on!

Our sparkling star was a Christian saint of Byzantine Syria, which is now part of Lebanon. Marina was an only child and, as her mother died when she was a kidlet, she was raised by her devout Christian father, Eugenius (who had the *genius* idea to marry her off the minute he was able, so he could retire peacefully at the Monastery of Qannoubine). Eugenius's plan was put in place to 'save his own soul' but Marina was having none of it. 'O my father, why would you save your own soul, and destroy mine?' she supposedly retorted, and if you aren't already head over heels in love with Marina then I'm not sure how to help you. (Ye of little faith!) If you can stomach any more discrimination then take note of the fact her father followed up his first bout of bias with the proclamation, 'What shall I do with you? You are a woman!' An announcement rather than a question because he genuinely couldn't fathom why or how Marina could do anything other than marry a man and serve said beau. *Shockingly*, Marina had her own ideas and a tongue in her head to say them – she would join him at the monastery as 'Marinus the Monk'. Despite her dad's threats that the devil would be on to her like a fox on a bunny hutch, Marina told him to simmer down – she would shave her head and dress as a man. Job done.

Marina and Eugenius fought the spiritual fight together for over ten years. She was a proper model monk and practically perfect in every way. Her devotion doubled when her father passed away and she began to pray, worship, fast and practise piety for the pair of them. These increased levels of asceticism only helped her to conceal her true sex. All the man monks went on like everything was gravy, putting her soft voice down to too much praying and her lack of beard to the fact she *must* have been a eunuch. To top it all off, the Coptic bible reckons that during this time she was so miraculous and superior she could heal the sick and dogfight away THE DEVIL. (So much for the devil being on *her* case, she was booting the brute off like an unsuspecting gnat in the path of a Sporty Spice backflip.)

There were forty monks at the monastery and every month four of the brethren were sent on a mission. I'm being vague here because it is only ever described as 'business'. (Perhaps they were spreading the monk-y message? Perhaps they were flogging discount grain and cabbages off the back of a cart? We'll never know so feel free to draw your own conclusions.) What we do know is that there was an inn halfway to this 'business' that the monks frequented and the night Marina stayed there was another guest checking in, a soldier from the Eastern Roman front. This rude boy was also checking *out* the innkeeper's daughter and could have saved himself the price of his room because he stayed the night in hers. The booty call ended in the conception of a young perisher and the soldier told the innkeeper's daughter to blame Marina (Marinus) for the mattress mambo that resulted in a child. When the girl started showing she spilled the embellished beans and her dad went tearing down to the monastery to confront the abbot. Marina was bawled out something chronic but she didn't deny involvement. Instead, understanding that this meant a young woman was in crisis, Marina confessed her 'sinfulness' and asked for forgiveness. She was now the official baby 'father' and got kicked to the curb (the *actual* monastery curb – she had to sleep and beg on its doorstep from that day forward). The innkeeper's daughter had a boy and Marina took the son on as if he were her own, making parent moves to provide for him such as kicking it with the local shepherds for quick access to free milk. She was perkier with 'fatherhood' than a pig in the proverbial.

Marina was a homeless single father for ten years until the monks took pity on her (*took 'em long enough*) and allowed her back on strict conditions. She had to perform hard labour, was forced to be a skivvy and then some. Eventually her boy became a full-blown monk himself but he wouldn't have his 'father' for long. Life was hard for Marina; the workload took its toll and she died at just forty years of age. As the monks prepared Marina's body for her funeral, they discovered that she was a woman and there was mass hysteria. All sorts of weeping, praying and soul-searching ensued. Apparently, a monk who was blind in one eye was even cured of blindness just by looking at her body. *The power of the vulva!*

Here endeth the story of the blessed Marina. Whether you believe all the devil beating, sick healing sort of stuff or not, I think we can all see eye to eye on the fact her life and personality was popping. Marina disobeyed in a time when most women could only dutifully obey; she showed determination, discipline, intelligence, strength and grace. To quote from the translated holy Syro-Antiochene Rite, (may we) 'emulate in perseverance and in endurance the manly woman so that our Lord may give us grace and mercy with her and the portion of the saints in the fearful day of judgement'. I'm pretty sure our 'manly woman' mopped up all the praise on her judgement day. Marina was considerably holier than most.

JOANNA OF FLANDERS
(1295–1374)

THE FIERY COMMANDER,
ARMY RAISER AND HELLRAISER

Joanna is often considered one of the most extraordinary women of the age and it is my absolute pleasure to explain why she blasted it. Strap in; this ride is sponsored by brazenness, nerve and a woman scorned – expect some major turbulence. To ease you in gently we'll start with some family blather – Joanna was Duchess of Brittany; bloodlines and succession disputes played a fundamental part in her story.

Joanna was born to Joan, Countess of Rethel, and Louis I, Count of Nevers. She married John of Montfort, half-brother of John III, Duke of Brittany, in 1329. John wasn't backwards in coming forwards and snapped up that Duke title quick-time when the 'third John' died without any male heirs. His claim to fame was disputed by Joan of Penthièvre (the Duke's niece) and her husband, Charles of Blois-Châtillon. To cut a long story short, the House of Blois and the House of Montfort thrashed it out to the bitter end and their battle royal became the War of the Breton Succession. To make a long story even shorter, Joanna made the defence of the dukedom pretty much her life's work – she had her eyes on the prize and was as stubborn as the pit stains on your favourite vintage shirt.

As with all wars, this one was a bloody mess, made worse because there was also a wrestle for the French throne going down, involving the King of England (which carried on for about a hundred years, so we neatly named it the Hundred Years' War). The French and English both promised to protect and support their respective sides and avoid any foul play – but Joanna already had an inkling there was going to be some punking among the ranks. She was right to be suspicious because when her husband went to be heard by the King of France, the snake imprisoned him on the spot. To add fuel to the fire, he then made the decision, along with the French courts, to declare the House of Blois the true heirs to the Duchy. (*Douche!*) The fire may have been stoked but it was nothing in comparison to the flames raging inside Joanna. In fact, from here on in she was most well known as 'Jeanne la Flamme' (or Fiery Joanna) and it suited her down to a tee. Charles of Blois started to prep his army to invade Brittany but our blazing Jo had her own agenda. By this point she had an infant son, who she declared leader of the Montforts (she knew she couldn't claim the title for herself but she wasn't about to let that one slide) and she made sure King Edward III of England was on side and could basically send her backup. She pressed on by rounding up THREE HUNDRED men and so her army was ready for battle.

Jo-Jo knew exactly who to use to her advantage, who to manipulate and who to KO. By getting old Ed, King of England, on side she could build an ally, avenge her husband and help legitimise her son's succession to the French throne. Around this time, Joanna swung many a wrecking ball into the battlefield but she is most well known for the Siege of Hennebont in 1342, when her fiery side came out with a vengeance. There wasn't a hell's chance in France she was going to let the men take all the glory. Joanna started by putting on her war paint, or in this case she took up arms and jumped into a male soldier uniform and armour. Joanna completely ran the show, conducting the whole town and telling its women to 'cut their skirts and take their safety into their own hands'. Ain't nobody got time to be in a skirt when there's a war to fight! In my mind, Joanna's got her skirt wrapped round her head and face like a balaclava'd ninja and she's using her breast girdle as a sling-shot to snipe unsuspecting enemies. But I've said too much already . . .

The siege lasted for over a month and Joanna showed mad skills as a military leader. In one of the most dramatic moments of the conflict, once referred to as 'the boldest and the most remarkable feat ever performed by a woman', Joanna conceived a plan to storm the enemy camp. She'd been up and down the watch tower more times than the Grand Old Duke of York on a hill, checking the situation and ensuring her defence was progressing. When the timing was bang on she ordered that three-hundred-strong unit to charge and led the way. To sum up, they killed everyone in sight, set the whole place on fire and skedaddled sharpish. Joanna went missing for days and the Blois boys presumed her dead. But our firenado was simply biding her time, getting some R&R at a CASTLE (seems she knew about the self-love club ahead of her time too). Jo had been lying low before heading back for more and this time she was stepping things up a gear. Her army was now five-hundred strong and she returned to Hennebont at the crack of dawn, keeping it casual, with a triumphant blast of musical instruments! Joanna could have gone hard or gone home but she chose to GO HARD.

Various complicated War of Breton Succession plot twists occurred after this but the most important detail to remember is that, thanks to Joanna, the Montforts were eventually victorious. However, sadly, by this time Joanna had started to suffer from mental illness; she was basically sectioned and confined indoors (but to another castle, at least). She died not long after her son won the Duchy but our girl went out in style. More recent evidence suggests there was nothing to say that she was actually mentally unwell – which makes you wonder if someone was trying to repress our role model. But again, I've said too much . . . Joanna's fire has got me all impassioned. She was daring, impulsive and courageous. A medieval author at the time described her as having 'the courage of a man and the heart of a lion'. Medieval misogyny aside for a sec, Fiery Joanna was certainly a lion, a king and roar she fluffin' well did.

ONORATA RODIANI (1403–1452)

THE FRESCO PAINTIN', DOUBLET WEARIN'
FIGHTER WITH FLAIR

The early Italian Renaissance was arguably the greatest period for art and yet, *I'll be damned*, phenomenal female artists of the time hardly get a snuffle of a mention in the history books. Thankfully, we can put this right because this book would not be complete without an ode to Onorata.

Known as 'The Warrior Paintress' or 'The Amazon', Onorata lives up to her blamtastic titles; there was certainly nothing basic about this paintbrush pro and the same goes for her artwork. Female artists were quite rare back then but there definitely weren't any women painting frescoes – Onorata's speciality. Creating huge works of art in the plaster of grand-scale walls and ceilings required scaffolding (apparatus *far too precarious for a lady!*) and the job meant long periods of time away from home. The expectations for women started and finished at being wives and mothers; these medieval misses couldn't just jack it all in and mooch off for a few months, leaving the men to fend for themselves! Not only did Onorata somehow swerve all of these traditional responsibilities and live footloose and fancy-free, she would have had and hired A MALE ASSISTANT. *Hold my beer* – yes, Onorata had a man obeying *her* orders and perspiring under the hard knocks of being second best. Now, I know what you're thinking, this woman seems too good to be true already, but there's *so* much more to unpack. *Pour me another beer!*

Although little is known about her early years, Onorata was certainly part of the emergent bourgeois class and there must have been some cash kicking about somewhere because nobody becomes a fresco pro overnight. Training was long and arduous and Onorata would have had to slog to learn and master the technique. It requires serious skill and discipline; artists can't afford to make a single mistake while at work otherwise they'd have to ditch the lot. And if you think that's stressful, wait until you hear what a famous art historian of the day had to say about Onorata's expertise. Giambattista Biffi thought Rodiani's frescoes were (among a shower of other subtly blatant backhanded compliments) 'good for a woman'. How can a man with the greatest name on the planet, *Giambattista Biffi* (a name that for some reason makes me want to hoover down gnocchi, prosciutto, pizza, tiramisu, gelato and red wine), be such an *EEJIT*?

Biffi might not have been bothered but Onorata got the ultimate commission from someone who was. Marchese (or *Italian nobleman* to you and me) Cabrino Fondulo, who lived in a palace in Onorata's hometown of Castelleone, asked her to paint the entire crib. To pimp it, Onorata worked flat out for months but there was also a workplace sexual harassment case to contend with. Usually it's men on top of scaffolding wolf whistling down to a woman (while demanding to see 'the twins' and dry humping the air) but this sex pest, one of Fondulo's esteemed courtiers, was heckling *up* to Onorata atop the scaffolding from the ground. The reversed levels clearly didn't make his behaviour any more acceptable or Onorata's tether any longer. This predator, let's call him *Harvey* (it just sprang to mind). Harvey was as incessant as the cheap 'Ray-Bans' hackers. He started with inappropriate comments and progressed to handsy behaviour before long. But it wasn't Onorata's *hands* Harvey was grabbing. Despite verbally putting him in his place many a time, Harvey wasn't getting the message. Onorata needed to get physical and after one too many narrow misses, dodges and pushes away, our fatigued fresco virtuoso snapped. It is thought that Harvey attempted to rape her and so lunging at him with a paintbrush wouldn't have been effective. Instead, she pulled out a knife. Onorata killed Harvey with a single shank.

Frightened for her life (Harvey was the Marchese's fave and she knew he was going to throw a giant wobbler), Onorata decided to flee Castelleone. It was a good decision; her boss flipped his lid all over the palace before coming to the realisation that he had a half-painted yard. Eventually he would go on to pardon Onorata because she was the best in the biz and he needed that fresco flair, but she was long gone. Disguising herself as a man, Onorata reinvented herself completely, off in search of pastures new, believing 'it is better to be honoured outside my homeland than to be dishonoured within it'. Onorata was remorseful about her actions but it's also possible that she got a bit of a taste for blood because she became a mercenary soldier in the cavalry company of a chap named Odoardo Lampugnano. (Another fine specimen of a name.) Women were well over five hundred years away from being able to sign up as soldiers or to fight, and so the only way for Onorata to do so was to continue living as a man. It seems like she got a taste for this too because she kept up her disguise and her sword swinging for *twenty-nine years*, only returning to her hometown when it was being invaded by the Venetians in 1452. Onorata led a troop of soldiers back into Castelleone like an absolute champ but sadly this was to be her last battle. As she lay on her home ground, slipping away, she was allegedly recognised by some of the locals who, after all that time, outed her as a woman. Some sources even say she found the energy to make a dad joke with her final breath by saying she was dying '*with Onorata*' (her name meant 'honour'). Let's just call this a fact because it's the most beautiful, poignant dad joke I ever did hear.

The legend of Onorata lives on in Castelleone despite uncertainty as to whether any of her artwork does. Although art history from Onorata's day rarely includes female artists (aneurysms all round), her life and actions are rich enough to paint a picture of a creative and heroic rebel with the guts to stand up, fight and even kill for what she believed in.

JOAN OF ARC (1412–1431)

THE ASS-KICKING SOLDIER SAINT AND INSPIRATIONAL UNDERDOG

Few medieval folk are as well documented as Joan; she has been adopted by new generations over the years and motivated all manner of mortals. Joan of Arc is a universally recognised historical female figure. School kids pole to pole will be able to rattle off all of the big players famed within their classroom; Joan has made the company of favourites such as Henry VIII, Florence Nightingale, William Shakespeare, Queen Victoria, Nelson Mandela and Ariana Grande . . . Joan is the star of umpteen books, plays, poems, works of art and films – and the name of a brand of brie and a line of kidney beans. It is even thought she inspired the 'bob' haircut. Until you've influenced a hairdo, cheese and/ or a tinned good, you have nuh-uh rights to say that you've made it.

As the write-ups about anyone working class always start, Joan was born into *humble beginnings*. The daughter of a farmer, residing in the peasant village of Domrémy, Joan was illiterate and expected to amount to jack squat. France was in a bit of a state at the time, the Hundred Years' War was getting pretty rowdy and the French army had not had any notable victories since forever-ago. But among the burning villages and suffering, Joan was chatting with the heavens. At around the age of twelve, J-of-A reckoned angels and saints started to visit her.

Domrémy was quite an isolated, dinky part of la France so any visitors at all must have been the talk of the town, but the spirits weren't just passing through; Joan believed they gave her a divinely ordered mission. By age sixteen, the archangels had properly got into Joan's head and she was adamant her sole job and purpose in life was to support the king (Charles VII) and save her country from English domination. Her fated life of farming and baby-making was going to have to wait.

Joan almost continuously wore men's clothing; it seems that, for whatever reason, she'd made up her mind that they were *her* and they were going to help her progress with her master plan. Perhaps she thought she would be taken more seriously the afternoon in February 1429 when she rolled up to the court of Charles VII to tell him God had sent her, in all her peasant-teenage glory, to save him and the future of France. The King of England wasn't getting off lightly either – he received a letter from Joan stating that: 'The Maid promises and certifies that if you do not leave France, she and her troops will raise a mighty outcry as has not been heard in France in a thousand years.' Joan wasn't playing.

The king and royal government granted Joan's wish to get involved with the Siege of Orléans (I'm not sure they had a choice) and she got her desired life leading and directing the French armies against the English for eighteen months. Until Joan started running the show, the morale among the French soldiers was about as low as an iPhone battery after a commute. Although J-of-A didn't have a scrap of formal training, her military leadership skills were rocking. It was like the soldiers were transformed by a cult; the men saw her as a saint and were literally willing to die for her. Joan would lead troops into battle with hype-girl-type rallying cries such as 'Let all who love me, follow me!' – and follow they did. Like the Justin Bieber of war-torn France, there was a frenzy wherever she went and she got swarms of new recruits signing up like fanboys. Joan was an inspirational mascot to those fighting; she brandished a banner rather than a weapon (although it is thought she could give a deadly left hook). It was her intellect, willpower and grit that seemed to have everyone hypnotised and she capitalised on it. Joan may not have shed any blood on the battlefield but she came to SLAY. She famously took an arrow to the shoulder, brushed it off (her shoulder *not* the arrow) and when she returned to fight, she did so wearing *double armour*. Genius.

Her efforts didn't bring the war to an end but they certainly had an effect on later commanders, who tried to copy her style but failed. Joan may have been one of a kind but her days were numbered; in May 1430, she was captured by the Burgundians, a political party in allegiance against France. After being handed over to the English and the Bishop of Beauvais she went on trial for a string of convictions, the most serious being 'a thing abominable to God' – *wearing men's clothing*. Joan was denied a legal advisor but she held her own until the (very) bitter end when she was found guilty of heresy and burned to death at nineteen. The Church may have made the final decision but they also went on to change their mind and make her a saint after she was retried posthumously and found to be not guilty nearly FIVE HUNDRED YEARS LATER. They caught on to her brilliance eventually. So, if you're being overlooked anywhere, firstly kick up a fuss about it now but, failing that, here's hoping you'll be recognised in a *few centuries' time*, eh? Some theorists reckon Joan escaped the fire and another woman burned in her place, others that after the fire went out all that remained was her heart, intact and pumping full of blood. Let's face facts (and biology), this is a crazy ass idea, but whatever happened that fateful day, Joan's heart certainly lives on in other ways.

The military has always been a male subculture but Joan changed the game, not only forcing her way into the boy's club but *taking control*. She lived fast, died young and achieved more in nineteen years than most do in a lifetime. Joan is a long-established underdog done good story but she didn't just do good, she did whizzer. She overcame her youth, sex, and social status and managed to be a hero for people on all

ELENA DE CÉSPEDES
(1545–CIRCA 1590s)

THE SEX-CHANGING, STATUS QUO RESHAPING 'OFFSPRING OF AN AFRICAN SLAVE'

At a very early age Elena's face was marked with hot coals, branding her an 'Andalusian slave', a permanent reminder that she was born to an African slave (Francisca de Medina), and she started her life as such too, in Alhama, Spain. Although she would never escape the stigmas surrounding her past, she did manage to put it on ice in other ways. Elena was set free from her master when she was ten but continued fighting for freedom her entire life. At sixteen she was trapped again, this time in an unhappy marriage. Her husband mistreated her and, in a trashy soap opera cliffhanger-type moment, walked out on her the second he discovered she was pregnant. Rather than set fire to his belongings as the violins and credits rolled in, or stare longingly at the door in his wake before sliding down a wall, Elena knew she had to fight the power.

When her baby was born, Elena left the child with family and began to move from town to town, travelling throughout southern and central Spain with nothing on her to-do list but to hustle. Success was the only option for Elena; she started to dress as a man and changed her first name to her surname to bag certain jobs that only people with the Y chromosome could bag at the time. As far as we can tell, her initial desire to wear 'male' clothing was born purely and simply from an awareness of the benefits being a man in society allowed. It meant she got left alone as she travelled and could pick and choose jobs as freely as Bullingdon Club alumni. Elena became a tailor, a hosier, a weaver, a manual labourer and a farmhand. For the latter, she was paid by a man named Antón Marino in small change AND BREAD. (Although this fact has nada to do with anything, I thought that payment by carbs deserved a mention and could perhaps give a generation that will scarcely afford houses something new to strive for.) For years, Elena lived as Céspedes and few people questioned her regarding her gender. At *some point* (to be clear because the history books aren't), Elena began to identify as intersex, then later as a male. Elena became *Eleno* and so from here on in that is exactly what we shall call him.

Eleno showed some serious industry and opportunism. He fought successfully as a soldier, rounded up sheep most expertly as a shepherd and even decided to learn surgery and have a bash at that for a while. Upon threat of being banned for *not actually being licensed* to cut into people, Eleno simply got further training from a Valencian surgeon (who *did* know what they were doing) and cracked on. With an entrepreneurial spirit that would put all the contestants from the entire back catalogue series of *The Apprentice* to shame, Eleno then found a town called Ocaña, which had no surgeons, so he could be the one and only and cash in yet again. This turned out to be a winning life move for Eleno because it was to be the town where he also met the love of his life. Eleno was rumoured to have had many affairs with women over the years, but it was Maria del Caño who made his palms clammy and his mouth as dry as a gluten-free flapjack. In 1586, the couple became engaged and Eleno asked the vicar general of Madrid, Juan Bautista Neroni, for a licence to marry. Juan was very suspicious of Eleno's lack of facial hair (his very own 'masculinity' barometer) and questioned whether Eleno was actually one of the female-flavoured variety. The vicar ordered nine doctors and midwives, lawyers and even some random people 'of good repute' he pulled in off the street to carry out tests on him and determine his sex. Eleno was confirmed as a male (stick with me) and the pair were allowed to marry. *Hallelujah!*

But, alas, a year later Eleno and Maria were arrested after a neighbour accused them of tricking the church and courts. *The opposite of hallelujah!* Eleno was tried for sodomy, bigamy, impersonating a man, mocking matrimony and having a pact with the devil. The supreme spirit of evil aside for the moment, the whole case became fixated on whether Eleno had a penis or not. For the inquisitors, 'maleness' revolved only around an appendage. Without that vital organ, Eleno was 'Elena' to them, no matter what he told them or how he felt. Upon arrest a second time, he was re-examined and found to have *no* penis. The original reports were rejected and the judge, Lope de Mendoza, believed he had bribed the medical professionals, or made a pact with the devil to trick them. The sodomy was put down to Eleno having made a dildo from wood and he was therefore categorised as a 'deviant woman'. Eleno himself is thought to believe that he grew a penis after childbirth and the reason for its disappearance was down to an illness. It is possible that he was born with both organs, or that he had an enlarged clitoris after pushing out a babba, or perhaps (on another planet) he was indeed homies with the boss of hell. Eleno at first professed 'I am a man and a woman', but later went on to say that he felt like a man and that was the reason he married Maria. He knew two women couldn't marry and he wouldn't have done so if he wasn't a *he*.

There were lots of oddities in the case and the scribe summarised Eleno's responses rather than giving his answers verbatim, so we can't know exactly how it went down. What we do know is the Spanish Inquisition most likely decided upon a guilty verdict because of their own anxieties about his gender, sexuality and race, and an uneasiness with how somebody like Eleno (somebody *other*) had created a prosperous, professional life for himself. They sentenced Eleno to two hundred lashings, an appearance at an *auto de fé* (public shaming and penance) and ten years' unpaid labour in a hospital. To twist the knife further, they stipulated that he must do it all in 'women's' attire. 'The Woman Surgeon' became famous and people came from far and wide to see Eleno at work for a time, before he disappeared completely from historical record. Eleno was a threat to the status quo so he was knocked down, but it didn't squash his ingenuity and ability to reinvent himself or break his spirit. He was roadblocked for trashing all stereotypes and expectations but now we can raise him up again for doing just that.

MARY FRITH (CIRCA 1584–1659)

THE SMOKIN', PICKPOCKETIN', FENCIN', CROSS-DRESSIN' ROGUE

I should probably be transparent from the top and mention here that she was also a gang leader, pimp and violent criminal – but we'll get to that bit (and you'll see why she still deserves a place in the #*GenderRebels* hall of fame when we do). *Talk about an awkward introduction!* Anyway, let's crack on – Mary Frith, aka Moll Frith aka Moll Cutpurse aka Mal Cutpurse, was the most famous female rogue in seventeenth-century England, hence all the titles . . . probably. Moll (or Mal) is basically ye olde way of saying someone was shady and the Cutpurse bit described her favourite pastime perfectly – she was an out and out thief! Much like street swindlers today, thieves back then would work in threes and stick to a patch. Mary's team would operate in the area around London's St Paul's Cathedral – the first made an obstruction, while Mary would literally cut the victim's purse strings and then another would leg it away with the loot. I told you this one was a character . . .

As a child, Mary was described as having a 'boisterous' and 'mannish' spirit. Historical biographies note how energetic, active, physical and *wild* she was – *FOR A GIRL!* It was seemingly complete madness that she preferred to roll around in the mud fighting with the boys, dressed in a doublet and baggy breeches, rather than in an apron slaving over a hot stove at home. *Facepalm* Her misspent youth might not have involved drinking in the park or smoking in the bushes (rites of passage with the 'youth of today'!) but her adulthood certainly involved copious amounts of both substances. If you were looking for Mary Frith in the early 1600s, you would find her either in jail or at The Globe Inn, boasting about her criminal activity, swearing, getting wasted and smoking a clay pipe. She is actually thought to have been the first English woman ever to smoke tobacco. Now, I know smoking is *so not cool* any more but it has to be said that there's something majorly boss about Mary's decision to lay to rest her last feck. Especially as these behaviours were viewed as 'masculine' at the time, frowned upon for a female and therefore entirely *undesirable*. But our Mary wasn't looking to be desired, she was looking for trouble.

Mary's family tried to reform her at sixteen, sending her off to America on a ship – a ship she proceeded to throw herself overboard from and swim home to continue living as she pleased. She was fearless, a rule breaker and law breaker and she kept it up for her entire life. The 'male' attire really came to force and became a permanent fixture after a dare. A local showman and Mary's friend bet her she wouldn't ride a horse across the capital, from Charing Cross to Shoreditch, dressed as a man. Mary didn't just do it, she did it blowing a trumpet and brandishing a banner! For wearing men's clothing in public (a crime for women then), Mary was forced to do penance at the doors of St Paul's Cathedral. Rather than repent whatsoever, Mary found the male attire to be rather a great convenience for her lifestyle and stuck it out. It apparently allowed her to ride her horse, fence and fight more freely and Mary was all about this way of life. She was even allowed to per-form shows at the Fortune Theatre as a man (without a licence), during which she joshed with the audience and sang songs. The fact that she continued with the breeches, performed in public and had a voice (and a loud one at that) reminds us how she constantly transgressed the traditional constructs of 'femininity' in early modern England. All of her opinions and actions were unheard of for women of the time and she was flaunting them.

Although the severity and frequency of her crimes made Mary a celebrity in the criminal underworld, in Mary's (warped) head she reckoned she was doing it all for justice and fairness. She may have made a living from selling received stolen goods from her very own shop on Fleet Street, *but she liked to sell the goods back to their rightful owners!* She was a pimp, the go-between who found the 'prostitutes' to be made into mistresses – *but she liked to track down any man that made them pregnant and demand the woman got money for their illegitimate child!* She was a highway(wo)man and held up carriages, stole money, shot riders and even horses if she needed to – *but she was a staunch cavalier and claimed her exploits were all for the king!* She was even supposed to have tamed and trained a parrot and monkey and taught them to do tricks to make money as a street performer. Never mind simply the first smoker, Mary feels like the first documented successful female freelancer with a love for a side-hustle!

During her time on the rampage, Mary was imprisoned on numerous occasions, tried and re-tried, sentenced to death and even incarcerated for 'insanity' in Bethlem Hospital (Bedlam). But she always managed to wriggle her way out and back to freedom. At the height of her 'career' she was worth over three thousand pounds but had only a hundred left by the time of her death – probably all the bail outs and bribes she had to shell out for. These sorts of facts about Mary have been questioned, debated and sensationalised over time and in the multitude of literature, plays, poems and novels written about her life – including Mary's own memoir, *The Life and Death of Mrs. Mary Frith*. The book laments her own 'genius' and is about the best example of tooting one's own trumpet you are ever likely to read. Mary wins all the points here for self-worth and essentially publishing a life-hack-style guide on how to be an accomplished criminal. What's more, women (and especially not lower-class women) were hardly known for writing memoirs then. Another forward-thinking feat by Mrs Frith.

Mary was often called a 'hermaphrodite' but she never referenced herself as such. Her true sex and sexuality have baffled and intrigued many historians, playwrights and writers, but the one truth that always shines through regardless is her individualism. Mary did Mary. She tried to disrupt the gender roles and seemed to forge her own identity as a reaction to her environment. Whatever the truth, she left this world happy: 'Merry I lived, and many pranks I played, / And without sorrow, now in grave am laid.' It probably goes without saying that, *of course*, Mary also wrote her own epitaph.

CATALINA DE ERAUSO
(1592–CIRCA 1650)

THE CONVENT FLEEING, FRAUDULENT
LIEUTENANT NUN

Heard the one about the Spanish, Basque, lieutenant nun extraordinaire with the unconventional attitude? *Ave Maria*, it's a cracker! In a pack of jam tarts, Catalina would be the only lemon curd; she always chose the road less travelled and she mostly had a fugitive status while travelling it. Catalina's life wasn't meant to be full of adventure but she made dang sure she flipped the system. Born in San Sebastián, to parents with a fair bit of dough (her dad was a bigwig military commander), Catalina had four brothers and four sisters but cock-shock-horror, the boys were treated *very* differently to the girls. Her brothers had the ability to splash a bit of that cash and (gender stereotypically) join the army. The sisters' only choice was marriage and kids or nundom (being an adult can be so disappointing). At only four years of age, Catalina was enrolled at the Dominican convent in her hometown and condemned to a life of submissiveness and silence. But Cat was wilful and wild and she didn't plan on sticking about for long . . .

The elder nuns had an uphill task controlling Catalina; she was restless, rebellious and had some seriously dirty *habits* (winky face emoji with its tongue out). She was split up from her sisters and sent to a much stricter monastery called San Bartolome, to clean up her act. At age fifteen and days before she was meant to take her vows, a final binding contract with Jesus Christ, Catalina stole the keys to the convent and bolted. In a nearby chestnut grove (howzabout that for attention to detail!), she refashioned her blue bodice into a pair of breeches and cut her hair short. It is thought that, later on, she even started to take some kind of herbal remedy meant to reduce her chest. She opted for the only safe escape she had, to become a man. Catalina would utilise more disguises during her lifetime than we all do trying to create multiple one-month free trial subscriptions. In her own words, she 'dressed up, and cut my hair, went hither and thither, embarked, went into port, took to roving, slew, wounded, embezzled, and roamed about'. As a 'man', Catalina had the freedom pass to pursue a life of danger, exploits and adventure and she held on to it, never appearing as a woman again.

There was major restlessness in Spain at the time – it was nigh on bankrupt and thousands were fleeing the country to live in New Spain (like the old Spain but better. And in Mexico). Now a fugitive, Catalina headed off in that direction too, to find employment and seek her fortune. The first person to take her in, a doctor and professor, attempted to sexually assault her so she made like a banana, stealing his moolah en route and continuing on the run, doing all she could to perfect her disguise. Catalina had more jobs around this time than I've had takeaways. She was a page boy in various households, a cabin boy on a ship, a store manager, a merchant, a sailor and a candlestick maker. (I lied. She was never a candlestick maker.) From Spain, Catalina travelled to and around South America and there are many lively accounts of her movements (not least those in her own autobiography, *Memoir of a Basque Lieutenant Nun*). She supposedly stole hundreds of pesos, fought duels, had several female lovers, gambled, pillaged, pilfered, murdered, escaped death on many an occasion and went in and out of prison. I know what you're thinking: this is *surely* the juicy bit, why is she skipping over the beef in a single sentence? By this stage, Catalina was gaining notoriety; the stories are so magnificently varied it's hard to decipher the truth. But we do know that whatever she did, she did it with all the rage and mania of someone who's accidently mixed Sudafed and rosé wine. And she did it as *Antonio de Erauso*. Or *Pedro de Orive*. Or *Francisco de Loyola*. Or *Alonso Diaz Ramirez de Guzman*. Whoever she felt like being on any given day.

In 1619, just when it seemed that Catalina had 'settled down' and got a little job in a shop, she got sacked for coming on to the boss's wife's sister (*quite* strongly). She didn't get a glittering reference, *quelle surprise*, and her job prospects were curbed. Our girl couldn't catch a break! But it was no sweat for Catalina – she decided to join an army battalion heading for Chile and fight in the War of Arauco against the Mapuches (she'd been getting enough fighting and maiming practice in, after all). Erauso gained a reputation for her (his) brutality as a soldier and quickly rose through the ranks, becoming a second lieutenant after only three years. This was to be her only promotion, however, as she let the beast back out once more and went on a very violent killing rampage, which landed her back in the slammer. After a messy period of robbin', fightin', killin' and trips to and from death row (you've probably recognised some behavioural issues and cycles by now), Catalina headed back to Spain.

In 1625, she presented a petition to King Philip IV, requesting that she be allowed a military pension and the Spanish government granted it. (If you don't ask you don't get, I suppose.) In another turn up for the books (well, this book thus far especially) Catalina also asked Pope Urban VII if she could have permission to continue to dress as a man. HE. SAID. YES. She seized the opportunity to make hay while the sun was shining hard enough to burn a beige person to death and it paid off. Catalina is our first gal actually allowed by law to 'cross-dress'! It is thought it helped that she was religious and a virgin (two of the Church's favourite things). Catalina's sexuality was seemingly also very chill with Pope Urban – as long as there was no penis penetration in the mix, everyone was just fine. (*Who takes lesbianism seriously anyway?!*) All of the aforementioned was obviously great for Catalina to carry on gadding about as she so desired, and this part of the story is only slightly overshadowed by the fact that the Pope was called Urban and I keep imagining him in a snapback cap.

Catalina sort of semi-retired and spent the last twenty years of her life in Mexico, driving mules (beats sit-down-jazzercise in a care home with a patronising teacher in neon legwarmers any day). Much like we are now, people still spoke about her escapades and she remained a seventeenth-century Spanish celebrity and luminary. Historians have pondered over the years whether she was asexual, a 'hermaphrodite', transgender or a 'transvestite'. The questions surrounding her sex and sexuality these days are very much the same-same but different. But who cares for labels? Catalina loved her life and relished the privilege of being able to live as freely as the men did. Find me another lieutenant nun you could say that about. (Don't worry, I'll wait.)

QUEEN CHRISTINA OF SWEDEN (1626–1689)

THE QUEER QUEEN WHO QUIT HER JOB AND QUASHED THE RULES

Queen Christina of Sweden's motto for life was *Fata Viam Invenient* (The Fates will find a way). I hate to disagree with any of our influential women wonders but I can't help but think Christina was either deluded or taking the pish with this one. Not a single decision in this woman's life was left to fate. Queen Christina of Sweden was defiant, tenacious, single-minded and hard-core. She called the shots and ordered them to be fired. Christina was determined to make moves from the instant she was born – so much so that she's our only woman to have even left the womb disguised as a male! The only hope to be heir to the Swedish throne at the time, her parents, King Gustavus and his wife Maria Eleonora of Brandenburg, were desperate for a boy. When the mid-wives announced her to be so, there was much elation – for all of about five minutes – until they realised there had been a mistake. According to Christina's autobiography, she was born 'completely hairy' and this appears to be the only reason for the confusion. (They'd be rattled if they caught sight of me from the neck down during the winter months.)

In the end, Gustavus decided they'd better *make the most of it* and raise her as the queen-to-be. 'Making the most of things' for her father basically meant raising her 'like a boy' – making sure she took a keen interest in 'masculine' pursuits such as, hold on to your hats, *the right to an education.* Hers was highly extensive for anyone at the time, and especially as (so she was continually reminded) she was a girl. She learned horse*man*ship and fencing and became quite the professional. When Gustavus was killed in battle in 1632, Christina became Queen of the Swedes, Goths and Vandals, Great Princess of Finland, Duchess of Estonia and Karelia and Lady of Ingria at only six years of age. Her title may have been lengthy but her time spent actually enjoying it was not – Christina sat very uneasily on the throne. By the time she had turned eighteen, she'd had more than enough of the rules and pressures of queening and was fed up of everyone trying to make her take a husband. Christina had a marked aversion to marriage and appeared to feel the same way about the idea of sex with men: 'I could not bear to be used by a man the way a peasant uses his fields.' We hear ya, Tina. *We hear ya.*

While Christina spent her days batting away the unwanted attentions of a string of male suitors, including her own cousin (what is it with these royals and their obsession with keepin' it in the gene pool?), her attentions were firmly fixed elsewhere. Ebba Sparre, or 'Belle' as Christina called her (cute), was her handmaiden and 'bed-fellow'. Christina was infatuated with Belle and frequently hinted at a sexual relationship – she told an English ambassador at the time that her 'inside was as beautiful as her outside'. *I mean,* there are hints and then there's too much information! She might as well have done a PowerPoint presentation detailing their every move. While some accounts say that she had several male partners throughout her lifetime, others reckon she avoided them like the plague.

Perhaps in pursuit of some of that *me-time*, in 1654, at age twenty-seven, Christina decided to spit out the silver spoon that had been choking her since birth, shake off the stifling royal rules and finally be who she wanted to be. This began with her (then completely and utterly scandalous) decision to abdicate the throne. Our girl wanted to wear what she pleased, sleep with whom she pleased, and believe in what she pleased (there was also the small matter of wanting to change the state religion of Lutheranism back to Roman Catholicism – an idea that, quite frankly, was as gratefully received as a turd tagine). The best bit was that Christina still wanted it all. She wanted to quit but keep a continued status of sovereign, money and power. And *you betcha* she managed to do just that. She decided to travel across Europe and the best way of doing so without being bothered by a bunch of boys was to disguise herself as one. Christina chopped off her hair and threw on the 'male' garments for which she had been slagged off for too long, smeared her face with grime, grabbed her sword, jumped on her horse and did one.

After leaving Sweden, Christina really dialled up the rebellion. She refused to receive influential people, came and went as she liked and openly made fun of everyone that crossed her path. She would reportedly sprawl her legs up on theatre chairs, was scorned for talking and snort-laughing aloud during Mass, mixing with poor people (*gasp!*), and even associating with Jews (*gasp times infinity!*). Her intelligence and wit meant she could shut down any criticism with a single gibe and if anyone upset her too much, she simply had them executed. Nobody messed with Christina, Queen of Sweden! In her later years, she even bounced back from the clutches of death more than once – she was a remarkable, unstoppable force to be reckoned with. Honestly, the only obstacle that seemed ever to get in her way was a recorded affliction of terrible menstrual pains, which were known to knock her block off for days at a time. Trust pesky periods to rain on a rainbow.

Pamphlets of the day labelled Christina 'a prostitute', 'a lesbian' and 'an atheist' because she 'walked like a man, sat and rode like a man, and could eat and swear like the roughest soldiers'. People were still obsessed with her sexuality even after her death – scientists exhumed her body in 1965 to try and decipher if she was, in fact, a 'hermaphrodite'. The results were inconclusive, which, let's face truths here, means OF COURSE SHE WASN'T. She just wanted to live her best life her own way but never got a minute's peace to do so.

Christina saw and described herself as a king (and the badger's nadgers of kings at that): 'I governed Sweden for ten years as a king . . . my auspices have been the most glorious and the most advantageous in the world for Sweden.' Her accomplishments during her lifetime were indeed subject to a great deal of extravagant praise, but she never saw how her sex had a part to play in any analysis of her rule or success. Looking back, she was a feminist before her time. A king and a keen sportsman, her watchword was always '*fair play*'. From her childhood, right through to the end of her days, Christina certainly smashed all that she set out to. Fair play, Christina. *Fair play.*

CHRISTIAN 'KIT' CAVANAGH (1667–1739)

THE 'MALE' DRAGOON WITH A PENCHANT FOR LOOTING AND SHOOTING

Christian Cavanagh was born Christian Cavanagh but she was also known by an all-you-can-eat buffet array of names along the way including Christian Welsh, Christian Davies, Mother Ross, The Pretty Dragoon and *Kit*. Three guesses as to which my weary typey-tappy fingers will select and proceed with?

Kit grew up in Dublin, Ireland, and as a teenager it seems she was a bit of a toerag. Her behaviour quickly spiralled and when Kit became more precarious than a sedated flamingo on a Segway, her mother sent her to live with an aunt who ran a public house in the city. Now, I'm not one to question a woman's judgement, but punishing a tearaway teen by banishing them to a *pub* does seem a dollop *doh* to me. Any road up, Kit continued her antics for a few years before meeting her first husband, Richard Welsh, and popping out a couple of bambinos. The good times were rolling for the pair until 1692, when one day Richard went out and never returned home. Believing him to have been murdered, Kit went into mourning for her husband for a full year before discovering he was, in fact, alive and kicking. Richard wrote to his wife from the

British Army, where he was serving against his will. There is some debate as to how exactly he found himself in this position, my favourite story being that he was press-ganged by an old schoolmate who got him so sloshed he woke up on a ship halfway to Holland. Now, I thought I had some drinking stories worthy of a film rights contract contest but this one takes the tequila. Never mind *waking up in Vegas*, imagine waking up a draftee! #*aboutlastnight* . . .

Without a second thought, Kit left her children with her family and set out to find her long-lost love. According to her memoirs, she cut her hair, quilted a waistcoat to 'preserve my breasts from hurt (which were not large enough to betray my sex)', put on a wig and went out to buy some 'silver-hilted swords' and 'Holland shirts'. Our steadfast lover was about to become an equally stubborn fighter. She enlisted with Captain Tichborne's company at the Battle of Landen and hid in plain sight as 'Christopher'. As the army crushed it across Europe on its crusades, Kit enquired after Richard at every camp, the bluff being that (s)he was looking for her 'brother'. Although she didn't find her hubs, 'Christopher' soon found a name for himself as a feral fighter and marauder. Kit relished the looting and plundering and ripped apart every town she stomped through. Nobody suspected that she was anybody other than who she flat-out lied to be. She mimicked her comrades, drinking and swearing (two of her most treasured pastimes anyway, so it was hardly a chore). She slept alongside the men and even urinated with them – using a 'silver tube with leather straps'. If you too have ever peed all over your gold lamé leggings and box-fresh kicks at a festival after attempting to spend a penny through a Shewee, you'll understand why whatever Kit's enterprising contraption was, she deserves a Walk of Fame star for it.

Kit's Christopher turned out to be a bit of a catch – so much so that in one town a woman accused Kit of fathering her child, but she wasn't resting on pretty or blue steel. Rather than skulk away or deny it and blow her cover, KIT AGREED TO PAY CHILD SUPPORT

FOR THE BABY. The sisterhood was strong with this one. In another town, Kit formed a close relationship with a young local girl whom she saved from being raped by a sergeant. Put in plain English, she saved her by *killing* the said sergeant. Nobody was going to mess with her 'sweetheart', no matter the cost. The cost turned out to be Kit's job but she refused to go back to her dishwater civilian life. Promptly after her sacking in 1697, Kit re-enlisted with the 4th Royal North British Dragoons, a role she adored and managed to hold on to a dab longer. There was much to-ing and fro-ing over the years but it would be an entire fourteen before Kit eventually found her HOMEWRECKER. Oops, sorry, I jumped the gun and wrote that with my sympathy broken heart for Kit, who on her return from the Battle of Blenheim in 1704 found her husband in the arms of another woman. Kit lost her excrement and flew at the pair, cutting off his fling's nose with a sword to spite everyone's face. After risking her life for him for so long, this wasn't exactly the *Notebook*-style reunion she had in mind. There wasn't a safety match in hell's chance Kit was taking Richard back – she wanted to remain a dragoon and made him swear he would keep her secret. Despite her bravado, it is thought that later, when Richard was killed in battle, Kit spent days turning over bodies to find him and give him a proper burial. No, *you're* crying.

Kit kept on keeping on, continuing to serve and even going on to have another child and marry again. Twice. It seemed no man nor musket ball to the right upper thigh could hold her back from battle. In 1706, she ultimately met her match in mortar, from an explosion that fractured her skull and ruffled her identity. The regimental surgeon spotted her breasts, which, it seemed, eventually *did* 'betray her sex'. Although she had to retire, her valour was honoured by Queen Anne herself and she received a pension for her services. Kit went back to Dublin for a bit and tried to run a pub but she had a colony of ants in her pants, goading her to stay on the move until the end of her days. Kit was given military honours at her funeral and was the first woman to be buried among the Chelsea Pensioners in London. It would be another two centuries before her female counterparts of later years would be able to experience the same respect and distinction. Kit could throw fifty shades of shade but she also had a 24-carat gold and courageous heart, one that, for once in this book of multiple woeful exits, was rightly revered when it ceased to beat.

JULIE D'AUBIGNY (1673–1707)

THE SEXUALLY AMBIGUOUS, SELF-WILLED, SWASHBUCKLING OPERA SINGER

Julie d'Aubigny was better known throughout seventeenth-century France as *Mademoiselle Maupin* or *La Maupin*. In fact, as an adult she was *only* known by that because people would literally be scared for their lives if they dared to call her anything but. So, I shall refer to her as Maupin for fear of waking up to find her towering over me, returned from the dead, squawking operatic trills in my face and holding a rapier to my throat if I don't. Think that sounds a tad OTT? Just you wait.

Maupin's father was the Grand Squire of France and he trained her up alongside the King's Squires as soon as she was out of rompers. You've heard of running before you can walk? How about *sword fighting before you can talk*? As a young woman, she was taught all of the life skills necessary to ensure her the right start in life – how to gamble, drink excessively, ride horseback and fight to the *actual death*. She learned fencing from the masters and, most uncommonly, she only fought men and on an equal footing. This 'manly' education also encouraged a taste for literature, history, opera and a love of exercise, which (rage and killing aside for a moment) was pretty unheard of and lucky for Maupin. Unluckily for Maupin, she was also married off as a teenager to a man named Jean, Sieur de Maupin of Saint-Germain-en-Laye. At the time,

Maupin was having a secret affair (the first of many) with her father's boss and it took her all her might not to poison Jean to death on the wedding night. Instead, it is thought she concocted a plan to send him off to do a tax collector's job in Toulouse. FOR EVER. (I told you Maupin was savage.) Armed with a new name and a wedding ring (which would allow her to enjoy all sorts of promiscuity an unmarried woman would never get away with), Maupin decided to do a runner to Marseilles and get to it already.

Maupin's sword-slinging ways soon found her in the company of a murdering fugitive fencer named Sérannes. Over time and after further training, the pair became quite the double act – organising fencing events, which the public would pay to watch. Playing on all her strengths – sword fighting, singing and her cavalier musketeer mentality – Maupin began cross-dressing to make some extra money. During their shows, she would sing songs to gather a crowd, then draw her sword and challenge anyone who thought they could take her on. If someone was brave enough to raise a hand, Maupin would cuss them through more made-up tunes and cause a right old ruckus. If anyone questioned her gender, Maupin supposedly responded by ripping open her shirt and telling the audience to 'judge for themselves'. Eventually Maupin and Sérannes got shut down by a local big cheese policeman who cottoned on to them. Maupin had a habit of stabbing people, slapping onlookers for no reason, and a reputation for being 'as sharp with the women as she was cruel with the men . . . the sting of her repartee was no less feared than the power of her arm, which could wield a sword with deadly effect'. She needed a cold shower and an ankle monitor.

Sticking with the men's clothing, Maupin went on to be the first contralto who wasn't a castrated male to sing with the Academy of Music at Marseilles. (What a career change!) She might not have had any professional training but she had a photographic memory and learned the parts too quickly to question. Maupin shone on stage and became one of the leading singers in French opera, playing all sorts of lead roles – male and female alike. A real hit with the audiences, Maupin's androgyny and talent enthralled the crowds but her temper offstage got her co-stars in a tizz. You can *sort of see why* when you dig a little deeper and learn she was sleeping with half of them, fighting with the other half and stealing a load of men's wives. In 1695, she had to leave the company for a time to let stuff thaw out after she openly made out with a woman at a ball and was challenged to duels by three different guys. She owned all of their asses. Well, to tell you the truth (and nobody likes *fake news*), she killed the lot of 'em.

I could write a whole other book about the relationships and sexual exploits of Maupin but there were so many I fear it could end up becoming my life's work. The headlines, however, would certainly include her seduction and passionate affair with a man she left for dead after he belittled her in the street and *oh, I don't know*, probably the time she DEBAUCHED A NUN. *Stay up for this one . . .* Maupin fell bum over noddle for a young theatregoer who used to watch her from the priciest box at the opera with her parents. She pursued her, despite the girl's queer-bashing parents shutting it down. Nevertheless, our renegade outlaw turned opera superstar persisted. Maupin would try it on and turn up at her door, dressed as a man, shouting the girl's name. Eventually, the parents went doolally and sent their daughter to a nunnery. They clearly didn't know who they were dealing with though. Maupin took Holy Orders just so that she could sneak into the convent. She put THE DEAD BODY OF ANOTHER NUN in her boo's bed and broke her out of there, setting fire to the whole place on her way. Maupin was charged with kidnapping, body snatching, arson, and failing to show up to court. She escaped the 'death by fire' sentence (charged to her as a 'monsieur') because she was untouchable, because she was *Mademoiselle frikkin' MAUPIN!*

Duels, murders, convent arson, escapes, love affairs, theatre, fame . . . Maupin certainly made the most of life. I could go on and tell you about the time she rode across Spain with a band of robbers, or her affairs with German royals, or her on and off alcoholism, or her suicide attempt after a love rejection – but for all the Maupin stories, we'd be here all day. She was a lover and a fighter (sometimes both at the same time) and she found and utilised the agency posing as a man allowed her. Ironically (after all of her nun fun), she wound up taking refuge in a convent and died at only thirty-three years of age. It is thought that Maupin's body was cast upon a dump because she was an actor and they didn't get to be buried on consecrated ground. Let's all start a campaign to get Maupin her own statue, her own town, her own theme park . . . I think you'll agree she deserves a legacy as outlandish as her life.

ULRIKA ELEONORA STÅLHAMMAR (1683–1733)

THE SWEDISH CORPORAL PUT ON TRIAL FOR MARRYING A WOMAN

Childhood was pretty cruisy for Ulrika. She was raised in a manor in Stensjö on the South Swedish highlands and born to aristocratic parents. Her upbringing was privileged although she probably never got a second to check it because she had seven siblings, five of whom were sisters. The house was busier than a mosquito on a nudist beach. Ulrika spent her adolescence outdoors – riding horses, hunting and shooting while her sisters stayed inside and embroidered. She was fresh to death and vivacious. Ulrika's friends and family used to joke that it was a shame she was not born a male and how unlucky she was to be female. I'm not sure if that was a 'funny ha-ha' or a 'funny HA-HA' joke but either way it would require canned laughter to land.

Ulrika's dad was a very successful and respected lieutenant-colonel but a train wreck when it came to personal finances. In 1711, he died, leaving his family destitute. Turns out *Noblewoman to Needy* is nowhere near as genial as *Rags to Riches*. And so in need were the Stålhammars that they had to beg, steal, borrow and marry people 'beneath them' to stay afloat. Her sisters were eloping with toads but it was a long time before an arranged match was found for Ulrika. Women who were 'past their prime' and enjoyed 'male' pursuits were clearly unpopular with the Swedish suitors back then. Nobody was prepared to woo someone only breaths away from their last and Ulrika was *nearly thirty, for Gawd's sake!* Her absolutely *wacky* levels of 'unattractiveness' were a blessing for Ulrika, who was biding her time and secretly applying for a passport. (A passport *outta there!*) Refusing to accept second best (or, let's face it, a life as depressing as pigeons eating puke), Ulrika raided her dad's wardrobe, stole a horse and headed for the hills. Breeched up, bright-eyed and bushy-tailed, Ulrika renamed herself Vilhelm (which is basically 'William', if you aren't Scandi) and set her sights on the big time. If you've ever tried to get a job when you haven't already had a job, you'll understand the chicken-and-egg dramas Ulrika faced. Not only was her CV barren, Vilhelm had neither contacts nor two kronor to rub together. Perhaps the 'good breeding' or the plum in her mouth were her saviour, because somehow Ulrika started to get odds-and-sods jobs. (S)he worked as a footman, a waiter and general dogsbody for fancy-pants people up and down the country, finally settling back in the south. But she wasn't planning on peasant-ing forever; all the while she was polishing floors, she was fantasising about her days galloping through fields, firing muskets. Once again, Ulrika was scheming and dreaming her escape.

Having racked up enough reputable character references and recommendations, Ulrika was able to apply for her number one job in the artillery regiment in the city of Kalmar. Enlisting in the army as an artillerist meant Ulrika could pursue her ultimate hobby – shooting stuff. And in this role, her pistols were upgraded to *cannons*. Sweden was a decade into the Great Northern War at the time and Ulrika would go on to serve as Vilhelm for the next thirteen years. Nobody suspected Villy (although the other soldiers did reportedly find it an iota unusual that he refused to sleep in the barracks and instead spent part of 'his' wage on checking in to nearby sleeping establishments to avoid having to be anywhere near them). In October 1715, Ulrika was promoted to corporal, a role that she strolled into without a fight or the need to 'prove' herself. She didn't even have to fisticuff for equal pay because nobody knew she was a woman.

Work upgrades may have been milk and cookies but Ulrika was lonely. The work/life balance scales were anchored down by her corporal-ing and she was scouting for a partner to tip it back the other way. Enter Maria Lönnman . . .

Maria was a local maid who Ulrika had caught serious feelings for. She didn't mess about either – in 1716, on New Year's Eve (*prototypal* proposal o'clock), Ulrika popped the question. They married quickly. Ulrika had got her girl but there was the small issue of Maria supposedly not knowing that her husband was, in fact, *her wife*. If you're wondering about sexy time then fear not – Vilhelm pretended to be impotent. It is also thought Maria had been violently sexually assaulted previously and so the most getting jiggy with it that went down was spooning like Pringles and 'laying upon each other's arms' (did somebody say *pins and needles?*). Later, Maria would vehemently deny knowing anything of her spouse's true sex but she certainly would once Ulrika's sister, Elisabet Katarina, and the long arm of the law got involved. Word had travelled through the Swedish grapevine that Ulrika had got hitched and *eight years later* Elisabet wrote to her describing how her being gay and cross-dressing was a 'sin against the will of God'. It was clear she was about to cause a stench. The current law and religious regime made Ulrika's marriage a crime punishable by death, and as such she had to leave her job immediately and seek support. Writing to her wealthy aunt, Sofia Drake, Ulrika begged for her help and Sofia begrudgingly gave it for the sake of the Stålhammar name. Ulrika was sent to live with relatives in the countryside in Värmland and ordered to start wearing women's clothing again. Maria became a maid and housekeeper at the aunt's mansion. Sofia made darn sure the duo were separated during this time and refused to let them communicate.

From her 'rehab' and as rumours were spreading, Ulrika was forced to write a letter of confession to the Swedish government, asking for pardon. Within days, Ulrika was being inspected by the courts and it was decided that she was most definitely a woman, despite being 'unusually flat-chested' (a rather unnecessary trial note that has withstood the test of time). The other reports document the most distressing court hearing, which basically witnessed Ulrika and Maria pour their hearts out over each other. All they wanted was to 'live and die' together. Despite the strength of their love, Stålhammar was charged with having 'violated the order of God' by 'cross-dressing, making a mockery of marriage' and for having married a member of the same sex. They were acquitted from the charge of homosexuality because the jury believed the testimonies about their sexless marriage. Weirdly, there were very few laws against homosexuality but mainly because people were scared that if they spoke about it too much in public, everyone would rush out and line up for 'gay sex'. And petrified they should have been! You know how the gays like to recruit! It's all anyone's in it for aside from waiting for the phase to pass and prepping for eternal damnation! *Badum tish . . .*

Sweeping the obvious under the carpet (no rug jokes please), the court decided Ulrika and Maria's love was 'of the purest, most spiritual kind, a union of virtue'. If this wasn't unbelievable enough, they also escaped the death sentence. Instead, Ulrika was charged with a month's imprisonment on bread and water alone and Maria to the same for two weeks. Their sentences ended up being reduced but heart-smashingly the pair were later forced to live apart once more. The love notes exchanged between them, until Ulrika passed away, were supposedly enough to make you snot your way through a *man*size box of Kleenex. Ulrika has become a hero in Sweden, especially with the LGBTQ+ community. There's no way of knowing which letter she most identified with, but we do know there was more love between her and Maria than a four-disc power ballad CD collection.

FLORENCE 'PANCHO' BARNES

DOROTHY LAWRENCE

SOMME 5K

HANNAH SNELL

ISABELLE EBERHARDT

MARY READ (1685–1721)

THE FEROCIOUS FEMALE PIRATE WHO FOOLED AND DUELLED FOR A LIVING

From her birth in London, Mary was disguised as her dead half-brother and brought up as a boy. Mary's mum had an affair after her husband became lost at sea and to cover up the illegitimate result (Mary) she raised her as her deceased son so as to continue receiving maintenance money from the legitimate in-laws (her only means of survival). The mother is known only as a 'young and airy widow' and funnily enough, we have nought more to go on apart from that *charming* description and the knowledge that she was shillingless. Mary was fundamentally her benefits fraud cash cow and it meant that as soon as she was able, she was sent to work to top up the funds. As a young *dude*, the world of work was Mary's oyster gorged seafood platter. By thirteen, she was hired as a footman for a loaded Frenchwoman and even though she was now making it rain shillings, she was bored. It may have been a winner financially but emotionally it was excruciating for Mary. She had the wanderlust itch and got her first scratch after running away from her job and finding a little earner on a boat. Mary's sea legs were soon shipshape. Much like your mum's downstairs bathroom, she got the feels for all things nautical.

Mary's ship work must have been a gig economy type deal because she was looking for the next position before long. Happily for Mary, she was still living as a 'he' so she swanned on in to the British army, ready to rumble as a soldier. Mary took to fighting like a sea monkey to water and powdered algae. It would also be the job through which she met the love of her life. While fighting at Flanders, she caught Cupid's bow for a Flemish soldier. Mr Lover Lover (let's call him 'Shaggy' for jokes) clearly shared her affections but was friend-zoning Mary, believing her to be a man. Shaggy couldn't allow himself to be gay – that would be *bombastic*! However, the pair became inseparable; they often shared a tent and Mary would volunteer for extra battles to stay close to the man she was willing to die for. Thankfully, she didn't have to as they got out of the army together a year later. After revealing her true sex to Shaggy, word spread among the ranks and the couple decided to marry and leave the army. It was the wedding of the year. The church was packed to the rafters with curious comrades who all came bearing monetary gifts for the newlyweds. Shaggy and Mary had enough cash to be discharged without struggle (and they didn't even have to put that 'asking for money instead of pots and pans' poem in the invite!). The couple settled in the Netherlands and opened an inn called The Three Horseshoes but, meanwhile, The Four Horsemen were on their way for Shaggy. The honeymoon period was cut dismally short when Mary's husband died unexpectedly. Preferring not to starve, Mary threw her boys' clothes back on, deciding to leave the rat-race restaurant trade for something more hair-raising. Mary was ready to jump ship. *Literally.*

Mary boarded a boat bound for the West Indies with a plan to make a new living, find solace in the glorious Caribbean sun and get wavy on rum punch. (I made that last bit up.) Taking to the seas during the golden age of piracy, it wasn't long before her ship was hijacked by a band of sea rovers. Mary was pressed into pirating by the crew and, despite at one point being given the opportunity for freedom, our thrill seeker chose to stick at it. Mary was quite the bloodthirsty buccaneer. When her pirate career was in full swing, she eventually came into the service of Captain Rackham (or the infamous 'Calico Jack') who tore it up all around Cuba and the Bahamas. It was in Jack's gang that Mary met the cheese to her macaroni, the equally acclaimed she-pirate masquerading as a he-pirate, Anne Bonny. Mary and Anne always get lumped together in the history books and as such have got sort of smushed together. It's about time each woman was allowed her own spotlight and so the next chapter is reserved exclusively for Anne Bonny. Most accounts written about the women unsurprisingly tend to focus on their alleged love affair. The evidence, however, is decidedly slim pickings and as such I'll give you the headlines (if lesbian pirate fan fiction is your thing, I'm sure you can fill your buckled boots in all sorts of corners of the worldwide web). So, Calico and Anne were an item but Anne was hot for Mary and Calico got jealous and threatened to slit Mary's throat. Anne told Jack that Mary was a woman and all was forgiven because suddenly she was *no longer a threat*. The End.

Mary was mad for it as a pirate. She was always the first to draw her sword and it got her into all sorts of tush-clenching scrapes. A lover we know for sure she had on board was a carpenter they had captured and forced to work for the crew (not the best start to a relationship). He got into a fracas with a fellow shipmate and (according to ye olden pyrate laws) they had to fight to the death on land. Knowing her boyfriend was likely to lose, Mary took charge of the situation and instead fought off the illustrious cutthroat by cutting his *actual* throat. Of all the scuffles, the crème de la crème ('à la Edgar!' for anyone fortunate enough to remember every word to *The Aristocats*) came in the summer of 1720, when Mary and her crewmates commandeered a 12-ton sloop on New Providence Island. The hijackers were caught by the island's governors and Jack wanted to surrender but Mary refused, instead firing willy-nilly, ordering her crewmates to come out and fight like men. It caused a mass brawl that would ultimately overwhelm them. The pirates were taken to Jamaica for trial and Mary escaped execution by 'pleading the belly' (she was pregnant), although she later died not long after being imprisoned. Asked by the judge what pleasure she could find by a life continually in danger, with risk of death by fire, sword or hanging, Mary's reply was that she thought it 'no great Hardship, for, were it not for that, every cowardly Fellow would turn Pyrate, and so infest the Seas, that Men of Courage must starve'. Mary chose piracy, she chose to support herself, she chose to prosper, she chose to thrive, she chose to survive. She started from the bottom – now she's in a book about top women!

ANNE BONNY
(AROUND 1697–1782)

THE IRISH PIRATE WHO PREFERRED
PANTALOONS AND PISTOLS TO PETTICOATS
AND PURSES

After that Mary whirlwind, this could feel like 'the difficult second album', but believe you me (there's never any need to crowbar 'you' in, is there?), Anne Bonny whipped it up like a Taz tornado too. Born in Kinsale, Ireland, our flame-haired hero(ine) had a childhood as equally fruitloop as Mary's. (You may have noticed I've purposely refrained from boring on about anyone's appearance until now as these women are all *so much* more than pretty faces, but for the sake of *true intersectionality*, redheads should *surely* get a mention? They're a dying breed after all! *#SaveTheGinges*.) Anne's dad, William Cormac, was a well-to-do attorney and he had an affair with his maid, Peg, who fell pregnant with Anne. (In many accounts, Peg is also called Mary but I one hundred per cent prefer Peg; it's more in keeping with our pirate themes.) William and Peg decided to continue their relationship but William's wife got her own back, making William's adultery public and causing a right hullabaloo, resulting in the loss of his reputation in Ireland. Anne was still a baby at the time and for some unexplained reason (with undertones and whisperings of future planned trickery and deceit), William decided to change Anne's name to 'Andy', later pretending she was a lawyer's clerk. But at this point the only real plan was to get the funk out of the UK and so the trio headed off for a new life in the New World – Charleston, South Carolina.

Despite sort of starting again from scratch, it wasn't long before Anne's dad made another mint and bought an enormous plantation over there. As she grew up, Anne was made to take care of the house and grounds but she had bigger fish to fry – whale-shark-sized, in fact. There might not have been much of a game plan in place but she was channelling a lot of rage. Poor old Peg died of typhoid fever when Anne was around ten and she seemed to build in anger every day in the aftermath. By twelve, she had a temper that would put an iPad-deprived toddler to the test and a newfound violence that was leaving anyone who got in her way half dead. One man came on to her and she had him hospitalised for months (that's one way to get rid of the harassers, I suppose . . .). At fourteen, Anne met and married a guy she didn't want to merk, a sailor named James Bonny. It's hard to say what attracted the impoverished Jimmy B to the heiress daughter of one of the wealthiest men in town, or the rebellious Anne to a man so 'lowly' he could make her dad weep. Unfortunately for pound-sign-eyed James, Mr Cormac kicked Anne out the minute he heard of the coupling and completely washed his hands of her. Anne and James upped and left for the Bahamas (as you do) but potentially not before setting fire to the plantation, an inferno that would leave it a teensy pile of ash. *Mimes sitting back and eating popcorn as the drama unfolds*

They settled in Nassau, known as the Republic of Pirates back in the day, and the pair had a lot to do with the comings and goings down by the harrrrrbour. (Had to be done.) But whereas Anne was making friends with the pirates and whiling away the hours in taverns with them over Barbadian beverages, James was snitching on them. Money-grubbing with all his might, he was ratting on the pirates in exchange for cash from the island governor, Woodes Rogers. Their marriage was already rocky but this sent Anne over the edge – she was disgusted with her spineless spouse and decided she was due an upgrade. Before long, her eyes had locked on to a target and it was love at first sight. James was as meek as Captain Hook's Smee and her new man was as hardy as Captain Jack Sparrow. You guessed it, Anne was big time into Calico Jack and the feeling was very much mutual for Rackham. To gauge just how much, picture this – Rackham even offered to BUY Anne from James! This was obviously illegal but common practice in pirate circles (*worse things happen at sea!*). Thankfully (for our sanity) Anne full-blast refused, going looney tunes at Rackham for believing her to be someone who could be bought and sold. He certainly saw Anne as prize pirate booty though (in all manner of the word) – it is said he pursued her much like he would take over a ship, with 'no time wasted, straight alongside, every gun brought to play, and the prize boarded'. (Big for your boots much?) In truth, Rackham was a second-class pirate. He mainly dallied about with small boats and found easy prey. He spent most of his time half-cut and was usually too goose-loose to joust. It would be Anne and our homegirl Mary Read who put Rackham in the history books; without them he would be a mere footnote.

Some doofus men started a bonehead rumour that women were bad luck on boats, so they were rarely allowed onboard. There was no way that Anne was going to stay ashore, leave her love and get FOMO, so instead she grabbed a cutlass and man-pirate uniform and hotfooted it down the jetty. Aboard *The Revenge*, it wasn't long before Anne had got her name on Governor Rogers' 'Most Wanted' list. As Anne and the crew pirated merchant vessels along the coast of Jamaica, Anne became notorious for firing her pistol like barmy and sending foes off the plank. Everyone was very impressed until someone spotted her breasts one evening and went berserk. But Anne went berserk-er, killing the pirate who was whipping everyone up over a couple of mammaries and chucking him into the sea. Once the secret was out, she became known only as

'The Captain's Woman' (please try not to throw this book in the sea). Miserably misogynistic nicknames aside for a moment (forever), as you know, Anne would at least have an ally in Mary and it was about this time the power couple was formed. Whatever happened that fateful day for the crew on the date of their capture, we know that most of the men were too weary after chugging back liquor, and Anne and Mary were the only ones who could hold their rum. (Or perhaps the opposite?) Whichever way, it only gave them more pyre to work together when stuff went south. Anne was supposedly so livid with her *ship*-for-brains crewmates' lack of courage or action that as she was being hauled off, she started to fire at her own men.

At the trial, Sir Nicholas Lawes, the Governor of Jamaica, announced Anne should be 'severally hanged by the neck till you are severally dead'. (We geddit, Nicky, no need to labour the point.) But Anne was pregnant – the perfect get-out-of-hanging card. Three cheers for wombs! Rackham was given special permission to see Anne on his day of execution but she gave him naff all sympathy, simply leaving him to die with the words: 'Had you fought *like* a man, you *need not have been hanged like a dog*.' (Let us apply some ice to that *burn*.) Anne's fate is not really known but it is most likely that her dad bailed her out and that was a wrap on her pirating days. Her career may have been short but it was big-league impactful. She could have lived and died as a scullery maid but instead she has lived on as a sensation. By hook or by crook, Anne Bonny did whatever she wanny.

MARY EAST
(APPROX. 1715–1780)

THE LOVELIEST LONDON LANDLADY WHO LIVED AS A LANDLORD

Mary East wasn't just the neighbour with secrets unknown; her life story can only be pieced together through a baby's handful of accounts and police records. Ask a Magic 8 Ball about Mary's childhood and it would tell you to 'Ask again later'. Mary's *teenage* years, however, are crystal ball clear and we know that by sixteen, she had already suffered so much man dramedy she had given up on dating them altogether. Mary had been courting (old-fashioned dating that wasn't based entirely on the mutual convenience of a lustful swipe) but she had been courting some right sorts. After a particularly shambolic highwayman and badman boyfriend, a guy who disrespected her and the law, she decided enough was enough. Mary didn't need to find a way out because, like many highwaymen then, he was arrested, tried and hanged for his crimes. After all the rigmarole and heartbreak, Mary swore she would remain single forever but she spoke too soon. Before long, a human of the *lady persuasion* caught her eye in the neighbourhood. History has regrettably scribbled out her name so I am prepared to get teed-up on power here and come up with one for us. *Thinks about the world's most influential gay women before remembering that, according to the media, there's an obvious, esteemed leader* And so, drumroll please . . . henceforth Mary's unnamed crush shall go by the name *Ellen DeGeneres*! Like Mary, Ellen never wanted to be with a man again because *reasons*. She was seventeen, as chipper as a deep-fried potato, ready for adventure and, as luck would have it, into Mary too.

A same-sex shack-up in those days was about as easy as Sudoku for someone with dyscalculia (not a prayer). The pair needed a plan and so '. . . after consulting on the best method of proceeding, they agreed that one should put on man's apparel, and that they would live as man and wife in some part where they were not known'. The decision as to which of them should live as a man came down to the flip of a coin (halfpenny), an overlooked method, I believe, much more trustworthy than Rock, Paper, Scissors. The lot fell on Mary and so it was settled – she would transform herself into a man. It is also possible that she always wanted to take on the male identity and bygone times have devised the penny bit to keep it all heteronormative and merry. Anyhoo, the pair had about thirty quid between them and they used some to buy clothes for Mary's new personality, 'Mr James Howe', and the remainder to Thelma and Louise on out of there (the running away, not the driving off a cliff bit). Their only plan was to be a success in love and business together and they found their starter whistle when they happened upon a pub to let in Epping. Ellen and James Howe became the new landlady and lord of the boozer, which had more locals than Moe's Tavern, and they wiggled right on in to the heart of the community. Everyone loved Mr and Mrs Howe! Apart from one young tippler who caused a bit of a fray in the bar one night and messed up 'James's' hand. Mary took the ruffian to court and received £500 in compensation. With their payout, Mary and Ellen decided to go where the grass was greener and the locals less aggy. They took on a new pub in the Limehouse area (known as 'Limehouse Hole' in those days but I purposefully left that out because it doesn't conjure that plush-and-promised-land mise en scène quite as well). Over the next three decades Mary and Ellen, cohabiting as 'man' and wife, ran a succession of celebrated watering holes across East London. Their final and favourite was The White Horse in Poplar, on the corner of Poplar High Street and Saltwell Street, where 'James Howe' is recorded as the landlord in 1745.

The Howes were good at the pub game. The White Horse made their game even stronger as it was in a very profitable position, being nearby the docks. Bram Stoker (the *Dracula* author) wrote a book called *Famous Imposters* and in it he describes how the couple 'throve exceedingly' during this time. Mary particularly (probably because she had far more agency as James) was very respected within the local community and even became a churchwarden. They lived in good credit and despite doing more masters of the public house swaying and drink clinking than a *Les Misérables* reprise, they managed to keep their private life private: 'It is remarkable that it has never been observed that they ever drest a joint of meat in their whole lives, nor ever had any meetings or the like at their house. They never kept either maid or boy, but Mary East, the late James How, always used to draw beer, serve, fetch in and carry out pots always herself, so peculiar were they in each particular.' I'm not sure what the meat or pot carrying was all about but perhaps, in light of the reveal that James was a female, the fact she was doing all these 'boy jobs' caused all manner of good griefery. I imagine she even OPENED JARS!

Whenever people are doing well, some fun-sponge or other tries to suck the elation from the situation. In Mary and Ellen's case, such a parade-rainer was a rather salty woman from Garlick Hill, known only as 'Mrs B'. Mary had known Mrs B previously: she was an acquaintance who saw through the James disguise and recognised Mary when they saw each other again in the late 1750s. Mrs B 'thought this a good scheme to build a project on' and began a tireless blackmail campaign against the couple, threatening them with exposure if she didn't get her cash requests. Over the years the threats and demands increased. I must solemnly announce at this point that Ellen passed away ahead of her partner and Mary was left to deal with the mean mugging Mrs B on her own. Swooping in on her while she was at her lowest, Mrs B sent two henchmen for Mary who pretended they worked for magistrate Justice John Fielding and feigned her arrest for a 'robbery'. As a community pillar, Mary knew she could rely on the kindness of her neighbours and she was forced to reveal her true sex, for the first time in over thirty years, to a local pawnbroker as she was being pulled out of her pub: 'I am really a woman, but innocent of their charge!' With the help of this confidante, Mary escaped the chumps and managed to switch it up so that *she took Mrs B to court* in Whitechapel. Hell hath no fury like a woman forced to masquerade as a man for thirty-plus years of her life so she could enjoy said life and escape scrubs like Mrs B . . . Mary attended court back in her Mary clothes, causing 'great diversion to all', and after getting at least a little bit of justice (we know that one of the accused was imprisoned), she disappeared to live the rest of her time as a woman. When Mary died she left all she had earned to her family, friends and the poor of Poplar. (*Who's cutting onions?*)

All that remains of The White Horse today is a lone white horse statue on top of a pillar on the site of the pub, which was demolished in 2003. I hope the residents of the Whitehorse apartments that overlook it know of its history, of the feats accomplished there by women who were simply trying to love each other and live their lives peacefully. Information about Mary East and her lover has been in as short supply as Mrs B's compassion, but Mary's purity of heart is always referred to. A *London Chronicle* article from August 1766, after the Mrs B trial, reported Mary's plans for a life without Ellen: 'After her house is lett or sold, and her affairs settled, she intends [on] retiring into another part to enjoy with quiet and pleasure that fortune she acquired by fair and honest means, and with an unblemished character.' Mary loved and lived honourably and her love for Ellen DeGeneres was as glorious as that first sip of beer on a hot day. Let's raise a glass to love.

CATHARINE VIZZANI
(1718–1743)

THE ITALIAN VICAR'S SERVANT WHO DIED FOR HER LOVE OF WOMEN

Catharine or 'Catterina' Vizzani may have a name reminiscent of a cocktail you'd pay £18 for and instantly regret when it invariably tasted like Listerine and disappointment, but her life was far from anticlimactic. Born in Rome, into a carpenter's family, we know little of her upbringing but we do know that she was quite the amorous teenager. By fourteen, she had certainly decided that it was the female of the species she was after and go after them she did. Catharine was about as subtle with her sexuality as a forehead tattoo: 'She was reserved and shy towards young Men, but would be continually romping with her own Sex, and some she caressed with all the Eagerness and Transport of a Male Lover.' (I'm sure you Sherlocks don't need these interjections by now but that description, comparing her exemplary love-making to that of a man it was so steamy, was, *of course*, penned by a *male* human.) The only thing Cat may have chosen to keep on the down low was the reported number of notches on her apparently termite-whittled-looking bedpost. 'Female sodomy' was punishable by death in Italy at this time and so she had to find ways to live and love as she pleased, and (you must have noticed a trending theme by this point) Catharine found she could carry on no worries *dressed as a man*.

It was around this age that Catharine also decided she wanted to settle down (nobody could blame Snapchat for her 'growing up too soon' in 1732); Catharine had found 'the one'. The woman of her dreams, Margaret, was a whiz with her fingers and yes, I will be pressing charges for the damages sustained after I fall over your minds in the gutter. Margaret was big into her arts and crafts and Catharine visited her 'under the pretense of learning Embroidery' – an excuse I love so much I'm not even going to ruin it with a quip. But their (air quotes) embroidery time was not time enough for the pair to practise what they truly desired. Knowing her butt would be in a sling if she was out and proud about Margaret, Catharine had to wait until the dead of night to make her moves. Like Romeo at the balcony in the Capulets' orchard, Catharine would visit Margaret's window in her ruffled shirt and waistcoat; the *Juliet & Juliet* scenes that followed were even more poetic and fairy tale. Catharine would stay until the sun started to peep, whispering sweet nothings that were everything to her love. This went on every night without fail for nearly two years until Margaret's dad found out and got an entire beehive in his bonnet about their relationship, threatening to report Catharine to the governor of the city and the courts (spoilsport). Absconding pretty swiftish, the heartbroken Catharine knew she would never again see her best girl and she was mad as toast. That first cut is always the deepest and Catharine wondered how she would ever recover. She decided she needed a hasty POA. If she wanted to get out alive and if she was ever going to find love again, she would have to keep up her male disguise. 'Giovanni Bordoni' was born.

'Giovanni' left for the ancient city of Viterbo (well, it's ancient now; it was still a young whippersnapper back then). Unfortunately, Catharine hadn't got that much further with her plan and it wasn't long before she was living at the 'bottom of her purse', the eighteenth-century equivalent to getting a text from your bank. Out of ideas,

Catharine returned to Rome where (s)he took refuge in the Church of Santa Maria, in the Trastevere neighbourhood. There she met a canon named Giuseppe Lancisi – if you're on board with my drinks analogies (and why wouldn't you be), there's no doubt he'd be a *cheeky little aperitif.* Giuseppe took pity on 'the lad' and offered him protection and work as a vicar's servant in the province of Perugia, an invitation that Catharine left no time to RSVP YES to. At first, this was a match made in holy heaven – Giovanni was respected as an excellent worker and the vicar was most impressed with his ability to do everything and anything, even trim his beard for him. Giovanni may have been teacher's pet but Catharine was secretly hating her life. It felt as though she was in the clink, not the church, she missed her heydays and started to rebel. The vicar didn't have a sense of humour and if he did it would most likely have been described as 'alternative'. He began to get very neggy with Giovanni and eventually lost it.

The cool kids of Perugia reckoned Giovanni was a professional womaniser and the best for miles. Reports of our reputed seducer hit the vicar's ears and he certainly wasn't patting him on the back, like all the other men, for his escapades. He wrote to Giuseppe, describing how Giovanni was 'incessantly following the Wenches, and being so barefaced and insatiable in (his) Amours'. In turn, the canon wrote to Catharine's parents, who disclosed her true identity to Giuseppe. Her old man replied to say 'this same Child of mine, whose Irregularities have made such a Noise, is no Male, but as truly, in all Respects, a Female, as the Woman who bore her . . .' The canon chose to keep Catharine's secret because he was a snazzy man, but things were getting iffy for 'Giovanni', so Cat decided to leave the vicar and headed for Montepulciano, where she found work as a footman. *And a new girl . . .*

Maria was the niece of the local minister and Catharine liked her enough to focus her attentions solely on pursuing her hand in marriage. A passionate love affair began and the pair were more into each other than Britney and Justin circa 1999. In 1743, she convinced Maria to run away together and marry her in Rome. This would need to stay a secret if they were ever to be free but Maria confided in her sister (who naturally told the whole town). The minister sent his chaplain and two servants to track them down, with the promise of a hefty fee if they captured Giovanni and returned Maria safely. The couple got off to a flying start, leaving earlier than planned because they were too love drunk and excitable to sleep, but they stopped in Lucca and were intercepted. During an attempt to surrender, Giovanni was fatally wounded, shot with a musket ball in the left thigh, four inches above the knee (*Run off and elope with your lover*, they said! *It'll be gorgeous and entirely risk free*, they said!)

On her deathbed Catharine was forced to remove the 'leathern contrivance' fastened just below her abdomen (i.e. her fake 'Little Giovanni'), and hide it under her pillow. Before she passed away she told a nun she was a woman and a virgin, ensuring that she would be buried and honoured as such. Remember, sex with women didn't count in their minds – as long as that hymen was intact all the peen-centrics were happy and Catharine could have a first-class funeral. After her death, she became famous once her biography was released. She was also part of the first scientific study on a female body to 'explain' her sexual orientation. Surgeon and professor Giovanni (Italians can't get enough of that name!) Bianchi dissected Catharine's body in the first English extensive study of 'the lesbian body'. His findings were published in a book with the snappy title: *Breve storia della vita di Catterina Vizzani romana che per ott'anni vesti abito da uomo in qualita di servidore, la quale dopo varj casi essendo in fine stata uccisa fu trovata pulcella nella sezzione del suo cadavero di Giovanni Bianchi professore di Notomi in Siena*. Bianchi was looking for a 'sexual anomaly' and *obviously* found nowt. It seems Catharine's father was the only one who understood that Catharine was born that way and that her 'constitution' could not be 'repressed'.

Although she might have been labelled a 'deviant invert' for her sexuality, Catharine still managed to throw 'appropriate female behaviour' out of the window. The Ts&Cs for women in eighteenth-century Italy may have only allowed her acceptance once she did a switcheroo from 'feminine' to 'masculine' behaviour, but she was in control and didn't care about breaking the rules. Catharine went so far against the grain she must have had splinters for days.

MARGARET 'PEG' WOFFINGTON (1720–1760)

THE IRISH ACTRESS WHO CROSS-DRESSED FOR WORK AND PLEASURE

Peg was one of the most famous actors in Georgian theatre and her life was equally as theatrical. (*Oh no it wasn't. Oh yes it was!*) She may never have done panto but the various existing and exaggerated accounts of her life make it sound like one. And so, 'Take your seats! Today's performance of *The Life and Times of Margaret 'Peg' Woffington* is about to start!' Peg has become somewhat of a legend in Ireland and as such her life story sounds like the result of a particularly lengthy game of Chinese Whispers or the Telephone Game, played in a meet-up group for persons hard of hearing. I'm happy to be the person at the end of this chain and I'm proud to hereby serve up the most captivating plot points. There's no interval, so stock up on snacks now.

Peg and her sister were raised by a single mum in Dublin; her dad was thought to be a journeyman bricklayer who died falling off a ladder. (Surely workplace ladder hazard awareness should have been *day one* of bricklayer school?) The family were desperate for dosh and Peg's mum had her working from when she was womb-fresh. An illustrious show person of the day known as Madame Violante had a much-publicised acrobatic act that essentially involved her crossing a tightrope walk with baskets of babies swinging off her feet. Peg was thought to be one of those babies. She was making money for her mother and sister before she could even remember and went on to continue to support them in a time when independent women weren't allowed to exist. Peg grafted like a good'un and when she was a bit older she did so in the posh part of the city, College Green, where she sold watercress (*beats crack!*). The impoverished Peg was a hit with the aristocrats in the area, who always came out to the streets to buy from her when they heard her cries of 'fine young salad for ha'penny!'. Sometimes Peg would even sing for her supper. She was a tough nut; she knew how to handle herself but also how to wrap the local Daddy Warbucks around her watercressy little finger. When she was around twelve years of age she bumped into Madame Violante again, who noticed a twinkle in Peg's eye. Violante was scouting for young talent and Peg was going to be the Leona Lewis to her Simon Cowell. She cast her on the spot as Polly Peachum in *The Beggar's Opera*; Peg was to join Violante as an apprentice in her company of juvenile players. It's people like Peg and stories like this that make cracking the acting industry look like a doddle. I blame her wholly for all the actors that have to endure the 'why don't you just write to Downton Abbey?' question from their Great Uncle Nobody at every family party.

Peg's Polly triumphed in the spotlight. Playwright Charles Coffey came to watch her perform and was enamoured by Peg from the moment she stepped out of the wings. He offered her work at Dublin's brand-new playhouse on Smock Alley, where she started out shadowing the players, learning her craft and dancing for the audience in the intervals. In the classic understudy twist, the actress playing Ophelia in a production of *Hamlet* got sick one night but Peg knew all the lines off by heart. She begged her way into her costume and into the lead role. Apart from a gap of around two to three years where we don't really know what Peg was up to (probably flogging double glazing in a call centre with all the other out of work actors), her career went from strength to strength. The dates are also questionable as she advertised her age as younger than she was because women aren't allowed to age. (Even now, most of my industry friends have been twenty-five every year for the last five because the industry tells them they have to be and yes, I'm dobbing them in because *seriously, why is this still OK?*) Age aside, our sprightly Peg became a bums-on-seats winner, and audiences loved to see her in action, especially in the comedy parts in which she thrived with her Dublin street-sharpened wit. It is thought that her surname was actually Murphy but she took Woffington as a stage name and it was the name on everyone's lips in theatre land. One of her most celebrated roles was Sir Harry Wilder in George Farquhar's *The Constant Couple*; she played it in breeches and it caused quite a stir at the time. These 'breeches roles' turned out to be Peg's speciality – the audience went wild for their favourite comedy actor playing a man and she would always bring the house down. Cross-dressing in the theatre world has been around since its beginnings because women weren't originally allowed anywhere near a stage and so men played the female parts. When women *finally* wangled their way in, it should seem revolutionary that women were allowed to play men, especially as women are *still* turning to male parts today for the opportunity to play characters with any sort of substance. However, I'm very sorry to have to report that these breeches roles were actually only a hit because the men found it extra erotic to ogle at the women's legs. Cue my screw face stage left.

The green room was often as dramatic as onstage and Peg's love life gave her fans a rollicking good gossip. She was connected by rumour to many men and some of the biggest names of the day, famous actors (such as David Garrick), playwrights, poets, colonels and diplomats. There was only one who Peg had on Bae Watch though – an Irish guy named Taaffe and friend of her co-star, who saw her in *The Constant Couple* and let it be known he was horny for her thereafter. His romantricks worked; Peg left for London with Taaffe in the early summer of

1740, where they set up home in stage land central, Covent Garden. The couple's golden days were, however, as short-lived as the tooth gem craze of the 1990s and Taaffe started triflin' and disappearing for days at a time. He was sniffing out some money (or rather *somebody*) elsewhere. Taaffe was honey-tongued and pinky-promised his life to Peg but was secretly seeing a rich heiress, Miss Dallaway, on the side. When Peg found out she hit the roof, went through the roof and carried on ascending. Peg plotted a plan to get her revenge on the love rat and it involved her new best friend, *breeches*.

With a Narnia-like costume cupboard at her disposal, Peg went to the theatre and picked out a red army officer jacket, a moustache, arranged her hair *en peruke* and headed to Dallaway's. She found the heiress at a ball in Vauxhall where 'he' caught Dallaway's eye and led her in a minuet. Obviously used to playing men, Peg dazzled in the role and the dance (although there's not much to it other than a bit of jigging). Before long Peg had ramped up the flirtation. When Dallaway mentioned she had a sweetheart, Peg made sure she knew he was anything but, asking the heiress if she had heard that Taaffe was infatuated with the famous actress Peg Woffington. Her love rival didn't believe the young officer but Peg had evidence – she showed Dallaway gushing love letters she had saved from the rogue Taffers. 'I see you love him too and I grieve to pain you,' Peg pronounced, making sure Dallaway knew he was a 'worthless fellow' and unworthy of her affection. Dallaway turned as white as a follow spot and fainted flat. It is reported that Peg kissed her forehead with the love of a sister and when she came around, Dallaway thanked Peg for saving her. Peg saved herself too; Taaffe switched on her for losing him a life of money and actually got locked up not long after for robbery. Peg went back to her only true love – the stage. *Bye, boy, bye!*

The show went on and towards the end, even though Peg's health was rapidly declining, she refused to ever let her understudy go on for her. In 1757, while speaking the epilogue as Rosalind in *As You Like It*,

Peg collapsed on stage. It was to be the last time she performed and her final words were 'If I were a woman, I would kiss as many of you as had beards that pleased me', which is from the monologue that begins: 'It is not the fashion to see the lady the epilogue'. It was so fitting to her feminist feats throughout her lifetime, it's *almost as if she planned it*. Peg was self-reliant, talented, provocative and audacious. Get up off your junk! Let's give the lovely Peggy another standing ovation.

MARY HAMILTON
(1721–UNKNOWN)

THE QUACK DOCTOR AND 'FEMALE HUSBAND'

If you look up Mary Hamilton in *The Oxford Dictionary of National Biography*, you'll find the definition 'sexual imposter'. *Face glitch* History hasn't been all that kind to Mary. The accounts of her life are so crazily varied (and on the whole damning) because they are mostly made up. The truth bombs are only really to be found from legal documents and depositions and so, like finding gold at a garage sale among the Princess Diana mugs, ice skates and crochet ducks, I've had to vigorously rummage. Her life is always described as 'notorious' or a 'curious case', but she was more than just a 'case': Mary Hamilton was a stonkingly strong but presumably massively misunderstood radical.

Here's the story. Mary was born in Somerset to Mary (senior) and William Hamilton. Her real father died before she was born and her mother remarried. When she was a toddler the family moved from Somerset to Scotland for no apparent reason (perhaps they preferred teacakes and whisky to scones and scrumpy?). Mary was an only child but instead of smothering her with love and gifting trips to Disneyland to save her from being sad, her parents stifled her with their strict rules and religious beliefs to 'save her soul'. It was a recipe for rebellion but

Mary didn't get a septum piercing, dye her hair green or hotbox her bedroom; she knew she was different and she needed to free herself from her family to literally be free. There was *something about Mary* (wink wink, nudge nudge) and at fourteen she ran away to find herself. Mary Houdini'ed her way out of the gender-constraint straitjacket she had been battling, dressed herself as the more liberated sex and made her way back to England, or more specifically, Northumberland. As *money makes the world go round* (and quite frequently grinds it to a hellish halt), Mary needed to find a way of bagging some. Mary Hamilton, single, young, uneducated *female* would have starved but *Charles Hamilton*, single, young, uneducated *male* was banqueting on the proceeds of the job 'he' waltzed into overnight. As Charles, Mary found work as an apprentice for two unlicensed doctors, Dr Edward Green and Dr Finey Green (as much as I would have loved the Greens to be a married couple I think we can all categorically, decidedly and darn' tooting agree that they weren't). Quack doctoring was the main movement in Mary's day and much like the cowboy builders of today, they'd show up, invariably make the problem worse and charge you out of your *derrière* for the honour. As it goes, Mary was quite the expert at pretending to be savvy with a stethoscope, syringe and scalpel and excelled at fraudulent medical professionalism. In 1746, she packed it in with the Greens and moved to Wells to set up her own practice as Dr Charles Hamilton.

Mary's new landlady in Wells was a woman named Mary Creed and she had a niece who Mary Hamilton thought was a piece, Mary Price. (There are more Marys in this chapter than at a Roman Catholic Church conference.) Mary Price took a fancy to Charles too. He was quite unlike anyone she had met before – self-assured, charming, and he swore like a montage of *The Osbournes*' best bits (and I imagine he had an intriguingly miscellaneous accent by now too, with all the bobbing about). Mary Hamilton fell hard; (s)he had certainly discovered herself by this point and felt the only way she could plunge fully but keep herself mortal was by continuing as Charles. The lie spiralled and in July 1746, Charles and Mary Price were married. The couple travelled around Somerset for two months (again, no reason given, perhaps they opted for a staycation honeymoon) but along the way they sold phony medicines together. Romantic. During this time, Mary Price found out that she was actually married to Mary Hamilton. The news spread like disease after a quack-doctor-prescribed 'cure' and 'Charles' was arrested. By October of the same year and after a stint in a 'house of corrections', Mary Hamilton faced the judge and jury at the Quarter Sessions court in Taunton. The exact charge on which Mary was to be tried caused the magistrates and media circus some confusion. Perhaps the latter were in town for the *teeny* claim the prosecution threw into the ring that Mary hadn't married one but FOURTEEN women. Well, it was a distraction from the fraud (something she was *definitely* guilty of) at least! Polygamy was much debated – what constituted polygamy and *how on this woman-hating-holleration-earth could it be a crime if it occurred between females?* There was also oodles of confusion about Mary's sex and when she said she had 'entered [her wife's] body many times' everybody assumed she *must* be a man. After much debate, the justices delivered the verdict that 'The he or she prisoner at the bar is an uncommon, notorious cheat, and we, the Court, do sentence her, or him, whichever he or she may be, to be imprisoned six months, and during that time to be whipped in the towns of Taunton, Glastonbury, Wells, and Shepton Mallet.' Sexual and gender ambiguity was clearly something the authorities were so ready to shove back into the closet that they were ambiguous with their own official, legal statement. It's a shame they weren't able to be as flippant as the he/she with the guilty/not-guilty decision.

Mary's case hit all the headlines from the *Bath Journal* to the *Daily Advertiser*, the *Ipswich Journal* to the *St James Evening Post*. Once in the papers, the story spun out of all recognition and Mary and her life story were suddenly catapulted and caricatured in people's imaginations, cemented as 'very gay, with periwig, ruffles and breeches'. (I'm pretty certain she wasn't happy in prison but she was *prettttty* gay and as for the overblown periwig, they may as well have written that she had a fruit bowl on her head and blew glitter through the bars.) Mary became a persecuted sexual outlaw and her freedom was dead but her new-fangled story lived on through press speculation, gossip and writer Henry Fielding's fictionalised account, *The Female Husband*. So successful was the book, it was later also republished as *The surprising adventures of a female husband! : containing the whimsical amours, curious incidents, and diabolical tricks, of Miss M. Hamilton, alias Mr G. Hamilton, alias Minister Bentley, Mr O'Keefe, alias Mrs Knight, the midwife, &c. who married three wives, and lived with each some time undiscovered: for which acts she was tried at the summer sessions, in the county of Somerset, in the year 1752, found guilty, and whipped four several times, in four market towns, and afterwards imprisoned six months.* Both stories were pamphlets, sensationalised and streamlined, even if the titles weren't.

Fielding made out he'd met Mary and got the story from her verbatim but that was quite obviously balderdash. Henry was out to make a quick buck – and he did, the work was as notorious as nits on a playground. Fielding had a bit of a history of getting hot under the collar in his work about cross-dressing women, worrying about unruly 'modern' females rebelling and revolting. But he was clearly conflicted about Mary – he made her both the villain and the hero, so there must have been something about her androgyny that had him torn. He essentially turned Mary Hamilton's tale into a scandalous lesbian romp with ludicrously 'symbolic' story points such as changing Mary's hometown to The Isle of MAN. (Hands up if you think Fielding felt threatened by all this *unruliness*!) Mary Hamilton was misrepresented, misconceived and although there is no doubt she was mistaken in some of her felonious activity, she lived in a time that gave her scarcity of choice.

HANNAH SNELL (1723–1792)

THE SEX-SWAPPING SEA SOLDIER AND CELEBRITY

The life of Hannah Snell has been so well documented (or badly documented, depending on how you look at it) that I've had to seriously dig deep to deliver you this masterful chapter of dreams. There are many romanticised or confused accounts changing her story over time and as such there has never really been a biography on which you could rely – UNTIL NOW. As a fellow West Midlands Massive associate (Hannah was from Worcester), I get the feeling she'd be good with me selecting the best bits and sharing them with your eyeballs. And so, *Big Red Book at the ready* Hannah Snell, *This is Your Life* . . .

Hannah's juniority was spent dressing up as a soldier and parading around. (I've never used the word 'juniority' before now but I think I got away with it? I'm a fan of how it sounds, like 'childhood's' trendier twin.) The eighth of nine kids, all of Hannah's brothers served in the army or navy and she looked up to them, imagining one day she too would get to wear suave uniforms and go on adventures. But as a female (*here we go again*) she was already predestined to stay indoors. Even at school, Hannah was taught some of the basics, but apparently writing was not part of that deal; it wasn't seen as essential learning for girls. (Note to editor: Perhaps this book should be printed with a blood pressure warning?) The city of Worcester was then bustling with the clothing trade and Hannah's dad was a hosier and dyer, so clothes-making became another of her hobbies. Dressing up, costumes, the army and navy . . . sit tight for the return of all her juniority pastimes later on in the tale! The gradual decline of the cloth industry in the area eventually left the Snell family purse pinched, and by the time Hannah was seventeen she was fed up of feasting on the scraps of life. She set off to London because, as we all know, *the streets are paved with gold!* (Even if it's the type that turns your skin green.)

Hannah moved in with her sister and brother-in-law in Wapping, on the dockside, where she also met her husband, Dutch sailor James Summs. The seaman floated Hannah's boat at first sight but there was something fishy about James, namely the fact that he transpired to be a gigantic commitment-phobe. When Hannah was twenty-two and seven months pregnant with their first child, James wigged out and sprinted from his responsibilities, abandoning Hannah without even a glance back. *Slow clap for James* As if that wasn't horrific enough, Hannah then lost her daughter, Susannah, when she was only a babe in arms. Rather than invite her friends and family to a pity party, Hannah decided to change her doomed serial and her first priority was to seek revenge on her yellow-bellied husband. Dressing herself in her brother-in-law's suit and nabbing his name, James Gray, Hannah adopted the disguise so she could travel safely and track him down. Falling victim to her own masquerade, Hannah's plan backfired somewhat when she ended up being so convincing she was pressed into the British army. She later discovered that karma had caught up with James Summs and he had been executed for committing murder in Genoa, but Hannah's childhood dreams were coming true and she wasn't ready to say goodbye to James Gray.

In the army of the Duke of Cumberland in the 6th Regiment of Foot, Hannah was a private in the forces of George II and stationed in Carlisle. She put her best *foot* forwards (no more *corny* puns, promise) and at first contributed the only way she really knew how – cooking and mending shirts for her comrades. But Han was out to seize the day and soon learned how to handle weaponry and handle herself. Despite being known these days as 'The Female Soldier', it is her time in the marines that she is famous for. A new recruit in her regiment put her disguise at risk (he was an old acquaintance from Worcester who might have recognised her) and so she had no choice but to move on. It's like those Facebook 'friends' from school who creep out of the woodwork to ruin your day by tagging you in photos from early noughties foam parties and perpetually posting the results of their kid's toilet training/ wack World Book Day costumes . . . but I digress.

In the autumn of 1747, Hannah moved to Portsmouth to join Admiral Boscawen's fleet in the marines and was sent to India on a sloop called *The Swallow*. The conditions on board were gross and the shipmates spent most of their energy avoiding scurvy, hurricanes, beatings and each other. There was no hope of privacy in the ranks; the sailors lived closer than close. Hannah may have been trouser-clad but to fully convince her shipmates she was a 'he', she had to tinkle through a leather-covered horn. That seemed to do the trick (although they did nickname 'James' Miss Molly, a jolly jape about her size and lack of beard). What she lacked in stubble and height she made up for in the mischief she could do with firearms – though she was but little she certainly was FIERCE. In the battle of Devicotta in 1749, India fought against France at Pondicherry. In the trenches, Hannah was shot six times in her right leg, five in her left, and once in the groin. Hannah somehow survived and it is believed she removed the bullets herself, she was so determined to keep her disguise under wraps. She may have also asked a local Indian woman to bring her some salve and lint or bribed a doctor to keep her sex schtum. Whatever the truth, her unlikely survival would have been enough to make Bear Grylls proud.

A few months after the battle, Hannah's unit returned to Portsmouth and once safely back on home turf she decided to gather her besticles, inviting them to a surprise party. In a London pub, Hannah finally got her secret off her bound chest, announcing that *she herself* was the surprise, 'Why, gentlemen, James Gray will cast off his skin like a snake and become a new creature. In a word, gentlemen, I am as much a woman as my mother ever was, and my real name is Hannah Snell . . .' She was whooped, cheered and lifted high into the air, revelling in her overnight fame and prospective fortune. For four and a half years she had been living as a man and now it was time to chase paper. Hannah was her very own PR prodigy; she got herself trending in London and beyond overnight without even a cheep of the blue bird or a hashtag. Within no time at all, copies of her portrait were being sold on every street corner (Instagram *schninstagram*), she was a pap favourite, she had her own sell-out show at New Wells Theatre and a serious number of real-life fans that *actually* followed her. Hannah even sold her story to the London publisher Robert Walker, who got it out there for the eyes of the nation, under the title *The Female Soldier*. The book was forty-six pages (so really more of a leaflet) but it was packed with exclusives and sold like an extra-value meal from a fried chicken shop after the school bell. Capitalising further on her new-found celebrity, Hannah made sure to hit the Duke of Cumberland with a petition for a pension for her services, which he granted without a jot of fuss BECAUSE SHE WAS HANNAH SNELL.

When Hannah retired she *still* refused to put herself in flight mode. Instead, she opened a pub named The Female Warrior in Wapping, married twice more and threw a couple of kids into the mix too. Despite the right colourful life she led, she died in the gloom of the famous lunatic asylum, Bedlam, of an unknown mental illness. Throughout her years Hannah gave custom the side-eye and stuck two fingers up at convention. (Although it's thought she lost a finger during her soldiering days so perhaps she just flicked the one.) The naysayers and her ex-husband can all swivel on it.

MARGARET ANN BULKLEY
(1789–1865)

THE TOP MEDICAL STUDENT TO TOP DOCTOR IN TOP DISGUISE

I could start at the very beginning (a *very good place* to start) but this is a book about women who rewrite the rule books and run the show. To purposefully skew-whiff the system (and my own format, to be fair), this chapter starts with the death of our defiant and disorderly subject to extra highlight their bangarang. Two months after Margaret Ann Bulkley died in July 1865, Elizabeth Garrett Anderson became Britain's first female doctor. This is relevant because I wanted the opportunity to shout out another feminist first but also because Margaret Ann Bulkley had already served as a much-celebrated physician and surgeon in the army for *forty-six years* before Elizabeth graduated. Have a guess as to how she managed to do it . . .

Margaret only lived as a female for approximately the first fourteen years of her life, during her time growing up in an impoverished family in Cork, Ireland. Margaret's mum, Mary-Ann, was the sister of a very well renowned and well-to-do artist of the time, James Barry, and her dad ran the local weigh house (a public building where people, from what I can gather, genuinely just went to weigh stuff). There was a bit of a revolutionary streak in the brood and Margaret's dad, Jeremiah, lost his job for his anti-Catholic beliefs, plummeting them into further poverty and landing himself in a debtors' prison. Margaret, her mother and siblings were well acquainted with the strugglehood. She had a brother, John, and a third sibling, Juliana, who crops up at some point but the details of her life are meagre because it is possible that Juliana was *actually* Margaret's daughter, the result of a rape when she was a very young teenager (when Margaret died, her body was examined and they found signs of her having given birth to a child). But enough of skipping to the end already – Margaret's was a jam-packed life, lived to the max and grasped fully once her female body no longer conditioned her circumstances. You see, Mags *was* the sharpest tool in the shed and her IQ thoroughly surpassed her shoe size. Because of the Bulkleys' power elite connections, Margaret was fortunate enough to have been educated by private tutors and finished her schooling by the time she was fourteen. As a lass, her work prospects were minus nil but her powerful pals believed in Margaret too much to let her talent shrivel up and die. The painter James Barry, General Francisco de Miranda, a Venezuelan radical, and David Steuart Erskine, 11th Earl of Buchan, had concocted a 'conspiracy' (or *bleedin' great master plan*, as I like to call it) to get their brainchild to university to study medicine. (It's not what you know; it's *who* you know . . .) Women weren't even allowed to *look* at an establishment for higher education then but Margaret had academia firmly in her sights.

In 1809 Margaret and her mum set off for Scotland on a Leith smack – a fishing boat, not a description of the drug of choice for the area (having lived in Leith for three years, *pre-gentrification*, I was surprised too). Margaret was only five feet tall and so she wore three-inch-high inserts in her shoes and oversized clothes but she knew appearing 'bigger' wasn't going to be enough to fool anybody – if she wanted to pass as a man, she would need to adopt a certain attitude. She chose 'entitled' and, *not surprisingly whatsoever*, it worked. Armed with a letter of recommendation from Lord Buchan and the two shillings and six-pence needed to matriculate (can you IMAGINE fees that low? By buying this book you have helped me pay back 0.0000001% of my student loan, so thank you for that), Margaret Ann waved goodbye to her mother and her former self and became 'James Barry', the 'nephew' of the famous painter and now first year medical student at the University of Edinburgh. Once in, Margaret studied solidly for three years. For obvious reasons she didn't mingle too much with her classmates and took extra classes to keep busy. James Barry may have known nothing of Freshers Flu, Strawpedoes or Jägerbombs but 'he' memorised all there was to know about chemistry, botany, anatomy, midwifery, philosophy, Greek and whatever extra curricula there were going.

There is no definite record of Margaret ever saying she went on to identify as a man (there are arguably some clues), but from here on in she really never strayed from being 'James'. It is true that Margaret was terrified of being found out – she even kept her cover in all of her correspondence back to family and friends – but equally she seemed to *transform*, as if Margaret never existed. For that reason, I will call her James from now on and if my pronoun switch doth offend we only have the male historians and oppressive gender 'norms' (abnorms) of society to blame for the confusion. James flew through his studies and the only thing about him ever to be questioned was his age rather than his sex. On the front of his final thesis he signed his work James Miranda Steuart Barry (a grateful nod to his patrons and supporters) and added the Greek Menander quote: 'Do not consider my youth, but consider whether I show a man's wisdom.' He stormed his exams and moved back to London to further learn surgery at Guy's and St Thomas' Hospital under the famous surgeon Sir Astley Cooper.

In July 1813, after successfully passing just about all there was to pass, James was commissioned (with a little help from his friends) as a hospital assistant in the British army. He may have been somewhat reliant on the leverage of others to get this far but James had the expertise and pep in his step to go it alone. He started in Chelsea and then joined the Royal Military Hospital in Plymouth, where he was very quickly promoted to assistant surgeon to the forces, a role equivalent to lieutenant. In less than two years, James was working on a posting in Cape Town where he became personal physician to the governor, Lord Charles Henry Somerset, after spectacularly saving his daughter's life. There was no stopping James after this; he climbed all the ladders and shattered all the ceilings. He worked in South Africa for ten years and not only saved people's lives, he made sure that he changed them for the better. James always championed the socially marginalised and made a point of treating the women, children, sex workers, slaves, mentally ill and disabled first. He campaigned for the humanitarian rights of his patients and managed to find time to improve the sanitation and water systems while he was at it. Not to mention performing one of the first known successful Caesarean sections in medical history. The child was named James Barry Munnik in his honour, a name that was so well respected in Cape Town, it was passed down to a later prime minister of the country. By 1827, he was promoted again to head surgeon to the forces and went on to travel to a long list of enviable vacation destinations for work including Trinidad and Tobago, Jamaica, Malta, Corfu, Canada; you name it, he had the T-shirt. His ethics, beliefs, activism and radical actions were revolutionary but they made him a controversial figure. Known for his bull-in-a-china-shop behaviour, James would make sure he got the change he knew the world deserved, no matter how tactless his approach or how many times it got him arrested. He even famously managed to flap the unflappable Florence Nightingale, who called him 'the most hardened creature I ever met' after a ding dong.

In many ways James was distances off the galactic scale ahead of his time. In others, he very much *was* a product of his time – he had to be a he to achieve a smidge and I can't not mention the fact that he had a black slave, Barry, who worked for him in South Africa and stayed with him until the end of his days. He would have worked and fought the good fight up until then if he could but ill health forced him to quit and he died of dysentery in 1865. Sophia Bishop, the charwoman who laid out his body, recognised that James was biologically female and the British army tried to suppress the story for the next hundred years. Although he got his wish to be buried as Dr James, he never received the knighthood anyone else of his reputation would have swiped. *Posthumous knighthoods are definitely a thing, let's make it happen!*

QUQUNOK PATKE (LATE EIGHTEENTH CENTURY – 1837)

THE PROPHESYIN', SEX-SWITCHIN', NATIVE AMERICAN TRIBE CHAMPION

If you thought Ququnok Patke was toilsome to get your teeth around, have a pop at Ququnok's surplus supernumerary of tribe names. Highlights include (but aren't limited to) 'Ko-come-ne Pe-ca', 'Qanqon Kamek Klaula' (Sitting in the Water Grizzly), 'Madame Boisverde', 'One-Standing-Lodge-Pole-Woman', 'Manlike Woman' and the as-it-says-on-the-tin classic, 'Woman Who Carried a Bow and Arrow and Had a Wife'. (But more on that later.)

Ququnok was a Bundosh warrior, born into the indigenous North American Kootenai tribe of the Rocky Mountains, in what is now known as Montana. Think about the most peaceful, zenergy-loving, mindful, anti-fly-swatting person you know and times their tranquillity tenfold – you have the people of the Kootenai. But there's always one bad egg in every *salade niçoise* factory (as the famous saying goes) and Ququnok was more of a disturber than keeper of the peace. As far as historians can tell, Ququnok had a pretty decent and loving upbringing; the tribe mentality meant they were 'one big family' and she was protected and cared for. There appears to be no 'bad childhood' reasoning for her to have caught an attitude but it's fair to say her gears were well and truly ground down. Ququnok's frustrations seemed to be knotted into a giant gender-inequality-based wrath.

In 1808, a band of Canadian fur traders invaded Ququnok's camp and one of the young voyageurs, Augustin Boisvert, took a shining to her. I'd love to tell you he saw through her teenage angst, recognised she was actually battling against her fated womanhood and felt compelled to save her from a life of subservience but, in actual fact, he was just after a slave wife. It's thought that Ququnok got the whole 'Lodge-Pole-Woman' nickname because she was tall and large and therefore an *entirely gruesome romantic prospect* for the men of the village. She was cheesed off about being fobbed off and so decided to go with Augustin and give an extra FU to everyone by leaving the tribe. At least she had the prospect of adventure with her trader (or so she thought); running away with him would save her from life as a dutiful wife or, indeed, a dutiful *second* wife. Once the pair had married, they lived in Althamer (British Columbia) at the north end of Lake Windermere for about a year before Ququnok had enough of her husband's demands and roared back. Nobody knows exactly what went down but it is reputed that Ququnok's 'conduct had become so loose' she was cast off by Augustin. I like to imagine she *loosely conducted* herself via the medium of flying kicks and death-drops.

There is a period of around twelve months before Ququnok returned to her people. Nobody knows what she was up to for that time but she obviously really found herself on that gap year. Life got very interesting in the Kootenai tribe when Ququnok thundered back in, declaring she was a man, dressed as such and boasting about how she had been given the gift of prophecy. Ququnok claimed that she had spirit powers and that her ex-husband had turned her into a guy: 'I am a man now. We Indians did not believe the white people possessed such power from the supernaturals. I can tell you now that they do – greater power than we have. They changed my sex while I was with them. No Indian is able to do that.' Her long-lost family thought Ququnok had gone quackers.

Ququnok changed her name to Kauxuma Nupika ('Gone to the Spirits'), took up hunting, running ragged, chasing women, and was never seen in a dress or without a weapon again. Whenever she encountered anyone she would perform a little dance, signifying her sexual transformation. (Lawd knows what the choreography consisted of but my money would be on it involving a thrust or three.) The Kootenai were kerflummoxed by what they considered Ququnok's possessed desire to be a man and a hero and it's true that, to them at least, it came rather out of the left field. Her dance-worthy metamorphosis could have been a cry for help, it might have been an awesomely elaborate explosion out of the closet, we'll never know – but we do know that it was a definite choice. Ququnok (Kauxuma) took to being a man like a duck to water and I'm so sorry for all the duck-related jargon but there's just something about the spelling of her name that is taking me there time and time again. *Fowl* I know.

The first thing on Ququnok's agenda was to find a wife and she made no qualms about it. In fact, her mistaken understanding of how men should approach women played out as if she had been rehearsing in a locker room. She came on to every unmarried woman in the vicinity, mimicking the 'pick-up' habits she had witnessed in her lifetime and vowing to cast revenge spells on anyone who refused her. Her entrance into the mannisphere was pretty mixed up but astonishingly she did find a partner, a local woman whose husband had left her. They didn't marry but they did move in together. This got tribe tongues wagging and the birdbrained tweet on the streets was their rumoured sexual relationship was 'made possible' by a buffalo leather dildo. However, the magic happened (and what two people do in bed is their own business) but the intimacy unfortunately didn't carry over into the rest of their relationship. Ququnok was thought to be well jel of anyone who came near her girlfriend and constantly accused her of sleeping around. Although that would be enough to make anyone run for the Rocky Mountains, it's thought the last straw appeared after Ququnok furiously pierced an arrow in her lover's arm mid-way through an argy-bargy. (That'll do it.)

Ququnok was exiled from her tribe but she thumbed her nose at them all and had the last laugh. Like an impoverished creative in an overcrowded market, she had to find ways to capitalise on everything and anything and she managed to, essentially working out how to make herself into a brand. The hills were alive with the sound of Ququnok's rites and prophecies and they made her one of the richest Native Americans of her time. She owned horses, properties and had the swishest canoe for miles. Superstition was as much a part of people's make up in her neck of the woods as the lie of the land – it was deeply rooted – and Ququnok saw a gap in the market. Although much of the stuff she was spouting was guff, she is best known for a series of doomsday prophecies from around 1809, in which she foretold a smallpox epidemic and kept on about a time when 'white men would kill Indians'. She was alarmingly accurate. For nearly thirty years she travelled throughout the Pacific Northwest as a man (and a successful businessman at that), working as a prophet, guide and sometime peacemaker, sometime warmonger. Despite being disowned by her people, Ququnok fought for the Kootenai against their ancient tribal enemies, the Blackfeet. She could speak Kootenai, Flathead and Blackfeet and became a recognised mediator among the Kootenai and Flatheads and an established war leader against the Blackfeet. Ququnok might have been banished by the Kootenai but they sure were happy to have her around when war was on. It is believed she eventually went belly up at the hands of the Blackfeet after deceiving them in battle by shielding the Flathead tribe.

Despite her evident anger management issues and tendency to chief people out of their cash, Ququnok died for the greater good. In her lifetime, she served as the warrior she knew she could be and the many strings to her bow (and arrow) were strings that would never have been allowed to her as a woman. Ququnok was inspired and inspiring and we should all remember ~~her name~~ her many names.

AMANDINE-AURORE-LUCILE DUPIN (1804–1876)

THE PSEUDONYM PEDDLIN', PANT WEARIN' PROLIFIC NOVELIST AND PLAYWRIGHT

In her lifetime, Amandine-Aurore-Lucile wrote over fifty books, 45,000 letters, ten or more stage plays, a memoir and even found time to have the courtesy to streamline edit her own hyphen-loving name for us. *Aurore* was born in Paris and enjoyed a liberal upbringing but in truth her prelude was rather misery guts. Her father died in a riding accident when she was four and she became a pawn in arguments between her grandma, Marie-Aurore de Saxe, and her mother. Aurore's granny won the fight even though she was probably too old to care for her (such a throwback she had to take a three-hour nap every afternoon) but her mum had no means to look after her daughter. On the plus side, Aurore got to live on a whopping great estate in Nohant and enjoy the privilege of an education. She was taught a bazaar of subjects by her dad's ex-tutor, François Deschartres, and found a love for writing at an age when most school kids were taking sick days because they were sick of learning. Before she knew it, Aurore was eighteen and married off to a guy named Casimir Dudevant and had two poppets, Maurice and Solange (I *KNOW*). Suddenly, Aurore was in her early thirties, bored and quarter-life-crisis-ing, hankering for more. In 1835, she divorced her husband and her lifeless life and bon voyaged back to Paris.

Keen to get working and earning, Aurore took a job at a daily newspaper called *Le Figaro*. She only made seven francs per column but it was a start. Her first few articles were satirical takes on politics; she had a brave voice, which chucked her in hot water with her boss, Latouche, and sometimes the law (especially when she made numpties out of the National Guard). Before you could say '*Vive la révolution féministe!*', Aurore was power-networking her way around Paris. She started hanging with some of the country's most prolific writers and personalities and even became the head and sole female member of a bookish elite. This was cowabunga at a time when women wouldn't even step out of doors after dark, never mind run a late-night literary group on their tod. One of the group members, novelist Jules Sandeau, became Aurore's marriage rebound and the pair began working together. There was more money in books than newspapers and Aurore wanted in, 'embarking on the stormy sea of literature' as she put it in one of her later letters. Her first published novel came in 1831: *Rose et Blanche* was a collaboration and written under the pseudonym 'J. Sand'. The duo went on to publish a few stories, later as 'Jules Sand', but it was Aurore's first solo novel, *Indiana*, a year later, that made her famous. And it made her famous as 'George Sand'. *Indiana* was written from the perspective of a male narrator and readers were hunky-dory with that because they thought it was written by a man. The book was about a woman fed up with a loveless relationship and how she escaped marriage. Familiar. *To her not me*, I should add (before my fiancée brings the noise). Aurore wasn't having much more luck with Jules IRL. He was totally sour grapes about Aurore's overnight success and sulked and moped about for an entire summer, feeling all emasculated and going on like a right strop-o-saurus. *Diddums.*

After sacking off Jules, Aurore had flings with a string of prominent men, including the writers Prosper Mérimée, Alfred Louis Charles de

Musset-Pathay, Charles Didier, Jean Pierre and Félicien Mallefille, the lawyer Louis-Chrysostome Michel, politician Louis Jean Joseph Charles Blanc, actor Pierre-Martinien Tousez and, most famously, the composer Frédéric Chopin. (Lists this poetic-sounding make me wonder why every man in Britain is called Dave.) Aurore was also linked to women but the only real evidence of this was a note to the actress Marie Dorval, stating Aurore was 'wanting [Marie] either in your dressing room or in your bed' (which I think would be enough to stand up in a court of law). But enough about her lovers, I'm boycotting my own paragraph here because there was a time when Aurore was only known (and later remembered) as 'Chopin's Mistress' and she achieved bags more than sleeping with Choppers. By this point, Aurore felt confident enough to drop the pseudonym but it backfired when her repute came into dispute over her new-found love of modelling men's clothing in public. Also, *most scandalously*, she had taken to smoking tobacco. Her excuse for that was that she could do as she pleased and as for the top hats (which she became known for), her excuse was exactly the same. Aurore reckoned the idea of 'polite living' and social codes of the time could cry her a river. She was comfortable, men's clothes were sturdier and less expensive than women's, and she could do whatever she so desired without being buried by a parachute petticoat. Most importantly, it gave Aurore access to places denied to her as a woman – nobody was going to throw her under a bus for having a bust if she went to the theatre alone or chose to meld in 'men's' spaces. Sometimes she opted for a student's attire: grey breeches, long frock coat and *bousingot* hat (worn by some political and literary rebels during the period). She wore whatever gave her power, despite being more powerful than any outfit.

When the 1848 Revolution began, Aurore stepped it up and started her own socialist newspaper. Her work grew increasingly political. She fought for women's rights and independence and often sided with the poor and working class because of her early years' experiences. Her inkings were winding the chaps up more than ever and one of her contemporaries, a critic named Charles Pierre Baudelaire, griped: 'She is stupid, heavy and garrulous. Her ideas on morals have the same depth of judgment and delicacy of feeling as those of janitresses and kept women . . . The fact that there are men who could become enamoured of this slut is indeed a proof of the abasement of the men of this generation.' (Charles, 'U OK hun?') But Aurore wasn't fazed by the haters; indeed, one of her most quoted quotes is all about embracing the opposite – *there is only one happiness in life, to love and be loved* – and she carried on spreading love until the end. After her death, there was a substantial period of time when people fixated on her cigarettes and significant others but that was all so insignificant in comparison to her career conquests and feminist victories.

Aurore made no apologies about who she wanted to be and said so herself: 'In some respects we make our own life; in others, we submit to the life that others make for us. I have told or given some inkling into everything that has come into my life of my own will.' I've spent the majority of this chapter worrying about which quote to end on as she has so many poignant, perfect and affirming ideas that sum up her super bonne life. I hope you agree with this one that gave me all the tingles. *The world will know and understand me someday. But if that day does not arrive, it does not greatly matter. I shall have opened the way for other women.* A factual conclusion that deserves to win tens across the board.

CHARLOTTE DARKEY PARKHURST (1812–1879)

THE WHIP-CRACKING STAGECOACH DRIVER WITH ONE EYE AND SIX HORSES

Charley's is often described as a 'stranger than fiction' story but twenty-four chapters into a book all about women choosing to emulate or become men to live a life without hindrance, I think we all know by now there is diddly squat weird about it. Although born 'Charlotte', she always went by Charley (and it's the perfect unisex name – *what luck!*). She was later known as One Eyed Charley (because, well, she had one eye) or Cockeyed Charley (because her remaining eye was cocked) or Six-Horse Charley (because she had six horses). Her parents both died when she was a baby and it's understood she spent the best part of her childhood in an orphanage in New Hampshire near the Connecticut River. The orphanage was run by Mr Millshark (who sounds loads more heebie-jeebie than Miss Hannigan, Miss Trunchbull and Miss Minchin combined) and perhaps subsequently Charley discovered she preferred animals to people, falling in love with horses, especially, from a young age.

When she was around twelve years old and still sporting two eyes, Charley devised a plan to run away. She stole some clothing from one of the orphan boys to escape detection and split. The Wild West didn't have many prospects for a girl on her lonesome and most girls (whatever their family circumstances) went on to be a wife, mother, teacher or sex worker, if they were fortunate enough to be allowed to work. Charley wanted more and, despite her rocky start in life, she was hell bent on getting it. From the day of escape, Charley chose to live the rest of her life as a male and so (pronoun change klaxon) *he* did. Following his aspirations led Charley to a Rhode Island livery stable owner named Ebenezer Balch, who took Charley in as a stable hand. He was put straight to work, earning his keep by mucking out, washing and cleaning the carriages. Treating and raising Charley like a son, Ebenezer spotted his potential and allowed him to watch the stagecoach drivers until he understood enough to have a go himself. Starting with one horse, and then attempting four, Charley ultimately learned how to master control of six horses and drive a concord (a stagecoach, not a horse-drawn jumbo jet).

After a few years on Rhode Island, Charley started to consider some strategical career moves and the next rung of the ladder seemed to be to go wherever the money was. California was attracting tons of people at the time, following the Gold Rush in 1849 – wherever there were gold diggers, there was bound to be gold. Although he didn't have the best start (he got kicked in the eye by a mare having a 'mare, resulting in his eye loss), it wasn't too long before he was stagecoach driving and earning his reputation as one of the best master whips on the West Coast. If Charley was your Uber driver, his five-star reviews would be as tight as a hotel bed sheet. He was kinder and more personable than the other drivers; he kept sweets in his pockets for the kids and even turned to his passengers before a run, asking 'Are you all ready, ladies and gentlemen?' Meanwhile, nobody knew he used to be the former and had elected the life of the latter. His runs took him all over the map; he did 'The Great Stage Route' (Stockton to Mariposa), Oakland to San Jose, San Juan to Santa Cruz and Sacramento to Placerville, and was sometimes even known to do return jobs in one day for double the dinero. He travelled the mountains so frequently he could understand the terrain by the sound of his wheels alone and smell a storm a mile off. (Anyone else imagining him licking his finger and using it like a weathervane? . . . No? Just me then.) People trusted Charley and as a result he made a lot of coin carrying mail, money, treasure and other precious cargo, as well as passengers. Charley's achievements were surpassing even little Charlotte's dreams.

Don't get it twisted when it comes to Charley's sweeter than a Bacardi Breezer customer service persona, mind – out of hours, Charley drank hard, spat tobacco, shot guns and gambled into the night. His alter-ego served him well out on the roads when he ran into trouble and, as stagecoach drivers were frequent targets for robbers, he often did. Charley drove for the bankers JP Morgan for a time and to give you an idea of the risk involved, there were over 300 robbery attempts on the JP lines between 1870 and 1884 alone. Alongside regularly dealing with the toenail clippings of weather, perilous trails and long hours, Charley had to handle himself in heists. After an early ambush by a notorious crim called Sugarfoot (which ended Sugarfoot one – Charley nil), he had to quickly learn to throw it down, and stories of his hold-up hostilities became decidedly more violent over the years. If he had a teardrop tattoo for every bandit he'd put the pistol on, he'd have appeared to be sobbing. Our whip had those baddies whipped! It's even supposed that Charley left one of the most infamous outlaws of the day for dead – Charles Bones aka Black Bart (although I'm sure 'Bones' would have been just as impactful and suitable). These sorts of killer stories (in both the murderous and impressive sense) followed Charley for the rest of his career and into accounts like mine. How could I not mention the time he made it across a collapsing bridge in a whacking-great rain storm with seconds to spare, saving himself, his beloved horses and the passenger who told him not to brave it? Or the incident caused by what one can only assume was a right rut in the road that chucked Charley clean out of the carriage? (Refusing to let go of the reins, Charley managed to steer the horses while being yanked along the dirt, saving his passengers and being rewarded a hearty twenty dollars for his bravery.) My favourite thought is that, in 1868, he may have been the first anatomically female (or indeed trans) person to vote in a presidential election in California. If this much is true then we should adopt Charley and erect him in statue form in every town and city.

As Charley aged and railway travel started to steal his stagecoach passengers, he decided to call it a day. One afternoon in the early 1870s, he stepped down from his box, handed the reins to a young fledgling in the area he admired and told his horses to 'Git alang!' This was the end of his long love affair with horses but he started one with chickens instead, retiring to a small farm near Watsonville. On the love affair note, he remained celibate his entire life and it was one of the only reasons people ever really suspected he had a secret. There were a few instances that suggested Charley dug women but he was on the whole a very private person, preferring his own company and a handful of close friends. Legend has it that when Charley died of rheumatism and tongue cancer in 1879, his great mates Charles Harmon and Frank Woodward took him on one last stagecoach ride across the Great Divide and it was on that trip they spotted Charley's ample bosom, which he would usually bind. After an examining doctor confirmed Charley was born female, the news hit the papers from the *San Francisco Call* to the *New York Times*. A headline from 1880 announced, 'Thirty Years in Disguise: A Noted Old Californian Stage-Driver Discovered. After Death. To be a Woman.' (I particularly enjoyed the dramatic usage of full stops in this one.) Regardless of gender, his one eye, his cock eye, or six horses, Charley could and should be remembered for his fearless accomplishments in the American Old West. *YEEEHA!*

THE BRONTË SISTERS
(1816–1855 / 1818–1848 / 1820–1849)

THE PEN-NAME PUSHIN' BAMFS OF THE BOOK WORLD

Are you sitting comfortably? You better be. Don't even think about slinking past this chapter because you reckon you've got a handle on the lives of the world-renowned literary sisters already. Did you know they had an exotic menagerie of animals including dogs called Flossy, Keeper, Rainbow, Snowflake and Grasper, a rescued hawk named Nero and two tame geese dubbed Victoria and Adelaide? *Neither did I!* (But holy cripes I'm glad we're all up to speed in the pets' department now.)

Charlotte, Emily and Anne (born in that order) may be known these days for being the ultimate book bishes but in *those* days the most important book in their lives (even if forced upon them) was the Bible. Born into the church, their da, Patrick, was an Anglican priest and their ma, Maria, was best friends with God. Writing seemed to be in the Brontë blood – the parents both left behind religious works. Some of Patrick's were published but Maria's never made it out of their parish home (I doubt she did either as she had SIX CHILDREN IN SEVEN YEARS). When the littl'un, Anne, was born, the family moved to a village between Bradford and Keighley called Haworth, a step that would have been considered social mobility in motion in those days (although Haworth had a life expectancy of below twenty-five years and no grub or sanitation, so curse knows what it was like where they lived before). The Brontë's new parsonage postcode was nestled nicely on the Lancashire border and the moors became their garden. At first, the girls found the moors creepier than a kid's party magician with a lazy eye and brandy breath but it ultimately turned into their playground – an inspiring backdrop that snuck into much of their work with all sorts of symbolic realness. Sadly, childhood wasn't all 'Here We Go Round the Mulberry Bush' for the sisters and they suffered much loss, starting with the death of their beloved mother in 1821. Not to go too glumly into the next paragraph, but you know how they say that catastrophes come in threes . . .

And so, for two and three . . . In June 1825 and within a month of each other, the Brontë sisters Maria and Elizabeth both contracted and died of tuberculosis. At only nine years of age, Charlotte found herself the eldest sibling. Charlotte, Anne, Emily and their brother, Branwell, became dependent on each other. They were like four peas in a pod and called themselves 'The Quartette'. Their reinvented family unit operated under their father's rigorous parenting and home-schooling regime and their new guardian's (their Aunt Branwell) tough love Methodist tutelage. Patrick Brontë was often thought to be cruel but when it came to taking care of their education, he made sure they had everything that they needed. He did, however, only teach his son Greek and Latin and expected his daughters to take care of the house alongside their studies. *Blink. Overly long pause. Blink* But let's not dwell on that too much. Patrick's own literary ambitions were never really fulfilled so instead, perhaps, he channelled it into his kids.

The Quartette became obsessed with reading. Every week they would schlep the eight-mile pilgrimage to Keighley to get armfuls of books from the Mechanics' Institute library. Their reading list would have knotted Matilda Wormwood's knickers. They loved Shakespeare,

Byron, Thompson, Goldsmith, Pope, all the greats and even some of the not so greats. John Greenwood's local news and stationery store found its most dedicated customers in the Brontës, who similarly dropped by at any opportunity to pore over the newspapers and magazines. The children's creativity didn't start and end with reading – they drew pictures, painted, wrote plays, poems, tiny stories in mini books the size of matchboxes for their toy soldiers and made up entirely new worlds and empires, creating maps and plans for them. The siblings may have lived a secluded life in Haworth but their imaginations were wider than a double garage and allowed to venture the globe over and beyond.

When the time came for jobs and 'meeting one's responsibilities', Charlotte, Emily and Anne faced the dazzlingly enticing options of becoming either school mistresses, governesses or wives. They may have spent their youth savouring their father's Celtic stories of great men achieving great things but all three of them were forced to take low blow salaried positions. In a twist of fate as heavenly as Oprah's iconic '*YOU GET A CAR!*' moment, our girls' ambition and talent found freedom through finances – good old Aunt Branwell (R.I.P.) left her three nieces a chunk of money when she died in 1842. The trio wasted no time in getting to it with their writing, each penning individual novels, but also a joint venture, a volume of poetry, which in 1846 became their first work ever to go to print. The elephant in the room at this point went by the name of the-absolute-arsepiece-prejudice-against-female-writers and the sisters agreed unequivocally to NOT get flattened by it. Charlotte will jump in here and describe how and why they managed to escape the fiend because she said it so well: 'We veiled our own names under those of Currer, Ellis, and Acton Bell; the ambiguous choice being dictated by a sort of conscientious scruple at assuming Christian names positively masculine, while we did not like to declare ourselves women, because – without at that time suspecting that our mode of writing and thinking was not what is called "feminine" – we had a vague impression that authoresses are liable to be looked on with prejudice;

we had noticed how critics sometimes use for their chastisement the weapon of personality, and for their reward, a flattery, which is not true praise.' While we're on the subject, I'll let Anne pop along to the doo too because she flawlessly described how 'All novels are or should be written for both men and women to read, and I am at a loss to conceive how a man should permit himself to write anything that would be really disgraceful to a woman, or why a woman should be censured for writing anything that would be proper and becoming for a man.' . . . How could anyone disagree with that?

Kick-starting their careers off their own bats before Kickstarter was a twinkle in the future's eye, Charlotte (Currer), Emily (Ellis) and Anne (Acton) funded the poetry book themselves and were published by Aylott and Jones in London. Guttingly, they only sold two copies, but both readers were thought to have thoroughly enjoyed it! (If you're going to nosedive you may as well nosedive with style.) From here, the journey to individual publication for the sisters was merciless and the rejections relentless but they never let the bleeps grind them down. Unfortunately, their brother, Branwell, did not cope so well with all the teeth kicks and got lost in the sauce, folding into a life of alcohol and opium. (Even though he was the first to get published, a poem in the *Halifax Guardian*, he struggled to get anything else away and his failings were the death of him in 1848.) Charlotte, Emily and Anne's hardballing saw them all commercial successes – the books (you *may* have heard of them) 'Currer's' *Jane Eyre*, 'Ellis's' *Wuthering Heights* and 'Acton's' *Agnes Grey* set the literary world alight with flamethrower pow. Everyone wanted to know who these mystery, mastermind 'men' were and the women enjoyed the anonymity for a time. Monsieur Heger, a teacher at a boarding school in Brussels that Emily and Charlotte attended for a short while, said of Emily that 'she should have been born a man'; he was baffled as to how she could be, as he described, 'a great navigator' with 'strong and imperious will' AND a woman. When Emily died in 1848 (not long after the trio revealed their true identities), Charlotte wrote that she was 'stronger than any man'. The Brontë babes knew about girl power even if the rest of the world hadn't caught on yet (it still mostly hasn't).

Charlotte ended up surviving all of her siblings but she, Emily and Anne all died much before their time. They may not have had long but they rinsed their days for all they were worth. They fought with the power of their minds to combat the limits of their world, tackled subjects that women weren't usually allowed to touch and left transformative work, which is loved and adapted the planet over. Brontëmania is as bigtime as ever and if they were about today, I hope they'd be humblebragging their heads off.

MARY ANN EVANS (1819–1880)

THE FALSE NAME FAVOURING, FORWARD-THINKING VICTORIAN FICTION WRITER

This chapter has got me feeling the stressure as Mary was a big part of my upbringing and now I'm *totally adulting* I need to do her justice. Don't contact me if you think I haven't. I grew up in Nuneaton, a place that has graced many a 'Top Ten Crap Towns in the UK' list over the years but is, thankfully, also famous for being the birthplace of *moi* and one of the leading British novelists and poets of the nineteenth century, Mary Ann Evans (sometimes known as Marian but most famously known by her pen-name, George Eliot). In her novel *Silas Marner*, she calls the Nuneaton of her day 'a rich central plain', but these days it's only rich with discount stores, bookies and pawnbrokers. I was born in the George Eliot hospital, studied George Eliot at school, drank in the George Eliot pub and understood the need for feminism the night I witnessed the George Eliot town centre statue vandalised by a local tough guy (the alcopop-tanked, teenie-bopper me saw red as she was covered in Silly String and given a jauntily angled traffic cone hat).

Mary Ann's father, Robert Evans, was the manager of a local estate named Arbury Hall and she was born on it at South Farm. A year later, the family moved to a building named Griff House, which is now a Beefeater steak restaurant cum Premier Inn hotel on a roundabout.

(True story.) Her childhood was strict and dictated by the rigid Methodist principles of her parents but she found an escape in books and was allowed access to a wonderland of them at the library at Arbury Hall. Even as a youngster, the world was looking at her as an object and it was decided that Mary Ann probably wasn't eye candy enough for marriage, so instead she would be educated. (Blessèd be the so-called *bugly*.) From age five to sixteen she studied at a number of schools across the county until her mother, Christiana, died in 1836 and Mary Ann was forced back home to play housekeeper. Undeterred by dishes and dusting, Mary Ann kept up her own private study and even stayed in touch with one of her ex-tutors, an Evangelist named Maria Lewis. Maria was intriguing to Mary Ann for her knowledge and 'those who can, teach' influence, but she was also charmed by the idea of a faith system so different from her parents'. Her religious doubts were only heightened when, at twenty-one, she trucked to Coventry and met the freethinking, rolling in it Charles and Cara Bray. Charles had made a packet in the ribbon industry but was more interested in changing the world. (Not that ribbon didn't – where would we be without maypoles and rhythmic gymnastics? Discuss.) The couple kept company with likeminded radical brains and Mary Ann enjoyed hanging at a house that welcomed debate and a woman's opinion. Our sheltered Midlands bab[2] must have found this yampy[3] at first but soon felt ready to say *ta-ra-a-bit*[4] to her old life.

Mary Ann didn't find true freedom until her father's death in 1849 – up until this point she had to play the dutiful daughter to keep from tangling his brain like a pair of headphones with her new-fangled notions. He left her a runty inheritance but she used it to travel with the Brays, most notably to Switzerland, where she spent her

---

2   A term of endearment.
3   To have a screw loose.
4   Goodbye for now.

days writing, sketching and people watching, which developed into an obsession with character study. If you felt someone's eyes on you from behind a bush, they were probably Mary Ann's. Upon her return, she knew she needed to be in London and had ambitions way larger than 'the norm', which would be to find a man to support her being there. In 1850, she moved to Wandsworth (where I now live too – there's a portrait of her in my local, which I 'cheers' every time). She got a job with an old acquaintance from the Bray house days as the assistant editor on a liberal quarterly journal, the *Westminster Review*. The publisher, John Chapman, had his name across the front of it as the Editor but (shellshock): Mary Ann did most of the work for a fraction of the pay or praise. In better news, the fact a female held this position at all was big enchilada then.

The other unwritten Victorian law she was calling out and kicking back at was monogamy, choosing to live with a married man, the philosopher and critic George Henry Lewes. Social convention might not have been having it but Lewes had an open relationship and they were devoted to each other. Some accounts of Mary Ann's life would have you think that she wrote no books and loafed about being men's mistresses. A Lena Dunham tweet I enjoyed from back in 2013 read: *FYI George Eliot's Wikipedia page is the soapiest most scandalous thing you'll read this month. Thesis: she was ugly AND horny!* It perhaps sums up why Mary Ann was always wary of biographies – they would fuel pointless gasbagging and distract from her wondrous work. Her relationships, in fact, could arguably have even been considered by her as secondary to her writing: she could never put down her pen. When Lewes died in 1878, Mary Ann didn't have the strength to go to his funeral. Instead, she locked herself in her bedroom for a week before spending the next two years completing his unfinished manuscript *Problems of Life and Mind*. She always found a way to immerse herself in her work. Many of Mary Ann's female characters are intellectuals with inspired vision; her feelings about women having their career wings clipped was glaringly obvious from her narration.

While at the *Review*, Mary Ann could pursue her career as a novelist. She wrote alongside her day job and it is here she decided to take the nom de plume George Eliot. She chose to use a male pen-name so as to be taken seriously as an author (an intelligent, witty, revolutionary female writer would have rendered men's heads to sheds back in't day!). She wanted to write without the supposed scandal of her love life interfering with opinion. Women were publishing books but they were largely frothy romances; she fixed to escape the stereotype and have male readers consider her a match to their own intelligence if they picked up her book. And buy them they did! The first full novel published with her name on, *Adam Bede* in 1859, may have been many years in the making but it was an overnight success. Everyone wanted to know who George Eliot was but she was as secretive as Banksy. When the real George Eliot did stand up (because an imposter was trying to claim the hard work as his own), people (men) had to suck it up and accept that women were more than capable of writing life-changing literature. It took a while but Mary Ann, her work and her relationship with Lewes were starting to be increasingly accepted by polite society – she even had Dickens and Queen Victoria as fans. Nobody could deny the popularity of her novels and she wrote books for days over the next fifteen years, including the smashers *The Mill on the Floss* and *Middlemarch*.

When Mary Ann died of kidney disease in 1880, she was not buried at Westminster Abbey, despite being one of the nation's greatest writers. As someone who publicly renounced Christianity and because she married, not long before her passing, a banker twenty years her junior named John Walter Cross, she was deemed too controversial. John and Mary Ann were as close as backside and bench but this wasn't enough for the purity-demanding Victorians. At her funeral, it is believed a local lad asked if the late George Eliot's *wife* was going to be buried.

He didn't know she was a woman, and shockingly, some still don't. In one of her letters, Mary Ann laments: 'I know very little about what is 'specially good for women – only a few things that I feel sure are good for human nature generally, and about such as these last alone, can I ever hope to write or say anything worth saying.' I can concur that she certainly did. Mary Ann Evans was unconventional in every sense. Our kid was bostin'.[5]

---

5   Awesome!

ELLEN CRAFT (1826–1891)

THE SLAVE WHO PRETENDED TO BE A WHITE MASTER WHILE CROSS-DRESSING HERSELF TO FREEDOM

It's true you can't choose your family and nobody would have ever elected to start life as a servant to their slaveholder father – but this was Ellen's bleak reality. Her keeper dad ('keeper' as in master, certainly *not* as in 'catch') was a rich cotton planter in Clinton, Georgia, called Major James Smith. Her mother's name was Maria and Maria was the Major's house slave, *not* the Major's wife. Plantation owners sexually violating and impregnating young slaves was not an uncommon story during the years of slavery in the American South and Ellen was most likely the product of such a detestable tale. The fact that Ellen was a constant reminder of her husband's infidelity had Mrs Smith forever feeling ballistic and so she decided there was nothing for it but to send her away. At the age of eleven, Ellen became the 'wedding gift' to one of the Smiths' daughters, Eliza, and joined her and her new husband in the city of Macon. When most children her age (most *white* children her age) were probably cheerfully pushing hoops round with sticks without care, Ellen had to take on all the domestic and childcare responsibilities of a busy household as Eliza's lady's maid. The laws surrounding slavery were repellent but the day-to-day reality for the humans stripped of all humanity, *the enslaved*, was worse. Later, Ellen would go on to describe how Eliza was 'decidedly more humane than the majority of her class' and, extraordinarily, Ellen was granted small mercies[6] such as the right to her own room rather than having to sleep on the floor or a palette at the foot of her mistress's bed. Oh, and exemption from rape and torture.

Emancipation for Ellen seemed like an impossibility. Of course, she wanted to tell her masters to put eggs in their shoes and beat it but the slave trade was untiring and hellish and she could but merely survive it. In the early 1840s, she met the duck's nuts of a sunshine ray in her sombre world, her husband and master-plan partner to be, William Craft. A slave and apprentice carpenter on an adjacent plantation, William was born in Macon but had been split from his entire family when he was sold to a new master to pay the gambling debts of his previous. Ellen and William had each other at hello and wanted to marry as quickly as they swooned but the slave laws had different plans for their love. Slaves from different plantations were not permitted to wed and beyond that, if they were to have children, they would be legally doomed to the same fate as their parents – they too would become slaves. Hoping and praying that conditions would improve, Ellen and William decided to struggle on, unmarried, and wait for white people to locate and engage their damn brains. After more than five years of continued tumbleweed in that department, our schnookums couple could hold on no longer and asked for special permission to marry. The consent to do so should have been the start of their happy ever after but it actually made them more anxious – the fear of separation was a daily plague. The conclusion for their lives together was callous but clear: the glimmering hope of liberty would only ever remain a glint if they didn't do something drastic. Much like their received stamp of approval to become Mr and Mrs, both Ellen and William had some sovereignty on their respective estates – together they could pool their pint-sized privileges to overthrow

---

6   Monster mammoth mondo mercies.

the oppressors. William was allowed to keep a sliver of his apprenticeship earnings; Ellen's private room was a perfect stash spot and her position in the household meant that eavesdropping opportunities were peak. All roads were leading to an escape plot . . .

Even when slaves *weren't* trying to run, they were flogged, underfed, overworked, tortured and beaten to death. Most fugitive slave stories commemorated those who had to claw and fight their way to freedom, but the Crafts' was unique in that they made a dash for it in public, in broad daylight (and travelled in first-class train carriages no less!). At first, Ellen was too nervous to action their plans but the laws under which they lived (existed) saw her not as a woman but a 'mere chattel, to be bought and sold, or otherwise dealt with as her owner might see fit'. The only way she could take control was to gamble their lives. As a mixed race, light-skinned woman, Ellen took advantage of her appearance and it was decided she would get out disguised as a white slave master and William, as her valet. Ellen soon found an impressive backstory and threw herself into character as if it was press night. She cut her hair, learned to stride like an entitled Caucasian persecutor and took the name Mr William Johnson (Johnson was a popular, low-profile surname but also used as a code, developed by abolitionists, to guide runaway slaves to safety via the underground railroad) – she was determined to be free. It was illegal for shops to sell to slaves without their master's consent; some did so, not because they sympathised with the slave but because the white word would always win over the black in a court of law. Going to different shops across town to evade suspicion, William managed to use all he had saved to buy a William Johnson-worthy outfit, including a top hat, cravat, jacket and tassel. Ellen had to do whatever was clever to avoid attention or questions; the pretence agreed was that they were travelling to Philadelphia for specialist treatment for Johnson's 'rheumatism'. As Ellen couldn't write (slaves were denied an education by law), she wore a sling on her right arm so she might not be asked to sign anything and a poultice on her face to dissuade strangers from talking to her.

In December 1848, their plan was put into action and the pair cruised out of Macon on a train to Savannah, continuing their journey via a combo of steamboats, trains and coaches. Their journey was by no means an easy ride; the stakes were read-the-rest-of-this-paragraph-through-your-fingers-with-your-hands-over-your-eyes high. At one point, a friend of Ellen's master, a man who had known Ellen all her life, sat next to William Johnson. Ellen had to feign deafness to put him off. (What with a sling, bandaged-up face like an effed-up McCain Potato Smile and sudden outright hearing loss, you'd think people would give the poor 'man' a break!) In Baltimore, when the end was in sight, the pair were ordered off a train by the guard and refused back on unless they could provide sufficient paperwork to prove that William was Ellen's slave. Again, ailments won over and the guard eventually took pity on Johnson's walking wounded woes and allowed them to continue. Against all odds, they reached Philadelphia on Christmas Day. They were kept safe there and later in Boston by a number of anti-slavery society members who opted for deeds over words and changed history as a result.

The Crafts' story spread like a starfish and they began to hit the papers and hearts and minds of millions as they joined prominent activist William Wells-Brown on his abolitionist lecture tour. Even after all they had achieved, Ellen typically stood in the wings while William told their story. It *weren't right or proper* for women to talk to mixed-gender audiences and so, once more, she was silenced. It is even widely believed that the book about their story, *Running a Thousand Miles for Freedom*, which became a major tool for propaganda against Southern slavery, was a joint effort by the couple, but published in William's name only. Reprints since the 1990s have listed both the Crafts as authors BECAUSE FINALLY. The Crafts had become the most renowned and influential activists in the abolitionist movement in the US and UK but they were never safe. In 1850, a Fugitive Slave Law was passed that was out to recapture escaped slaves. William and Ellen became the top prizes for the government and they had bounty hunters and bloodhounds up in their grill until the end. They found asylum in England for nearly two decades, where they had five children and continued moving, shaking and influence peddling, but the Crafts eventually ended up back in Georgia in the late 1860s, after the American Civil War. The people who had been enslaved may have been liberated but they were in dire need. The poverty and illiteracy levels were all-consuming and despite many setbacks and much opposition, the Crafts founded an agricultural school for newly freed slaves, the Woodville Co-Operative, on an 1,800-acre plantation, paid for by their blood, sweat and tears and helped along by their supporters.

When Ellen died she was buried by her favourite oak tree on the plantation; she was forever proud of her roots. Hers was a life full of confronting oppression with fierceness, and she dedicated it to anti-slavery activism. She defied the expectations of her race, class and sex by not only having a public voice but letting it ring out loud and clear. She believed she could so she *obliterated* it. Put that on a tote bag!

LORETA JANETA VELÁZQUEZ (1842–1923)

THE CUBAN SPY AND CONFEDERATE CON ARTIST

If Loreta was around today she'd be a big whoop reality star on the rise, rocketing like all the Mentos in a Diet Coke ocean. Everywhere she went, Loreta was a walking press release – she created her own myth and got the media dizzy. During the Civil War she made herself the Confederacy's first (and arguably only) celebrity. We know everything about her time in the forces by her own account, although, unlike the influencers of today, no information regarding her breakfast preferences seems to have remained. Throughout her lifetime she used many aliases, her family background specifics are a fraction flaky and some believe she wasn't who she claimed she was at all, but rather a 'prostitute', stick-up artist and scammer. Either way, she led a technicolour life and the doubters would do well to remember that history is inconsistent at the best of times (wake me up when the world starts believing women). We *can* be certain, for she wrote 'I have no hesitation in saying that I wish I had been created a man instead of a woman', that she understood the wrongs done to her sex and sought to make them right. Her book, *The Woman in Battle*, called out 'utterly vile' corrupt soldiers and the dirty tricks of men at war and celebrated the versatility and strength of women – so you can see why the men might have been miffed . . . Rather than bring on a hernia trying to find holes in the story, we should do as she says, which was ask for her words to be treated with 'impartiality' and 'candour'. You heard the woman!

Loreta's family history was stated noble with an ancient Castilian twist. She was born in Havana to an affluent Spanish aristocrat father and French-American mother and sent away as a nipper for schooling in New Orleans, where she lived with an aunt. Privileged education aside, Loreta was naturally gifted – she had the smarts and curiosity enough to know her own mind and fix herself a boss sandwich. Mingling with American peers who loved to spout about living in a 'free country', plus her learning and her mettle, meant Loreta questioned *everything* about her Catholic upbringing and culture. When a 'marriage of convenience' was organised for her by her family to a muggle named Raphael, Loreta decided it was more of an *inconvenience*, actually. Instead she ran off and eloped with her true 'love match', a Texas army officer named William, at the age of just fourteen. Rebelling had given her family the red mist but they didn't manage to send Loreta to a convent or back to Cuba and she was eventually cut off from and disinherited by her parents for the decision. Together, Loreta and William lived at various army posts and had three children, all of whom, horribly, died young. Loreta was the driving force in their union, rising above the grief by immersing herself in politics and affairs of the state and persuading her other half to renounce his commission and join the confederate army. When the Civil War broke out, William was to be posted to Florida to train the troops and Loreta wanted to do the same but he shut her down. She didn't simply want to follow her husband to the Sunshine State and play wifey; Loreta wanted to be a part of the battle. Fed up of having to sit back and watch the dangle fest take all the glory, Loreta announced that she would join the troops herself, dressed as a man she was already calling 'Harry T.

Buford'. (Let's just agree that the T stood for *The Best Decision She Ever Made*.) William was having none of it but it only made Loreta zero in more on enlisting: 'I was obstinately bent upon realising the dream of my life, whether he approved of my course or not.' Her Negative Nelly husband thought he was protecting her but she was looking for a sword, not a knight.

When William left without her, Loreta went gung-ho with getting her disguise together. She visited an old French army tailor (the only one she could trust wouldn't go all Neighbourhood Watch on her) and requested her Harry T. Buford clobber. He helped to make her a suit of fine wire net shields (which she could wear under the clothes to hide her shape) and straps for her chest and shoulders, to wear under a silk shirt and keep it all in place. Loreta had even invented a banded contraption, fixed by eyelet-holes, to go around her waistband and help her hips take refuge. Once she'd braided her hair, owned her wig and moustache and tucked her pantaloons into her boots, she was ready to fight for the Southern cause. If you're going to do something, you might as well do it properly and as such Loreta resolved that she wasn't just travelling to Arkansas to raise a battalion, she was also doing it as A LIEUTENANT! Keeping to her word and after enrolling *two hundred and thirty-six men in four days*, Loreta headed to Florida and gave William the shock of his life. Only days later he was killed in an accident but having to go it alone was no stress; Loreta went on to serve in several regiments and become a master of mayhem. She fought in numerous battles including Bull Run, Fort Donelson and Shiloh. (They may sound like levels on *Sonic the Hedgehog* but they were battles more bloodcurdling than any final boss stage.) Loreta loved her military life; it was *nearly* all she had hoped for, but her fellow comrades were beginning to trampoline on her patience. She had come to realise that they talked the big talk but that bravado never carried itself on to the battlefield. Loreta's disdain at their camp banter had her describe them as men 'whom it would be a stretch of courtesy to call gentleman'.

Bored of braggadocio, Loreta decided to reinvent herself as a spy. She borrowed a local farmer's wife's clothes and headed to Washington, D.C., where she could gather intelligence for the South. Her spy disguises were as inventive as her soldier's – she switched between male and female threads whenever she saw fit, even hopping back to Lieutenant Buford when it was helpful to her surveillance. Loreta was as spunky a spy as she was a soldier; and her audacity had her rubbing shoulders with all the big men on campus, including President Abraham Lincoln. The life of a double agent suited our adrenalin junkie – she kept it up until the end of the war, but especially after her sex was discovered back on the front line. Giving up her uniform to focus solely on espionage, Loreta travelled freely between the North and South, reaching as far and wide as Canada, London and Paris for her love of the cause. Loreta organised rebellions to aid the escape of confederate prisoners, and stole, forged and contrived every ounce of ammunition she could to spar for what she believed in. This resolute determination continued once war was over; she turned her ambidextrous hand to political journalism, books and business schemes surrounding the railroad and mining industries. I haven't even mentioned the fact that she found the time to marry three more times during proceedings. Much like her career and the line-up of the Sugababes, Loreta reinvented herself time and time again. She was a seasoned survivor and for that we can probably thank her fearless intelligence. Of her heroic life, Loreta cited Joan of Arc as an inspiration: 'My soul burned with an overwhelming desire to emulate her deeds of valour, and to make for myself a name which, like hers, would be enrolled in letters of gold among the women who had the courage to fight like men – ay, better than most men.' If you've got any spare gold lying around, make sure to enrol Loreta Janeta Velázquez in it (before you realise you've got spare gold lying around and cash it in).

LILLIE HITCHCOCK-COIT
(1843–1929)

THE SKIRT LIFTIN', GAMBLIN', SHOOTIN', HONORARY FIREMAN

Holy smokes, Lillie Hitchcock-Coit is so good you're going to pop a synapse. Please take that as your official disclaimer (myself or Amazon Publishing do not accept responsibility for any ill health or inconvenience caused by erupted synapses induced by the story of Lillie Hitchcock-Coit, a woman who is guaranteed to leave you firing on all cylinders). Gird your nervous system.

Lillie was an only child but certainly not a lonely child. Her youth was spent surrounded by adults who treated her as if she was fully grown and she was 'accustomed to the society of men who commanded and took part in the affairs of the nation'. As her dad was an army doctor, Lillie was born at West Point (a military academy in New York) and moved to California at seven years old, when Dr Hitchcock transferred to a new post. Her mother was a herculean stampede of a woman and a writer, described as having a 'ready tongue and fluent pen' (which I'm going to steal for my CV strapline.) Her father had received a cumbersome inheritance from his parents but chose to keep working, keen to show Lillie that slacktitude was not the attitude and that she should pursue a career. She was a rich kid and a real brainbox but Lillie and educational establishments went together like OJ and mouthwash. At thirteen she was sent to a convent school in San Jose, an experiment that lasted all of four days before the sisters called the Hitchcocks and begged them to collect their daughter (when you've got on the last nerve of a nun, you've taken home gold in the Misbehaving Olympics). They tried her at a regular school but after an 'unexplained accident', Lillie got a pencil jabbed in her eye and had to drop out. Who knew all that wanging on parents did about objects 'having your eye out' might carry some weight? At the end of the day (as people who are trying to prove their point but have run out of intelligent-sounding words say), Lillie still passed her exams with flying colours and would *always* know what to say. She had a scholarly voice and noodle.

Lillie's city, San Francisco, was built entirely of wood then and as such was quite the fire hazard. Lillie learned all about the risky business of that highly flammable metropolis when the family first moved there and the hotel she was staying in caught fire. She was saved from its top floor by a volunteer team of firemen called the 'Knickerbockers Number 5'. (I haven't screwed up by not calling them 'firefighters' before you all take to Twitter, they were men then, and only ever men.) In a complete and utter admiration and respect way (not in a *hubba, hubba, Magic Mike* way – behave yourselves), Lillie was hooked on firemen. From that day, whenever there was a blaze in the city, she would pitch up to cheer the men on. Lillie made such a scene that crowds gathered to cheer her cheering them. Her parents couldn't stop her from bolting out of the front door when she heard the Knickerbocker No. 5 engine siren (not quite as catchy as 'Mambo No. 5' but Lillie's earworm all the same). So in love was she with firefighting, she sometimes beat the firemen to the fire. The volunteer groups were elite, their officers were the upper crust of the city's boys and naturally heroes for the local school kids. *You can't be what you can't see* didn't mean a thing to Lillie – she didn't just want to admire them, she wanted to join the ranks. In 1858, she gave it a whirl when the Knickerbocker red shirts were short of men as they responded to a fire on Telegraph Hill. The engines used to be pulled by ropes and all the water pumping was done by manpower too, but when Lillie saw the men struggling she brought her *womanpower*. This was not a drill, Lillie was as serious as the flames and screamed 'Come on, you men! Everybody pull and we'll beat 'em!' at the other volunteers. The fire was extinguished but the one in Lillie's belly was roaring.

Over the next five years, Lillie did so much for the firemen of the city that she was seen as their patroness. She attended every fire, every gala parade, every fundraiser and became the mascot the men never knew they needed. On 3 October 1863, Lillie was made an honorary member of the Knickerbocker company, a distinction she took so determinedly that she sewed a number five into all her undergarments. She constantly wore the gold badge they awarded her and was even allowed to model the uniform when she joined them in formal parade or on duty. Instead of black pants with the shirt and tie, Lillie had to wear a skirt. (The men may have been open-minded about having a woman as an honorary member but they weren't *possessed*!) Lillie's dedication to the fire service wasn't just an adorable phase she went through as a youngster, it continued for the rest of her life. Even when she grew up and travelled extensively, she would always come back to San Fran and to her Knickerbockers in all their glory.

In 1868, Lillie married a prominent member of the stock exchange board, Benjamin Howard Coit. He was fat-catting but so was Lillie – she had been made an heiress when her grandfather died and saw fit to spend it wisely, travelling and venturing. Her fortune allowed her to go far and wide; she even became a notable figure at the court of Napoleon III and a Maharaja of India. If years of having to lift her skirts to chase after fire engines had taught her anything, it was that living as society expected you to as a woman was as dry as January. Petticoats and such were as inconvenient as a trip to a Portaloo in a jumpsuit for Lillie and she felt her clothing had been holding her back for far too long. 'Firebelle Lil' Coit went on to make quite a name for herself wherever she went, smoking cigars and wearing trousers – frequently going the whole hog and disguising herself entirely as a man to participate in pastimes reserved for the men only. There's an 'eccentric' in every town and in San Francisco, particularly along North Beach, Lillie was considered the local loopster. She was an expert poker player and often held games at her home or dressed as a man to hit up the casinos. She was always the only female at the table and knew how to come away with her pockets packed. Lillie also loved to hunt and everyone in the valley knew her for a 'dead shot'. Her new wardrobe even allowed her to become an accomplished carriage driver – she shocked some of the best old male stage drivers on the coast with her knack at the reins. Lillie had given up on the 'rules' thoroughly and perfectly, and it's such a mouth-watering prospect I want to dip it in hummus. Her husband wasn't as enthralled with her disregard for law and order – he began to treat his marriage vows with the same indifference and got a bad case of the wandering eye. The Knickerbocker number 5s turned out to be Lillie's only true ride or die love.

When Lillie passed away, aged 86, you wouldn't have felt like you were parroting platitudes to say 'she lived a good life' if you attended her funeral, because she really did. The Knickerbockers didn't just attend her funeral, they guarded her body until it was time to lay her to rest, then led the procession to Grace Cathedral. At the steps, volunteer firemen Samuel Baker, Captain J. H. McMenomy and Richard Cox became her pallbearers and they sent her off with her precious number-five badge pinned in place. In her will, Lillie left a third of her estate ($225,000) to the city of San Francisco. Her ashes were placed in a mausoleum, along with some of her most prized firefighting possessions, and two memorials were made to remember her by. The Coit Tower on Telegraph Hill and a firefighter statue in Washington Square Park now honour her memory. In 2004, Joanne Hayes-White became the first female fire chief in San Francisco, a day that would have made Lillie happier than the morning sun. From the convention-defying heights of Lillie's giant shoulders, Joanne told her city that she thinks Lillie was 'a pretty phenomenal gal'. (What she said.)

CATHAY WILLIAMS (1844–1893)

THE ESCAPED SLAVE AND BUFFALO SOLDIER

Covering my back by telling you that the details of some of these women's lives is hazy by now must be more annoying than the number of big yawn, stale, pale males with podcasts. However, much of Cathay's background is truly unknown because she was born into slavery and she was a black woman in American society, so she had to seriously shake things up to make a mark. Lucky for us, she beat the lemons given to her by life to a pulp.

Cathay was born near the cruelly named town of Independence on the outskirts of Jefferson City, Missouri. She was owned by a farmer with more ching ching than sense or humanity, a plantation owner named William Johnson (not the Ellen Craft William Johnson!) for whom she had been a house servant since she was old enough to hold a duster. The ancestry of slaves in the Upper South hailed from the agricultural tribes of West Africa. Traders brought them over in chains and exploited them and their skills for the insanely profitable business of developing the plantations of the New World. Cathay's hometown marked the start of the Santa Fe Trail, the transportation route to New Mexico, used by thousands to head for a new life on the frontier and a road that would prove to be kind of a big deal in her life. Her parents were not married, nor did they associate because they weren't allowed to. Her mother was a slave but her father was (very unusually) a free man and an exception to the rule. Growing up a girl with no rights or expectation of ever escaping bondage, Cathay could only imagine what liberty looked like. She found strength in religion; slaves would organise secret prayer meetings and sing songs to keep their mind and spirit free, even if they could not be. Cathay learned from other enslaved people about her heritage and culture and dreamed of embarking upon a new life in the American West. She never gave up hope. But simply hoping for change wasn't enough – she couldn't just wish an emancipated future into existence (sorry *The Secret* et al), Cathay had to work herself to the bone for it.

Having spent all of her life in Missouri and only knowing a tiny, bigoted corner of the world, you can imagine how freaked Cathay's bean was when, at sixteen, the Civil War descended and her town became occupied by the Union. She was surrounded by federal soldiers from Abraham Lincoln's army (and the majority of them were anti-slavery abolitionists) and the takeover meant that she was now FREE! However (and I hate to drop in a 'however' after such boomshakalaka news), in a sadistic twist of fate, the 8th Indiana Volunteer Infantry Regiment were moving in and if slaves weren't working for them they were considered 'contraband of war'. Cathay was no freer than she was as a slave and she was being owned by law once more based upon skin colour alone. Don't refresh your browser, no unexpected errors have occurred here: Cathay was free for all of about five minutes before she was pressed into service as a cook and then laundress. Military life was rock hard but cushy after a life of slavery. Cathay was given a small wage, food and drink rations and marched with the soldiers through Arkansas, Louisiana and Georgia. After four intense years, the Union finally won the war and Cathay found herself back in Jefferson, where the local barracks were being used as a recruitment centre for the post-war army. Cathay needed to figure out her next move; there were fudge-all opportunities for women, especially not single black female ex-slaves. She watched thousands of male ex-slaves enlist and knew that a black man in the army would earn more money than a black female cook or laundress. Cathay wanted to 'make [her] own living' so she put two and two together and I hope you're all good with basic math to work out her answer. Cathay decided to serve her country, exercise her right as an American citizen and get paid as much as the men did, *please and thank you kindly*. Aside from a friend and cousin in the area, Cathay was on her own and empty of pocket. She needed a hero, so that's what she became.

At five-foot-nine tall and with muscles that would put the group of irky men who loiter at my gym and try to teach me how to use machines I'm already annihilating to shame, Cathay didn't need too much of a disguise to fool the recruiters. She had her hair short, wore baggy clothes and opted for a slouch hat to hide her face (*kitsch!*). Thanks to her years of service in the Union she knew what was expected of her and how to behave and so successfully enlisted in November 1866 as 'William Cathay' (see what she did there?). 'William' was given a rifled musket and the standard-issue blue infantry uniform and was assigned to the 38th United States Infantry Regiment (one of four all-black regiments under white leadership organised after the war). Serving in the ranks as a 'buffalo soldier', Cathay became the first and only documented African American woman to serve in the US regular army while it was illegal for her to be there. The posts given to the buffalo soldiers were often the worst; the conditions they were subjected to were even more heinous and yet they had the lowest desertion rate in the entire army – these were true troopers indeed. Cathay travelled broadly and widely with the regiment; journeys were long and one was recorded to be 536 miles – enough to blow the motherboard of any Fitbit. As a 'guardian of the plains', Cathay and her comrades had to protect the Santa Fe Trail and she risked her life every day to do so during the Indian wars. There is some discrepancy as to whether her sex was ever identified but we do know that she was in and out of hospital during her time for what was probably diabetes (or viruses caused by reduced immunity as a result of diabetes). Some think she was never exposed, which, given the amount she was in hospital, says something about the level of medical care at the time but also the treatment of black soldiers. Her health could also be another reason for her discharge. Either way, we do know she was wily enough to pass as William for nearly two years.

After her service, Cathay struggled to get work. Manual labour was the only option for black women and by this point she had lost toes to her illness and was walking with a crutch. She filed for an 'invalid pension' but the army inspectors rejected her claim. The post-war pensions success stories of women posing as men were usually pretty right on; this was perhaps yet a further example of the prejudice she faced. Cathay's country had betrayed her once again. Around this time, a historian named Frederick Jackson Turner became famous with his frontier thesis that left out the part about minorities and women as if people like Cathay had nothing to do with it. And we wonder why stories like this have been whitewashed for all these years . . .

Cathay settled in Colorado where she married but she married a ballbag who stole from her, so she had him arrested. After all that she had been through, he was the last thing she needed. Rather than hit a wall (because she'd spent her life bulldozing them), she became a serial moonlighter instead, taking odd jobs and working like she had done all her life to survive. Cathay had an unbreakable will and was resilient to the end (which, morosely, came not long after her pension denial). It may not seem like the story of a happy life but Cathay took her life out of her 'owner's' hands and firmly into her own. She made her own version of the American Dream come true. Cathay dared to dare and take up space and we're *living for it!*

JEANNE BONNET (1849–1876)

THE SEX WORKER SAVIN', SHOPLIFTIN', FROG CATCHIN' MOB LEADER

If you're chapter bopping and have landed on this account for the title alone, I can't say I blame your let's-have-a-lookie-loo intrigue. Jeanne or 'Jennie' or 'The-Little-Frog-Catcher' Bonnet was born in Gay Paree, into a family of French actors who largely performed at Dumas's Théâtre Historique. Jeanne followed in her parents' footsteps, treading the boards with a gift for the stage that kept on giving at the box office, for she was immensely popular with the punters. Jeanne often played the young coquette (a vapid part made up almost entirely of giggling at or getting hit on by boys) and although her roles were bland, life as a young player was a thrill-a-second. It's no wonder our young French fancy fancied herself as a VIP and developed a 'strong distaste for domestic drudgery or running a sewing machine'. Child actor ego or otherwise, I think we can all agree that defying convention was a great choice by Jeanne (and I don't reckon Macaulay Culkin ever had to negotiate an overlocker or turn and stitch a seam). While her head could still fit through a door frame, Jeanne's family put their show on the road, following their theatrical troupe to San Francisco, the city that would become Jeanne's forever home. Unfortunately, the lights weren't burning as brightly for the group of French performers as had been promised to them. They began a tour of the poorer theatres – always a tough crowd, but they continued to put on shows for deadheads and whoever else would lend them their ears. France was a hard act to follow and Jeanne's days of chewing up the scenery and breaking legs would hit their finale before she was even a teenager . . .

The Bonnets began to fall apart after the early and unexpected death of Jeanne's mother, Désirée Leau. It hit Jeanne's only sibling, her elder sister, hard. She was sixteen at the time and became suicidal, which would see her committed to the State Insane Asylum, where she also died. Jeanne went so far off the rails she would have lapped a runaway train. Her life began to feel hopeless, she felt short of options and out of control. Before her father, Sosthène, eventually gave up altogether and moved to Oakland, emotionally drained, he sent Jeanne to a reformatory (a form of juvenile detention) called The Industrial School, when she was fifteen. Girls and boys were taught separately but it didn't stop Jeanne often heading on over to the male dormitory and attacking the squarest jawed 'macho' man, just to prove that she could. If the game 'Snog, Marry, Kill' existed back then, Jeanne would only ever pick options for 'Kill' – she was an angry young woman and her temper was never handed in to lost property. By now Jeanne 'cursed the day she was born a female and not a male'; she cut her hair short and continued on her rage-filled spree without purpose. Although she was 'up to here' with the restrictions set aside exclusively for her sex, there is no record of Jeanne ever changing her name, identity or clothing or attempting to live as a man during these teenage years.

When Jeanne was finally released from her 'educational' lockup, she found that all she had learned prepared her perfectly for a life of petty crime, a career she was triumphant in, for a time, before she began thumb-twiddling for more. Jeanne decided to hammer down and get a proper job – she wasn't stupid, she knew how to sort the sheep from the goats and so that's what she did. Around 1873, she began shepherding in San Mateo, a role for which she was first arrested for 'misdemeanour in male clothing'. As far as we can tell, Jeanne simply had an easier time scaling the hills and herding sheep in pantaloons, a vest, shirt and cap – reasoning that holds water. It also meant she could frequent a saloon of her choosing for a post-work tipple (anything *but* water). It was technically illegal for women to be anywhere near such establishments at the time but the pantalooned Jeanne could drink the bar dry. The alcohol may have been doing it for her but the sheep weren't; by now she knew downtown San Francisco like the back of her hand and sought to utilise her French connections in 'The Paris of the West'. Jeanne began catching frogs, an unusual but worthwhile business that she leapfrogged right on into and quickly became notorious for, not least because she was frog catching in *un pantalon* rather than trailing skirts. Hunting the waters of Lake Merced, Jeanne would spend her days seeking and scooping out the slimy croakers before selling them to the surrounding restaurants. Besides Paris, San Francisco had more French restaurants than anywhere else in the world and if you ordered *cuisses de grenouille*, chances were that Jeanne had snipered and delivered them to the kitchen. Jeanne's attire not only made wading through the waters easier, negotiations and trade with the male restaurant managers was a picnic in pants. She was respected in her new culinary circles but got bugged by the police for it round-the-clock. There are countless records of her arrests for 'promenading the streets in pantaloons' and 'making a spook of herself' (my new favourite phrase). Her assured non-conformity landed her in trouble at least once a month. With time, the convictions and sentences got progressively worse; most fines were around $35 but there was one reported in the *San Francisco Chronicle* in December 1875, listed at *$200*. It may have been a typo but it's also possible that the judge got huffity puffity on our girl to try and teach her a lesson and keep her out of there. It would never work. Jeanne told the courts and the papers that she would just have to keep getting convicted for her man's apparel because she had no other clothes, 'therefore if she didn't wear it she would be convicted too'. (*J'adore Jeanne.*)

Among the cross-dressing charges, Jeanne was arrested for being drunk and disorderly and getting into fight clubs without rules with French pimps. By 1875, Jeanne had begun visiting brothels, some believe to also 'visit' its workers, but she had similarly made it her business to actually *save* the women and teach them to make money in other ways. In fairness, she was encouraging them to leave one life of crime for another (she taught the women to shoplift) but she was incensed by the exploitative pimps. She wanted the women to have nothing to do with men and live by their own means. At first, she managed to recruit a couple of girls and three was a charm for a while before Jeanne was leading a twelve-strong all-female gang. Losing their girls obviously knocked the pimps senseless but our 'strong-minded, social outlaw' (the then code for describing Jeanne as a feminist, which, lesbehonest, also meant *gay* to them) wasn't going to quit. She became very close to one of her gang members (again, the jury's out as to *how* close), an ex-circus girl and then ex-'prostitute' and erotic dancer turned thief named Blanche Beunon, whom Jeanne met in Chinatown. Blanche was always described as a 'soiled dove' by the papers (*I know you are but what was Blanche!*), but Jeanne saw her purity and was determined to set her free. Stomping around with Beunon led to never a dull moment for Jeanne – Blanche's past was out to get her and her ex-lovers and pimps wouldn't leave the pair alone. They had to go into hiding together when one of Blanche's ex-boyfriends threatened to throw acid in her face, so they moved into McNamara's Hotel in San Miguel for safety. It was here, on 14 September 1876, that six gunshots were fired through the window, killing Jeanne in an instant and nobody ever knew if Blanche or Jeanne (or both) were the killer's true target(s). But here's the thing: the assassin escaped unseen and so the case went cold. To this day, Jeanne's murder (known as the 'San Miguel Mystery') remains unsolved.

The evidence surrounding the case – and for and against the idea that Jeanne would have ever preferred to be male – is a fact vs fiction storm, brewed expertly via the usual shower of dreadlines and craptions from the press. She was made a villain, degraded and debased, and the fact she was a working-class French immigrant unrelentingly got a mention to boost these suggestions. Her male garb became the focus and blame for her murder, although there was no evidence to prove anything of the sort. Stories of note included 'Woman's Mania for Male Attire Ends in Death' and ideas such as 'Her career and fate furnish an illustration of the difficulties under which women labour when they undertake to disregard the conventional rules' were rife. If all of this newspaper swirl hasn't made you die eyes first, then please join me in rewriting a few headlines to respectfully and factually report Jeanne's life. I'll go first with 'ENTREPENEURIAL, HARDWORKING, NON-CONFORMIST AND KINDHEARTED JEANNE BONNET LIVED AHEAD OF HER TIME BUT TRAGICALLY DIED BEFORE IT'.

VIOLET PAGET (1856–1935)

THE FAKE-NAMED WRITER AND 'DANGEROUS' BRAIN

During a time in Violet's life when she was exercising resting-scowl-face more than she was smiling, she adopted the motto *Labora et noli contristari*. It means 'work and don't be unhappy' (although Google Translate converted it to 'snacks and do not be sad' for me – which I must remember for my gravestone). It sums up a woman who devoted her life to the creative grind and pursuit of inner happiness. She believed in the power of art, and her own artistry was integral to her wellbeing and personality. Intrigued? You should be. Rather than carry on with vague fortune-cookie-sounding hogwash, I'll explain our wizard gal in more detail. Get a brew on and I'll *spill the tea* . . .

Violet was born in Château St Leonard, Northern France, to British parents. They had a nomadic lifestyle but preferred to be known as 'movers' rather than 'travellers'. There was money in the family, derived from Violet's mother's side, and the Pagets enjoyed jumping about every six months or so. They made homes in Switzerland, France, Germany and Italy, and Violet had some of the best tutoring that money could buy along the way. She developed a passion for reading, languages and music. Hers was not a blackboard and textbook education – in fact, some of it sounded downright daft. For example, her music 'lessons' would start and finish with being made to sit and watch her mother and governess play the piano for hours on end (if only I could sit on a beach in Gran Canaria for a summer, downing vino tinto, and magically learn Spanish . . .). Somewhat of a child genius, Violet had an imagination without lid and was described by her father as having the 'gift of the gab'. Gloomily, her mother, Matilda, was far less complimentary and clearly preferred Violet's half-brother, Eugene, who got all the attention. Matilda always thought Eugene was the best at everything and he rubbed salt and vinegar into the ulcer by later securing a place at Oxford. (Show off.) Violet spent all her time trying to impress her mum, who ended up ruling over her for her entire life until her death. Even Eugene felt it in the end and the fact that the paralysis he later contracted in the run-up to Matilda's death was suddenly cured when she bit the dust was *not* a coincidence. (*Yeesh!*) Violet's mum was eccentric and difficult – two adjectives subsequently used to describe Violet. (Although we're supposed to have reclaimed 'difficult', right? Let's just say that her ma could be a bit of a *schmuck*, never schmucking for betterment, and the effects on Violet's psychology were dreadful.)

The emotional instability of her childhood manifested itself through a series of adulthood breakdowns but somehow Violet managed a life full of achievement. She acquired surrogate mothers such as Henrietta Camilla Jackson Jenkin, a woman who couldn't decide on a surname but was a published novelist and big inspiration for Vi. In women like Henrietta, she had discovered her vocation and was ultimately saved by her craft. Violet found she was always peachy keen when she was working, writing and creating. Having fallen in love with the pen *and* the city of Rome, Violet produced her first publication aged fourteen, all about ancient coins in the golden age of the Roman empire, complete with footnotes on Roman history and all written in French. (Niche.) She had caught the writing bug and it seems she was riddled. Violet developed a fixation with history and she chased her next publishing hit hard, egged on by her dad, who was a closet wannabe writer himself.

At first, she failed to get her work in any English journals but she could also speak fluent Italian – Violet was brilliant in many languages and she wasn't going to wait for the Brits to catch up. By now she was already an engaged feminist and had started dressing *à la garçonne*, so inventing a male pseudonym for herself to progress further was no biggie. Plus, it seemed *a necessity* for a young woman tackling beefcake subjects. Her chosen name was 'Vernon Lee' and as Violet described herself, 'it has the advantage of leaving it undecided whether the writer be a man or a woman' and 'I am sure that no one reads a woman's writing with anything but mitigated contempt'. Her assumed name was used for a series of articles for the Italian journal *La Rivista Europea*, about contemporary female novelists (our friends George Eliot and Charlotte Brontë get a mention), and it was quite clear she was as proud as a peahen of their achievements. (Peahens are female peacocks BTW – they have all the confidence of the male peacocks without needing to make a song and dance about it.)

It wasn't long before Vi had overthrown the gatekeepers in English journal land, and from age nineteen onwards she never had a year when she didn't have something in English, American or European periodicals. Her letters to the publishers show a woman who was serious about her work and money; she made sure she got her worth and we salute her for it. Although she primarily wrote for an English readership and made many visits to London, she spent the majority of her life on the continent, particularly in Italy, having a lovely old time in Florence, Lake Como and the likes. Violet wrote across many genres (history, art, music, travel, supernatural, you name it, she penned it). She consistently bandied her way out of boxes and refused to be a one-trick pony. This, coupled with her supposed lack of cultural identity from all her roaming about, left her too ambiguous for the critics, who were petrified of her versatility and intellectuality. (Women using their brainpower to the best of its capabilities? *When will this madness end!*) The mind of a genius is often a complex one and nobody trusted a woman oozing with IQ.

Once Vernon Lee was revealed to be Violet Paget, the clap-backers tried to cremate Violet further – her work was critiqued with enragingly shirty one-liners such as 'an amazing production for a woman, and especially for a young woman'. Her peers felt the same – the author Henry James remarked that she was 'as dangerous and uncanny as she is intelligent, which is saying a great deal'. Henry is *cancelled*.

Violet had a number of open relationships with women but it was the Scottish writer Kit Anstruther-Thomson she really fell for. Their relationship was thought of as a marriage 'in all but the literal sense', and they were inseparable work and life companions for twelve years. Together they wrote about aestheticism and published their findings in *Beauty and Ugliness* in 1912, but the work was not taken seriously in their circles because they were in a same sex relationship. Rather than smash my laptop through a window at this point, I think it best we round up on some more praiseworthy positives. Violet wrote more than forty books in her lifetime, alongside plays, short story collections and essays. She lived a life without apology and quoted poet Walt Whitman in one of her last books to make it be known: 'And if I contradict myself, why, I contradict myself.' Violet herself believed she was here before her time and pushed back against Victorianism, even though she was born in the age. Upon coming to the end of my research I found her to have once said, 'I absolutely prohibit any biography of me. My life is my own and I leave that to nobody.' But when she met her maker she also left instructions for her life's journals, letters and private papers to be released fifty years after her death for future study of the period. We can only hope she is happy with her renewed fame because Violet was one of the most hell yes things to come out of it.

MARY ANDERSON
(AROUND 1841–1901)

THE 'MAN ABOUT TOWN' POLITICIAN WHO
BEAT THE BALLOT BOX BAN

Ma heid's mince[7] at the pure dead brilliant story of Mary Anderson, a Scottish lassie from Govan who got up to some serious globetrotting at an early age. The exact details are as vague as a politician's promise but we do know that she was an orphan and left completely alone when her last remaining relative, her brother, died. She was perhaps as young as six, yet somehow knew that she wasn't going to survive on her own in a 'man's world'. Dressing herself in her brother's clothing, she stole away to Edinburgh and decided upon life as a boy. When she was a 'young man' (and yes, I am well aware I've gambolled over a great chunk here but this is all we have to go on), Mary decided she wanted to be a politician. She had been living as a man for years, so ambitions like this were tickety-boo achievable. Not content with just wanting to become a politician, she wanted to become an *American politician*, so she went to America to do just that. (Don't ask me any questions.)

---

7   My brain is fried.

Settling in New York City as 'Murray Hall', Mary didn't find work straight away so instead she made her own, opening an employment agency on Sixth Avenue near Twenty-Third Street (detail this deep had better make up for the opener). She also worked as a professional bail bondsman for Jefferson Market Police Court and her work was profitable, although she did get into some dodgy dealings. Mary was the secret belle of the brawl and it seemed that these skills, coupled with her silver-tongued charm, lent themselves perfectly to politics. 'Murray Hall' became a very powerful and prominent member of the infamous general committee of Tammany Hall, a democratic party that controlled state politics at the time. In a party notable for its corruption, Mary had a riot in her role as 'ward heeler', which basically meant that come election day, (s)he had to get constituents to the polls in the Greenwich Village district by *any means*. Fists were thrown, bribes were paid and threats were made. Mary's stereotypical reputation on the political scene might make some of our cabbage-head male politicians look half decent. She was notorious, known as a 'man about town' and famed for being able to 'drink his weight in beer and stand up under it' in the city's saloons. She always had the regulation black cigar hanging out of the side of her mouth, she played poker with the city and state's most flagrant politicos and generally behaved abysmally around women. We can only imagine (pray) she was doing it to keep down with the 'bro code' and was fearful of being unmasked. One incident on record depicts a night when she entered a bar on Greenwich Avenue with a girl on each arm, practising some earnest PDA. The bartender, clearly cottoned on to what would madden him the most, asked 'Murray', 'And what will you have, little old woman?' Mary got very upset indeed and smashed a bottle in his face. *Boys will be boys!* (Said with all the complicated, multifaceted irony of Alanis Morissette's 'ten thousand spoons'.)

Mary managed to get away with being Murray for more than twenty-five years. She always wore baggy clothes and a long coat, even in the summer. Her colleagues were forever mocking Murray for his falsetto voice, his smooth face and the fact his feet were so small he had to custom order his shoes, but somehow nobody twigged. Mary even married twice; the first ended in separation (perhaps because she always had other women draped over her) and the second was similarly tempestuous. Mary was irrationally overprotective of her wife around men (or perhaps rationally, if you think about what she knew) and it caused domestics loud enough for the curtain-twitching neighbours to report them. We don't know if Mrs Hall was privy to Murray Hall's secret but we do know that she was twice as big as he was and people found that amusing (because women are supposed to be petite and adorable to make men feel like spartan warriors). Together they adopted a daughter named Minnie, although never legally and nobody could be too sure of the details. Holding down a home, a family, a job and hiding such a secret must have been exhausting for Mary. Over the years, and especially towards the end, she would buy volume after volume of medical books and surgical studies. The fear of exposure left Mary studying these books, self-diagnosing and treating her problems in a time before Dr Google had graduated sham med school. It was an ingenious but lonely existence and further proof that she truly took a belt and braces approach to her life as Murray Hall.

When Mary ultimately died of breast cancer, her doctor (Dr William C. Gallagher) discovered her biological sex and it was reported by the city coroner to the whole of New York. The revelation smoshed everyone's minds, particularly those of Mary's political cronies and her daughter, Minnie, who all-out refused to believe it – Murray was her *father* and that was that. When the obituary hit the *New York Times* on 19 January 1901, Mary became the national political scandal she never wanted to become. The headline read MURRAY HALL FOOLED MANY SHREWD MEN and the presumed brainiacs kept on calling Murray a 'he', never quite admitting that they'd been had. There was one incident that nobody could ignore, however – the time Murray *cast a vote* and there was photographic evidence to prove it. One of Mary's arch-enemies and opponents, smarmy State Senator John Raines, took enormous pleasure in (what he saw as) her ballot box blunder, lambasting 'I don't wonder you pull such an overwhelming vote down there, when you can dress up the women to vote'. Mary had beaten the men in a game they thought was only theirs to play.

There may not be any evidence to suggest Mary identified as a man but there's certainly lots to prove she loved women. The general consensus is that she was 'passing', a term used to describe gay women who passed as men to assert their political independence, make money, live freely and avoid people with appalling opinions. We'll never know but we do know that Mary managed to be a political leader and VOTE in a time when women may as well have been issued muzzles at birth. Mary didn't just *pass*, she SURPASSED and SASSED and I for one am in all respects GASSED about it (hence all the yelling).

CLARA MARY LAMBERT
(1874–1969)

THE MILITANT SUFFRAGETTE WHO SNUCK INTO THE HOUSE OF COMMONS

Clara was a Londoner and an Eastender through and through. Our china plate[8] was from a flat-broke, working-class family; they had a pony and trap[9] quality of life and often went Hank Marvin.[10] One of nine children, born to George and Elizabeth Lambert (who raised the lot on George's paltry odd-job-man wage), the family moved about and were recorded to have shared accommodation with other families in West Ham, Walthamstow, Hackney, Bethnal Green and Rotherhithe. By 1905, one of Clara's brothers, Arthur, had a successful laundry business in Catford and it saw the Lamberts with a bitty more bangers and mash.[11] Clara was thought to have worked for Arthur, alongside her siblings, as a collar-dresser for a time before swapping seamstress-ing for some serious suffrage-ing.

---

8   Mate.
9   Crap.
10   Starving.
11   Cash.

Clara was an original member of the Women's Social and Political Union and conceivably one of the most fervid and fire-cracking. Clara was considered a 'dangerous woman' to the parliamentary police (so she had to use various aliases, including Catherine Wilson and May Stewart) and dedicated her life completely to the militant suffragette movement. Her women's rights rampage over the years records her rabble-rousing at the forefront of much of the Barney Rubble,[12] always protesting like she was out to win suffragette Top Trumps. The whip was a weapon of choice for many suffragettes and Clara cracked it like a homicidal dominatrix across the capital and at anyone standing in the women's way. She famously even hounded the British Prime Minister, Herbert Henry Asquith, with one. When she missed him, she was so aggravated she set fire to a haystack (a twentieth-century rage vent that I imagine had similar steam let-off to a Boxercise Bootcamp two days before you're due on). Another time, Clara was arrested for pelting an 'over-ripe' tomato at the Public Prosecutor, Archibald Bodkin, in an act of defiance so deft I think we should all *ketchup* with Clara's clout and start leaving the house armed with punnets of the things. Or maybe *searches for the world's heaviest fruit* ATLANTIC GIANT PUMPKINS! (Someone find out how I can import all that Atlanta has and I'll see you in Parliament Square.) Clara was one of the 300 suffragettes at the voting rights for women demonstration on 18 November 1910, known as Black Friday. Along with more than a hundred others, she was arrested and suffered brutality at the hands of the police. The government were determined to stop the suffragettes – Clara *did* get their memo but she ignored it. Any retaliation from them only incited her and the WSPU women further. She involved herself every which way, including printing their magazine, *The Suffragette* (later known as *Britannia*), and moving the printing press from the safe houses of one sympathiser to another.

---

12 Trouble.

In March 1912, the group began a campaign of window smashing across London (*in case of sexism, break glass?*). During one particularly smashy weekend, which overwhelmed the police, Clara concealed a hammer in her hand muff (LOVE HER SO MUCH), shattered the windows of the Strand Post Office and its neighbours, and was sentenced. In and out of prison for a series of similar raids over the next couple of years, Clara never lost her kick and always went down fighting. On one occasion she left court screaming, 'I shall come out [of prison] more determined than ever!' On another she commented upon her sentence, 'I shall do the hunger strike, and if it means my life to save the thousands of other women, it must be so.' (Clara's hunger strike medal contained three silver bars, which showed that she had indeed endured such punishment three times, in 1912, 1913 and 1914.) As women were not allowed to be on juries until 1919, any time Clara stood in front of one, she stood in front of a panel of men. She knew she would only be sent down. My favourite outburst documents her feelings on that matter perfectly – she simply told them, 'I have not come to appeal to your intelligence because I have come to the conclusion that men do not have any.' Clara survived this string of arrests and purgatory punishments by the skin of her pants. She was twice released under the 'Cat & Mouse Act' (a temporary discharge for ill health after starvation) and continued to evade arrest by hiding in sympathisers' houses. They would help her get better until the police came a-knocking again at the front door (meanwhile, Clara was usually getting piggy-backed out the back).

Satirical drawings of suffragettes often portrayed them in men's clothes to mock the women and hint at lesbianism. They would be depicted in accessories such as ties and pork pie hats, items traditionally associated with women who loved women (a link that makes about as much sense as a Furby with low batteries). The suffragettes were so powerful and enduring, men settled that they had to be either gay or entirely 'unwomanly' to carry on the way they did. Cross-dressing as a tactic was more unusual among the suffragettes than the previously mentioned whip but Clara was certainly no sheep; instead, she led the herd. On 16 March 1914, she had a brainwave and the result saw her stroll into parliament, disguised as a man, with one of their iconic weapons in her left overcoat sleeve – ready to whip like wild. The House of Commons was out of bounds for women then. There was a special 'Ladies' Gallery', way up above the chamber, with a burly metal grille across it and no light (as it was decided the occupants should not be seen). It would be so refreshing by this point in the book to give even a sniff of a valid explanation for this female veto but the women were hidden because they were considered far too much of *a distraction* to the men. Of the gallery/ventilation shaft in the ceiling, Millicent Fawcett wrote that the grilles were like 'using a gigantic pair of spectacles which did not fit, and made the Ladies' Gallery a grand place for getting headaches'. (Sorry if you too are having a sympathy headache worse than those inflicted by a top knot and four double espressos at the injustice of this exclusion.) But Clara was on the ground, she had made it inside and was meddling among the men! Unfortunately, Special Branch had somehow got wind of the plot, tipped off the parliamentary police and Clara never got to have her fun. When she was caught and charged to six weeks' hard labour, she told Inspector Rogers, the arresting officer, 'If I had carried out my purpose they would have had it hot!'

Clara carried on dressing up, hotting up and destructing at any opportunity (phew). One episode in April 1914 stopped the press. Clara charged into the British Museum in a long tweed costume and coat, and 'appeared to be studying the antiquities' before brandishing a *meat cleaver* and making mincemeat out of a display cabinet of porcelain. At Bow Street Court the next morning, she subwoofer-ed her way through the hearing, hollering at the magistrate, while being restrained. She told the judge she would not sit down while her associates, including Emmeline Pankhurst, continued to be tortured. After this, Scotland Yard issued a memorandum to all the police stations in the country, warning officers to either avoid her like the ghost gang on Pac-Man or lock her up on the spot. It described how she had recently been found in the House of Commons 'in male attire with a rising whip in her coat pocket for an unlawful purpose'. I'm thrilled to announce that it didn't stop her and she kept up her self-willed ways until the WSPU dissolved and the First World War was well under way. What's more, in 1915, in the most paradisiacal role reversal ever, Clara became one of the first female police officers in Britain! She joined some of her fellow suffragettes in the Women's Police Service and met her lifelong companion, Violet Croxford, while on assignment in Wales. After the war, the pair opened a hostel for 'unfortunate ladies' in Kent. (*Those females are strong as hell!*)

Us 'ladies' today are *more than fortunate* to have had Clara and her cohorts go before us; we can be eternally grateful for their fight for equality. Clara carpe'd that diem with a concoction of rage, bravery and pugnacity that eventually changed our worlds in ways too monumental to sum up in a few closing sentences. Thank you, Clara.

QIU JIN (1875–1907)

THE WOMEN'S RIGHTS SUPPORTIN', POEM PENNIN', CHINESE REVOLUTIONARY

Qiu Jin's life and times absolutely lived up to one of her most famous lines of poetry, 'Don't tell me women are not the stuff of heroes.' I could very easily leave that pearl right there and down tools (especially as it sums up everything this book is about in ten words rather than 75,000). But without a full-fledged #*GenderRebels* style rundown, answer me this – how would you have ever known that Qiu's name, when translated from traditional Chinese, means 'Woman Knight of Mirror Lake' (the best name meaning yet)? Or that our Woman Knight didn't just live in a time of great political awakening among women in China, she was *the reason* for it?

Qiu had a comfy upbringing in Eastern China, in a province called Zhejiang. She was allowed to swordfight, she was allowed to tear around being 'boisterous' (ugh), she was allowed an education, but her atypical privileges weren't going to last forever – she *wasn't allowed* to be free as an adult. Once a teenager, it didn't matter to her family that she clearly had a career-worthy aptitude for poetry and writing. Nobody gave a flying fanny that she dreamed of changing the world like her martial hero and our old mucker, Hua Mulan. Qiu was going to be an obedient wife and fire out kids at a rate of knots like every other woman. A marriage was arranged for her to do just that when, at nineteen, she was handed over to a wealthy official's son named Wang Ting-jun. He was nice enough but I mean that in the most insulting sense of the word. While Wang went about his married life being 'nice' to everyone but his wife, Qiu had an insatiable thirst for knowledge and hunger for change. This wasn't simply a case of the munchies – if Qiu didn't do something to satisfy her needs and escape her constant state of cringing, she would explode. She joined a secret society known as the Triads; they opposed the ruling emperors of the Qing dynasty and were out to take back control of their country. Qiu and her consociates knew that the patriarchy in China's society would exist for as long as the country avoided a Western-style democracy. They were stuck in an almighty time warp but Qiu's ambitions for a feminist uprising and reform were mightier still. Her faith in the power of freedom, equality and universal love was not going to be discoverable while she was chained to the stove with Wang and their two kids in tow. She tried to leave the man she said 'treats me as less than nothing' but divorce didn't exist in China then. There was nothing for it but to *leave* leave.

In 1904, Qiu pawned her jewellery (the first small step to financial independence) and painfully unbound her feet (a giant leap for independence both physically and symbolically). Her feet would have been bound at around the age of five years old and part of the reason was to prevent women doing anything like Qiu was about to. The practice was supposed to make women 'sexier' to men, it was supposed to keep women 'in their place', it was supposed to keep them quiet. But Qiu wasn't going to pipe down any longer, she was louder than an airhorn and ready to blow. En route to Japan, where she planned to study, she wrote: 'Unbinding my own feet to undo the poisoned years / Arousing the souls of a hundred flowers to passionate movement.' This movement would continue through her work and she would spend all of her pent-up energy speaking out against arranged marriages and foot-binding, and fighting hard for women's financial and educational rights. In a time when many women were left illiterate, this power of speech became just as integral to Qiu's advocacy as her poetry and essays. She could use her voice anywhere, at any time, for free and without restriction. Public lectures became a vehicle for political pro-paganda and allowed her to speak truths like this about binding: 'If one day we succeed in wiping out this horrible blot on our civilisation, our bodies will begin to grow stronger, and the steps we take in walking will become a pleasure instead of a pain. Having thus regained their natural energy, the whole sex will progress without difficulty, and an endless store of happiness will be built up for thousands of generations of women yet unborn.' (If only there was the option to subscribe for more content.)

In Tokyo, Qiu joined another anti-Qing society known as Guangfuhui; she was jamming with revolutionaries and planning a revolution. If people had been shocked by her actions to date, they were certainly *not* ready for her new-found fashion. While studying under the writer and rebel wonder Utako Shimoda at the Girls' Practical School in Kōjimachi, Qiu decided to make men's clothing her signature. 'My aim is to dress like a man! . . . In China men are strong, and women are oppressed because they're supposed to be weak.' Qiu and 'weak' were incompatible. If anything, she looked the strongest in her uniform of second-hand dark-blue business suits, green necktie, brown shoes and blue hunting cap worn at a (frankly reckless) angle. Wearing Western clothes and keeping her hair short in a 'foreigner style', which was banned in China, Qiu was an eyegasm of tenacity and influence. Her two years in Japan were spent sharing ideas, lecturing, writ-ing about and stirring up revolt.

Upon return to China, Qiu lost no time in putting those ideas into practice. She became the principle of the Shaoxing Datong Sports Teachers School, an establishment so far-out it taught women to *read*! While masquerading as a school for sports, it was being used as a covert training ground for revolutionaries. They taught women how to fend for themselves, they learned marks*man*ship and even bomb-making (Qiu didn't choose the thug life, the thug life chose her). With her friend and fellow poet Xu Zihua, Qiu started a radical feminist news-paper called *China Women's News*. It's thought they managed only two issues before the authorities caught wind and party-pooped it. Around this time, Qiu was also plotting an uprising against the Qing dynasty with her male cousin, Xu Xilin, but *behold the seventh circle of what the actual hell*, the authorities were on to that too. Xu was betrayed by one of his fellow rebels and was subsequently executed the day after his capture, in July 1907. Qiu knew that they would be on to her but she had resolved to die for the cause and spent her final days doing all she could to ensure that once she was gone she would become a martyr for it, emboldening more to rally as a result.

After the officials found Qiu and some incriminating evidence (most likely *the explosives*), they attempted a stint of barbarous brutality for rebel information. Qiu stayed true to the revolution until the end, which came only a few days later when they beheaded her publicly in her home village. Her final words were 'Autumn wind, autumn rain, fill my heart with sorrow' and my heart is so sorrowful right now it hurts. Although Qiu was not given a proper burial, two of her closest friends, Wu Zhiying and Xu Zihua, organised a memorial service, which gathered hundreds of attendees and became a public protest. For their actions (and association with Qiu), the pair found themselves on the government's wanted list. We know shrimpy amounts about Qiu's personal life after she left her marriage but some believe Qiu and Wu Zhiying exchanged love rings in a commitment ceremony, not too long before she was put to death. Around Wu she was happier than Larry has ever been and, either way, Wu saw that Qiu was celebrated with respect and dignity and that's true love story enough for me.

Qiu composed our round-up for us when she wrote, 'The young intellectuals are all chanting, "Revolution, Revolution", but I say the revolution will have to start in our homes, by achieving equal rights for women.' This is but one of her teachings that she could rest assured in her day wasn't about to be stolen from her and HEpeated. It did, however, lay the groundwork to ensure that, over time, those offending HEpeaters learned to SHUT UP AND PAY ATTENTION TO WOMEN.

ISABELLE WILHELMINE MARIE EBERHARDT (1877–1904)

THE CLOAKED AND COSTUMED SWISS EXPLORER AND TRAVEL WRITER

If you thought your family (and/or your multiple non-stop family WhatsApp groups) were vexatious, you should thank your lucky stars you weren't born the illegitimate daughter of Russian anarchist nihilists, whose parenting style might be described as a reign of terror at best. Isabelle's mother, Nathalie Moerder, was a member of the Russian aristocracy and her father, Alexandre Trophimowsky, was an ex-Orthodox-priest turned atheist who channelled all his rage and revolutionary zeal into Isabelle. Her childhood in Geneva, Switzerland, was certainly *different*. Trophimowsky was rather an intense chap. He didn't trust the government (I'm sure we can all empathise with that bit) and staunchly accredited the education system with the downfall of the human race. Trophs squared the circle by home-schooling Isabelle with similar levels of ferocity, resulting in Isabelle becoming Chatty Patty fluent in six languages, including Arabic, by the time she was sixteen. She studied all the subjects – along with some subjects that, by the sound of them, I reckon Trophers made up. Everything Isabelle did was critiqued and scrutinised severely and her dad hated weakness of any kind. He believed in the theory of the Russian revolutionist Mikhail Bakunin that 'every child of either sex should be prepared as much for a life of the mind as for the life of work, so that all may grow up equally into complete men'. I tried switching the Bakunin quote off and on again but it's broken (it still only says 'men' at the end). As such, Isabelle's dad didn't bat an eyelid when she began wearing male clothing, enjoying the roomy, airy (and I imagine chafe-free) liberty it gave her as she was made to perform hard labour alongside her learning. Isabelle's beatnik upbringing was liberating in slight ways but, in the main, super sheltered. She wasn't allowed out of the house and would daydream of a life beyond her garden wall. It's no wonder she spent the rest of her days, once she had escaped, trying to stay lost, deciding: 'I shall remain a nomad all my life, in love with changing horizons and unexplored distances.'

By the age of twenty, Isabelle was free. She had become bewitched with the idea of living in Africa and answered the ad of a French officer stationed in the Sahara who was after a pen pal. Accounts of how and why Isabelle ended up in Algeria vary but we can be sure that her letter-writing desert pal helped turn her African fantasy from mirage to reality. Her parents might have been moneyed but, on her own, Isabelle's only currency was her mind. Cross-dressing to help her go cross-cultural, Isabelle found work as a Marseille dockhand and earned enough to afford the ferry over to North Africa. A woman would never have been allowed to do the journey but for 'Arabic student' Si Mahmoud Essaadi (Isabelle, in case you aren't keeping up), it was plain sailing over to Algeria. Isabelle knew that Muslim women were not permitted to go out alone or be unveiled but the burnous and turban she had adopted as 'Si' meant she could roam as a 'he' and as she pleased. Interestingly, it is thought that few were actually fooled by Isabelle's disguise and her cross-dressing was far more accepted in her new home than it was in Geneva. Her decision was respected among the Arabs, especially as she had converted to Islam. The French settlers in the country were less accommodating – nobody laid out the welcome mats because they didn't have a clue why a woman would want to live among Arabs over her fellow Europeans. They convinced themselves Isabelle was a spy because they could see no other reason for her being there. It's quite a cruddy conclusion given that, at this point (and despite apparently embracing the Muslim way of life), Isabelle got very '*Lads! Lads! Lads!*' as Si; she was a fan of dive bars, brothels, binge drinking, smoking kief (hashish not chicken kiev) and sexual promiscuity (*her body, her choice!*). Now, I don't know if you're ready for this jelly, but rumour has it that Isabelle also *got a kick from cross-dressing* – it became a firm feature in her sexual experiences and fantasies (no kink shaming in this forum, please). All of this absolute freakum might go some way to explaining why Isabelle is often thought of as 'the first hippie'.

Between the benders and blowouts, Isabelle began publishing short stories under the pseudonym 'Nicolas Podolinsky' (there is usually some explanation as to where the pen-names have derived from but Si and Nicolas seem to be plucked from the fuzziness and why the heff not?). Her first published work, *Infernalia*, had some positively dark necrophilia-erotica-type themes that I'm sure only Isabelle herself could explain, so I won't try to. Later, her work began to echo her travels and wherever she went, she wrote extensively and insightfully about her experiences, in a variety of styles and formats. Isabelle went to Paris for a time to try to become a full-time writer but it belly-flopped. It would take the world a little longer than Isabelle had to recognise her talent. While in Paris, Isabelle met the widow of the politician Marquis de Morès, who was believed murdered in the Sahara in 1896. She was amped that Isabelle had an expert knowledge of the area and commissioned her to travel back, become a spy for her and investigate the murder. Isabelle took the money because she couldn't be hooped with Paris anymore but the investigation bombed. During her travels, Isabelle became involved with the mystic Sufi Muslim sect named Qadiriyya, who were strongly opposed to the French colonial rule. She had found her tribe but was deep diving in some heavy-duty politics – working for them as a writer, journalist, sometimes spy and frequent informant. For all of these reasons, a man with a sabre (most likely sent by the French authorities who had blacklisted her for her unorthodox ways) tried to murder Isabelle in 1901. She survived the assassination attempt because her will was so iron it should have had its own theme tune.

A year later, Isabelle met and fell for an Algerian soldier named Slimane Ehni. Finding love in a hopeless place, her physical and mental health was, by this point, deteriorating. She continued to write (particularly about the Bedouins, a nomadic Arab clan) but spent the majority of her time getting into pickles. A wine-thirsty ASOS account holder would have nothing on Isabelle's spending habits; she pawned all she had, took loans and squandered whatever was left on tobacco and books. It rendered her homeless (but very well read). By 1904, Isabelle and Slimane were living in a mud hut and Isabelle died the night of a freak flood in the desert, during which she drowned. Some biographers have questioned if her death was suspicious, especially as she attempted suicide a number of times in her final years. Although she was epic, she *might* have been hard-pushed to raise a flood (but she may not have run from it). Many of her writings, travelogues, diaries and manuscripts were saved and published posthumously. Writing was her passion project and despite dying an obscure writer, her work is now famous for being as radical and undefinable as her character. Isabelle stayed in her own lane and I don't know about you but rather than keep at a safe distance or avoid that lane, I'd swerve to join her.

DOROTHY LAWRENCE
(1896–1964)

THE JOURNALIST WHO BECAME A WAR
CORRESPONDENT ON THE FRONT LINE

Ready for another account of a woman who overturned and outsmarted the dicktatorship? Of course you are! (And that was a rhetorical question.) This one's a hot off the press, prime scoop, headline conqueror. Dorothy was *Extra! Extra!* And you can read all about it . . .

We know less about Dorothy's childhood than we do about baby pigeons but we can be certain she was born in the southeast of England in Middlesex. Her mother was unmarried (someone call the police!) and for reasons unknown, gave her daughter up for adoption, leaving Dorothy with the church when she was around thirteen years old. Her guardian was well respected but, in later life, Dorothy would tell medical professionals that she was raped by another churchgoer while in her care. I wish I could bring you news of a childhood crammed with treehouses, pick 'n' mix and Hide and Seek, but this is as much as we know about what were supposed to be 'the best years' of Dorothy's life. Her abject adolescence might explain how Dotty got to be more workaholic than me (writing this at 5 a.m. after being woken by the smell of my brain cooking her chapter).

By the outbreak of the First World War, Dorothy was living in London and paper chasing, trying to be the best journalist on the block. That *block* being Fleet Street. Dorothy was scraping a living and was laughed out of every office she approached. She had been published in the broadsheets once or twice but she wasn't writing to be fish and chip wrapping, she was writing to change the world. Dorothy's mind was set on becoming a war correspondent and it made her butt heads and become the punchline in every editor's office in the capital. In turn, and with a vitriol-inflamed point to prove, she travelled to France in 1915 to try to join the Voluntary Aid Detachment, a position from which she planned to report undercover. When they refused her, for reasons unknown, she changed tactics and instead decided to bung herself smack dab into the middle of the war zone, her only plan being to simply call herself a freelance war correspondent if anyone asked (and I've just had a pang of sad that I'll never be able to go for a pint with Dorothy Lawrence). Two miles away from reaching the front line in Senlis, Dorothy was seized by the French police and arrested. She was going to need a Plan C. (Answers on a postcard if you can guess what that might have been!) She was dead set on wanting to see 'what an ordinary English girl, without credentials or money can accomplish . . . I'll see whether I cannot go one better than those big men with their cars, credentials and money . . . I'll be hanged if I don't try.'

When Dorothy fled the police, she was met with a crock of you know what from a ton of those men yet again. She started by idling around coffee shops in Paris, hoping to eavesdrop an exposé or inside story, but she was rudely manterrupted by groups of bored soldiers who couldn't comprehend how a single woman in public *wasn't a 'prostitute'* (but we don't have the time or patience to pull this thread right now). Two British privates with a modicum more egghead than blockhead about them decided to help Dorothy (if only out of sympathy because they thought she was bampot). Dorothy went on to name them her 'Khaki Accomplices' because they smuggled her out parts of their uniform, piece by piece, over the next few weeks, with their washing. In the meantime, Dorothy did all she could to work out how to transform herself into 'Private Denis Smith', the man she had to become to achieve the dreams that should have been firmly in her sights. Creative and nifty to the core, Dorothy constructed a homemade corset and used sacks and cotton wool to bulk out her shoulders. She cut her long hair short, practised using a shoe polish tan to dirty up her face, learned to drill and march and even shaved her cheeks to get the razor rash look (the *Lynx* effect). The only thing she didn't get her hands on was the underwear but having to go commando among the commandoes was the least of her worries. Leaving her petticoats in a field felt like such a release. Clothed in a blanket coat so nobody would catch sight of her female form or lack of undercrackers, Dorothy forged her papers and was ready to face the Western Front. If you're getting a celebratory finger-snapping-in-the-air-vibe from this symbolic moment in Dorothy's story, you'll be even more delighted to know that she chose to cycle the hundreds of kilometres from Paris to Somme (sleeping in ditches and haystacks along the way), a parcel full of her boots, braces, cap and uniform dangling from the handlebars as she went.

As our Dots pedalled her way closer and closer to enemy fire, she met a lush Lancastrian Sapper named Tom Dunn, who offered to help her out. Tom found her work alongside him, as Denis, in the 179 Tunnelling Company, 51st division of Royal Engineers, and gave her a place to stay. Truth be told, he was ill at ease with the idea of Dorothy being a lone woman sleeping between his peers and wanted her nowhere near them come nightfall. The abandoned cottage in nearby Senlis Forest wasn't much better than the trenches but Tom would bring her any rations he could spare. ('Food-sharing!?' What a guy!) The risk of being attacked by men may have lessened but Dorothy was attacked by the entire insect population instead, plus the harsh weather and the damp – leaving her with constant chills and rheumatism. The job itself was just as gruelling and Dorothy (Denis) was part of the team that dug the tunnels underneath no man's land, preparing them to be laid with mines. They dug dug dug dug dug dug dug from early morn to night, they dug dug dug dug dug dug dug up everything in sight. Denis kept 'his' head down and went undetected but after only ten days in the tunnels, Dorothy's feverish symptoms had multiplied. Following a fit of fainting spells, Dorothy (for fear of causing problems for Tom and a few others who'd helped her) gave herself up to the commanding sergeant. It wasn't the report ending she set out for but she had a story by now that would make the journos of Fleet Street look like dum dums. And the army appeared to feel like a shock of those too ('shock' from this day forward being the collective noun for 'dum dums'). Dorothy was immediately placed under military arrest, declared a prisoner of war and taken to Calais for interrogation at the army headquarters. The high command had egg on his face and beetroot cheeks – he was a man who had clearly never heard of plates. The thought of a TEENAGE GIRL *CYCLING* to the front had pushed him beyond the brink. Dorothy later wrote that she couldn't help but bwahaha laugh in everyone's faces during the cross-examination: 'So utterly ludicrous appeared this betrousered little female, marshalled solemnly by three soldiers and deposited before twenty embarrassed men.'

The army were fearful that more women would want to do 'male roles' in the war if word got out and, as such, Dorothy was banished to a French convent and forced to sign an affidavit to swear not to talk or write about her experience. When she was finally sent back to Britain, Dorothy had an abracadabra chance meeting with Emmeline Pankhurst (who better to bump into on a ferry in your time of sorority need?). She invited Dorothy to talk to her suffragettes, who were all desperate to contribute to the war effort. Dot was champing at the bit to speak and write about the front line and finish what she'd started but the War Office silenced her again, not allowing her to do so until after the Armistice in 1918. By that time, Dorothy hadn't just written a few articles on her experience as a private, she'd written a whole book. *Sapper Dorothy*

Lawrence: The Only English Woman Soldier was published in 1923 but it was so heavily censored by the authorities, it didn't make Fleet Street spontaneously combust as planned. She ignored the injunctions and redrafted it but, by this point, she was broke as a joke and enduring mocking by critics such as the *Spectator*, who called her 'a girlish freak' (if you've got nothing nice to say, *Spectator*, don't say anything at all). Dorothy's mental health came into question and from 1925, up until her death, she was institutionalised. Nowhere in Dorothy's medical records were any visitors mentioned during her nearly *forty-year* incarceration. We're all with you now, Dorothy, WE'RE ALL WITH YOU NOW. And lest we forget.

UMM KULTHUM
(CIRCA 1898–1975)

THE 'VOICE OF EGYPT' AND ARABIC 'STAR OF THE ORIENT'

There must have been a monster-truck load of pressure on Umm Kulthum's shoulders. If you've ever been put on a plinth or rolled out because you 'tick a box', you'll know how it feels to end up the hesitant spokesperson for everyone else that's been shafted into that same box. Imagine: Umm was thought of as 'The Voice of Egypt'! Not only was she expected to represent the entire population of a country, she was even dubbed 'Egypt's Fourth Pyramid!' It wasn't rare enough that she was the most successful *female* singer in the Arab-speaking sphere. *No!* Umm was supposed to personify an ancient wonder of the world too! If you've not had a sufficient amount of melon twist already, now try and comprehend that she sold over 80 million records! Umm had success and stardom so staggering, it has made me use more exclamation marks in one paragraph than will ever sit comfortably with my style. (!)

Umm grew up in the village of Tamay e-Zahayra in the Nile Delta, in a mud-brick house – a story-arc winner that would delight anyone (me) trying to creatively document her life from the *actual* ground up. To conceptualise the scene, Umm once said that the greatest display of wealth she remembered was that someone local owned a horse and carriage (such an unknown extravagance in the area that there was only one road wide enough to fit it). Her father was an imam at the local mosque; he taught her to recite and memorise the Qur'an in full. Her mother was a full-time mum, who taught her the importance of honesty, humility and trust in God (her ideals of a 'good' Egyptian woman). While Umm was being all truthful and docile and God reliant, the boys in her family – her dad, brother Khālid and cousin Ṣabr – were out making money and memories through music. Umm was not allowed to be a part of their performing family music troupe because she was not a he and that sucked more than a vacuum on a mucky rug because she had a one-track mind, stuck on singing. The commercial recording industry was booming and phonograph record players were being shared between the coffee shops and public spaces in the village. Umm spent this goosebump-making time for music learning every song she could get her hands on by heart. Much like me and Hanson's 'Middle of Nowhere' (*Zac n Anneka 4eva 9T7*), she knew the lyrics, she knew the harmonies, she knew every break and beat. When she was twelve, the songbird could no longer be caged and she started to sing twenty-four seven and nobody could deny her voice was stunning – it needed to be heard. The problem was (and feel free to join me in a communal eye roll), women very rarely performed. If they did, they had to be veiled and weren't allowed to sing any religious songs; even the audiences were majority male. Performing was seen as a disreputable profession anyway but this was predominately a male-only space, associated with debauchery – *no environment for girls*! One night, Umm's brother felt too unwell to perform at one of the group's functions and a plan formed so that Umm could take his place. Her dad knew he would face disapprobation if he let her join him in the group – in Umm's words, 'The idea that his daughter should sing in front of men he didn't know, was difficult for him to accept, but my singing helped support the family. So, he dressed me in boy's clothes, and I sang this way for several years.

I realise now that he wanted to convince himself, and the audience too, that the singer was a young boy, and not a young woman.' Umm was dressed in a long coat and head covering, like a real Bedouin boy, and thrust centre stage.

With Umm as the star, the family kitty was soon heavier than a birthday card your nan's sellotaped five pound coins to. The band audience sizes blew up bigger than the weddings and local dos they had been used to. Before long they were travelling back and forth, booking gigs far and wide. At first, they had to journey on foot but as their demand and radius grew, they began touring on boats and requesting rock and roll riders such as asking to be met at ports with donkeys to transport them to their venue. Eventually, Umm didn't need the disguise anymore; her talent sang for itself and surpassed the age-old chapter and verse about female entertainers. When she lost the performance persona it then became a novelty for people to see a girl on stage, another trick that seemed to work for them, and the gigs grew grander still. Umm started to get noticed and began singing solo, making several trips to Cairo in the early 1920s to warble for some seriously exclusive circles and influential patrons. Her family were reluctant to let her move to the capital permanently at first but Umm knew it was a vehicle for upward mobility – our village girl may have had a no-frills childhood but she was ready for a bit of lux. When she made the move a few years later, she kept her nose to the grindstone and became the most sought-after, best-paid success story and woman of note in Egypt. The industry loved her conservative, humble and 'asāla' (authentic) appeal but Umm's superpower was probably her extrovert networking skills. She didn't just add a load of people on LinkedIn and hope for the best, Umm made lifelong friends with the most powerful cultural leaders, journalists, composers and fellow musicians of the time, all of whom played a part in her meteoric rise in commercial recording and, later, TV and film. Umm's music spoke to everyone. After sell-out tours across the Middle East and North Africa in the twenties, by the thirties her concerts were broadcast live on the first Thursday of each month. Families and friends would gather around those coffee house radios to hear Umm. Her singing reached every ear in Egypt and continued to do so for almost forty years.

Unlike most of her contemporaries, Umm mixed her Egyptian-Arab musical heritage and frequently used religious material. Throw in her tendency to improvise, endless emotional energy, plus projected chastity and you can understand her magnetism at the time. Ni'mat Fu'ad, one of Umm Kulthum's main biographers, wrote that, 'When she stood up to sing, there was in front of her an invisible sign that read Do Not Touch.' (I wanna get me one of those! I might even laminate it and add some clip art too.) Umm was out of reach but also absolutely graspable. Her music covered the universal themes of life that forever top the charts and she never sang a song the same way twice. She had her fans hanging on her every note and nobody ever had anything but love for her voice. In fact, her nasality (*ghunna*) got a thumbs-up – although not always celebrated in the West, hers made her sound like a double reed instrument and everyone deeply adored it. Her fans included the King of Egypt, Farouk I, who gave her a knighthood (*nishan el kamal*) in 1944. Her relationship with the royals and the Egyptian president, Gamal Abdel Nasser, only furthered her popularity, especially during the time of the Great Depression in the thirties and the Egyptian revolution in the early fifties. Umm was influential and she used it to get political. One of her songs, '*Wallāhi Zamān, Yā Silāī*' ('It's Been a Long Time, O Weapon of Mine'), was even adopted as the Egyptian national anthem later down the line. Our patriotic Egyptian, devout Muslim singing sensation had cultivated a public image that was immaculate and morally sound and she defied patriarchal restraints. Even I'd sign up if she offered me first dibs on a clearly flawed *pyramid* scheme.

Not the type to have a duvet day, Umm never *officially* retired but she did gradually start to slow down and limit her performances. When she died at age seventy-six, her funeral became a national event and *over four million* people lined the streets to celebrate her life. (I hope they weren't all at the wake – that's *a lot* of cheese and pineapple on sticks to prepare.) Umm now has museums, street names and all sorts of wotnot in her memory and is a national symbol. She was a role model to women and girls who could never imagine a career in the public eye until she came shimmying out of the shadows. Group hugs all round that she did because Umm Kulthum was certainly not made to be subtle.

FLORENCE 'PANCHO' BARNES (1901–1975)

THE STUNT PILOT, PARTY ANIMAL AND AIR-SPEED RECORD-BREAKER

Most people who have been strapped inside an airborne metal tube and force-fed homogenised stew (while rushing headlong through time zones at 35,000 feet) tend to rank themselves quite highly on the scale of one to antsy. But for Florence 'Pancho' Barnes, flying made her feel like 'a sex maniac in a whorehouse with a stack of hundred-dollar bills'. I can't even excuse her controversial use of language in this analogy because I am *dead* and cannot be revived. And there's plenty more Pancho sauce to go round . . .

As a kid in San Marino, California, Pancho was raised in a mansion with twenty-five rooms (the sort of house that today would have been split into a minimum of 400 'luxury' apartments). Her parents clearly weren't short of a bob or two and paid for her to attend the finest private schools in the area. She was raised by her father and grandfather as the boy they wished she had been and by her mother as the debutante she was strong-arming her to be. More interested in racing her horses until she zonked, Pancho's behaviour was not for 'correcting'. The family tried her at a religious school for a short time but she ran away (or rather, *galloped* away on horseback); she had to have the sound of the wind whistling in her ears. When she was ten years old, her grandad, Thaddeus S. C. Lowe (a pioneer in American aviation and later thought of as the Grandfather of the American Air Force), took Pancho to an air show and gave her an instant taste for gasoline and power. Although she became locked in on pursuing a life in the fast lane, at nineteen she was left on the hard shoulder with four flat tyres after her mother arranged her marriage to a local clergyman, Rankin Barnes, to tame her tenacity. Pancho was domesticised by wifedom and a son and had to put up with her clanger of a husband until it eventually gave her a nervous breakdown. She lost herself, never truly finding her spark again until her mother's clogs had popped – but *when Pancho came back*, she came back in a big way.

In 1927, Pancho cut her hair, threw on some men's duds, tied a bandana in a knot, stuffed it in her jeans and waved goodbye to her ball and chain. Feeling a new lease of wild and ready for adventure, Pancho renamed herself 'Jacob Crane' and headed to San Pedro Harbour. 'Jacob' was signed up as a crew member on a banana boat, which Pancho discovered (only once offshore) was running guns and ammo to revolutionaries in Mexico. She travelled around Mexico for seven months, disguised as Jacob (who by this point had gained the nickname Pancho), island hopping, running from the authorities and keeping her nose seriously sullied. Once home, Pancho's newly revived sense of independence and confidence was not in keeping with the ways of the church or her husband, who she tried to divorce. This would have been a shocking move to make at the time, and when her husband refused, Pancho shocked further by riding up to his church, naked, on a white horse, to stun him into signing. Now quids in after receiving her parents' inheritance, Pancho looked to the next adventure and turned her attention skyward.

During this golden era for aviation, more companies were making planes than they were cars. They were the ultimate status symbol and

Pancho wanted in. She first took to the skies with her cousin, Dean Banks, and in 1928 managed to persuade his flight instructor to give her lessons. After only six hours of formal instruction, she was solo flying and dive-bombing her ex-husband's church in South Pasadena during sermons, leaving him looking up to his God and signing the cross over his chest. There were around 5,000 registered pilots in America by this point but only a handful of females – the authorities were actively trying to prevent them from gaining their licences because they thought they'd keep crashing and put the industry in disrepute. They didn't want to risk having women in the air or at the deck, especially if *they were on their periods* (stick a fork in me for I am DONE). Pancho wasn't having it; she wore men's clothes for her pilot licence photograph and tricked them into welcoming her to join 'their' club. A year later, she was competing in air races and had beating Amelia Earhart's world women's speed record in her sights. The 1929 'Women's Air Derby', the first of its kind, was seen as a novelty and stunt by the press, who labelled it 'The Powder Puff Derby'. There were even cases of men sabotaging the engines out of spite and killing the female pilots around this time. Nobody was taking them seriously but Pancho soon proved them wrong, a year later smashing the speed record in her most treasured possession, a Travel Air Type R Mystery Ship plane that set her back thousands of dollars but propelled her fast forward into history with the title of the fastest woman on earth.

Once Pancho *believed she could fly*, she believed she could touch the sky and she had, she moved to Hollywood to become a stunt pilot. She flew in some of the most-watched films of the 1930s, including *Hell's Angels*, and formed a union for aerial stunt pilots in the industry, to ensure they stayed safe and were treated with the respect they deserved. Pancho lived the life in the Hollywood hills. She liked fast cars, powerful planes and young men: 'I don't want to shock you but pretty much all we did was fly, fight and f*ck!' (She married three more times after the Rev; one of her spouses was even younger than her son.) Her drinking parties were legendary (don't forget this was during Prohibition – she was flying alcohol in illegally from Mexico). Her generosity was above and beyond and she was buying friends property across California alongside wazzing her money up the wall – but there was a sell-by date on her riches. The Great Depression hit and by 1935, Pancho was forced to sell everything, even her treasured Mystery Ship. Refusing to give it all up and let go of her flying career, Pancho traded her last assets and got herself a 180-acre ranch in the middle of nowhere in the Mojave Desert. She was a single mom, starting from scratch, but she was a single mom starting from scratch *who always had more in the tank*.

'The Happy Bottom Riding Club' was built in no time on the money she made allowing her Hollywood friends to use her land as a filming location. Pancho had an airfield, gambling hall, bar, restaurant and hotel, and the first entry in the guestbook read 'Anything can happen here and usually does!' The Happy Bottom had so many wealthy and influential pilots flying in from across America during these years, it is said the air 'practically shimmered with testosterone' (I hope nobody's eating). Pancho knew that these were men who liked planes, hooch and women and so she hired model hosts to serve them. The girls were watched by Pancho like a fresh ex on social media; she made sure the men kept their hands to themselves and gave the girls codenames so they never had to give their true identity. If anyone crossed Pancho or her girls she would spit out her cigar and become the sort of person you'd never want to put on speakerphone. Equally, she hated anyone to belittle her pilots (she knew some of the greatest test pilots of the day, including Buzz Aldrin) and if anyone disbelieved they were frequently breaking the sound barrier at Happy Bottom's in return for a free steak prize, Pancho would tell them 'they could fly up your ass, tickle your eyeballs, fly back out and you wouldn't even know what happened until you were farting shockwaves'.

Like all good fun, Happy Bottom's had to come to an end and in 1952, Pancho got herself into a court broil with the United States Air Force, who claimed ownership of her land. When she refused to give up what she rightfully owned, they involved the FBI and had them make out that she was running a brothel, a house of loose morals and ill repute. The court proceedings went squiff for Pancho on more than one occasion and despite managing to sue them for defamation, the government finally *did* get hold of her land. She was left a forgotten woman in the desert with minuscule money, failing health and only the memory of her supersonic glory days for comfort. She was always looking for the next scheme but nothing could ever compare to her ranch.

When Pancho died of breast cancer, her ashes were spread over the site of the Happy Bottom Riding Club with special permission from the Air Force. A crosswind came up and swept the ashes back into the aircraft, to fly her off again. Pancho belonged in the cockpit and it defined her, even after she was gone. I've started to think of Pancho whenever I see the trail of a plane in the clouds and so long may her memory soar because the world needs more Pancho. *Be more Pancho.*

DOROTHY TIPTON (1914–1989)

THE DOUBLE LIFE LEADIN', SUCCESS SEEKIN' JAZZ MUSICIAN

This chapter is proudly brought to you by the foot tapping, finger clicking, hip shaking, swing music era and one of its greatest admirers – Dorothy Tipton. Growing up in Oklahoma, Dorothy was socially awkward and her 'You Can't Sit With Us' peers were mean. She joined the local drama club, 'The Masqueraders', at Southwest High School to try and crack out of her chrysalis but it was through music that Dorothy finally found her shebang. Her parents were exhibitionists with a similar love of soul but they were neglectful and Dorothy was essentially left to her own devices. The family were mostly united through ragtime, swing and blues, known as 'race music' in the South at that time as it had been gifted to the ears of white folk like the Tiptons by black musicians and artists. Dorothy's mother played the piano by ear and so Dorothy learned to do the same. She taught her how to rag (improvise) but Dorothy's interests soon transcended her mother's knowledge and she had to teach herself to read and arrange music properly. During her early teenage years, Dorothy went to live with her Aunt Bess in Kansas and the dreams that she dared to dream really did come true. Music was taken very seriously in Bess's household and she was Dorothy's main musical cheerleader. Dorothy was enrolled at the Gertrude Concannon School of Music where she studied violin and saxophone and mastered classical piano.

At eighteen, and encouraged by Bess, Dorothy travelled to Oklahoma City to find work as a jazz musician. It was a competitive industry and more or less impossible for a woman. The jazz scene was overwhelmingly male and nobody wanted to hire or tour with a female, no matter how talented she was. Dorothy's job hunt became more painful than the devil's baby teeth and she ended up one step away from all that would have been expected of a dollar-depleted woman – *having to sell sex*! Dorothy's cousin Eilene remembers that one day Dorothy blew a gasket. Endless rejections take their toll (see: my frown-marked forehead) and Dorothy had just had the final door shut in her face (see also: the battened and ledged, braced, glazed, flush, laminated and solid core iron cast door that has replaced my face). Dorothy bellowed, 'Well, if I can't go as a young woman, maybe I'll go as a young man!' She took a sheet and wrapped her chest as tight as a pig in a blanket, asking Eilene to fix it in place with a giant safety pin. Necessity saw Dorothy slick back her hair and present in white double-breasted blazer and trousers, shirt, tie and boutonnière. She adopted her father's nickname, Billy. The sock she likely stuffed down her underoos would go on to be upgraded for a prosthetic, her five-foot-five stature would be increased with a small shelf in her heels, her trousers would become more pressed and her style more dapper, but this was all Dorothy needed for now – and she bagged a job in a jiffy. At first, she only brought out Billy for auditions and performances but by 1940, Dorothy was completely wiped out. Many of Dorothy's musician friends had believed her to be gay up until this point and although she hadn't denied it, she found life was easier as Billy. It's impossible to know if this was something Dorothy had always wanted for herself but it was clear to see that as Billy she could have it all (and why shouldn't she?). Apart from two loyal cousins, everyone else all but disowned Dorothy. Even Bess tried and failed to 'straighten her out'. It was difficult but Billy learned to blank them back; Dorothy was dead but Billy was here, *he* was ready to have a career, find a loving partner and make sweet music in all the ways possible.

For the next ten years or so, Billy toured with a number of groups and there was good money to be made playing local radio, supper clubs and private members bars, where men could legally gamble. Bands would back tap dancers, magicians, strippers, whatever act was bringing in the money at the time (*usually strippers*). By the mid-1950s, Billy was playing solo piano gigs in Washington and started his own band called The Billy Tipton Trio. They were talent scouted by Tops Records in California and recorded two albums, *Sweet Georgia Brown* and *Billy Tipton Plays Hi-Fi on Piano*. Both were successful in their own right and got the band quite the following. From here, fame and fortune could have skyrocketed for The Billy Tipton Trio but Billy turned down two of their most lucrative offers and opportunities. He graciously declined sponsorship and the chance to support some of the biggest acts of the day, including his hero, Liberace, in Reno at the Holiday Hotel as their house band. For anyone brain-buffering as to why he wasn't giddy about this after all his hard work, it's believed he was petrified that fame would out him as a woman. Billy had already had four wives by this point (although no formal ceremony took place, they all called themselves Mrs Tipton). A couple of his ex-wives went on to reveal that he would only ever make love in the dark and while partially clothed. He blamed his chest binding on a car 'accident' that had left him with broken ribs. Even during his relationships, when he should have been able to be his most vulnerable and intimate, his secret was holding him back.

By 1960, Billy had moved to Spokane, Washington, and settled down with his fifth wife, Kitty, whom he met while the trio were playing at Allen's Tin Pan Alley nightclub. The band continued to play but audience numbers dwindled and the band had requests to mainly play swing standards over jazz, which would have been a blow to the jazz-veined Billy. He often added to their sets by performing skits or impersonations, his favourites being Elvis and (kick a man while he's down) *Liberace*. To keep from going under, Billy took a secondary income job at the Dave Sobol Theatrical Agency, where he booked musicians. This must have been as exasperating as a twisted bra strap (or jockstrap) for Billy. He avoided becoming a few patatas bravas short of a decent tapas selection by immersing himself into the community. With Kitty, he adopted three sons and they busybodied themselves in the local PTA and scout groups. They were the sort of parents that volunteered themselves to help out on the school trips and then proceeded to sit by their child and rub sun cream into their face while all the other kids got crunk on sugar and pulled moonies out of the windows. No bake sale, charity fundraiser nor gala passed them by (mainly because Billy organised them all).

When Billy died aged seventy-four, he had been refusing to see the doctor for months, if not years. The first his family knew of his assigned birth sex was when the paramedics came to try to resuscitate him and one of his sons, William, saw his breasts beneath the bandages. Kitty either knew deep down or was scared stiff of the attention because she rang the funeral directors and local newspapers almost immediately, asking for the news about Billy to be kept hush hush. But it was too late. Billy's story made the news all over the world – Jerry-Springer-esque tabloid headlines such as 'My Husband was a Woman and I Never Knew'. TV producers hounded the family to appear on talk shows and give the public the dirty laundry. Billy became the poster boy for debate about sex and gender identity but he hid so many of his tracks before he left us, there's no way he would have wanted to be.

In one of his nightclub skit scripts, the 'straight man' character asks Billy how many sexes there are. Billy replied, 'Three. The female sex. The male sex. And the insects.' This may have been a simple joke for the audience but Billy spent his whole life masquerading behind the theatrical. So, *I'll say it again for the people at the back*, Billy said THREE. He didn't want to be defined by his sex alone, he wanted to be remembered for his talent and contribution. The insects were clearly a cover-up for something much deeper than vaudeville and anyone who disagrees can buzz off.

JUNE TARPÉ MILLS (1918–1988)

THE FIRST FEMALE ACTION HERO COMIC CHARACTER CREATOR

I'd bet my red-star-embellished crown that you've strutted about in a Wonder Woman costume, with your hands locked on your hips (or fused round a bottle of frizzante) before now. In fact, if you're not sitting reading in full-on Wonder Woman get-up this very second, you should question your dedication to feminism. But how many of you have a Miss Fury costume up the loft or stuffed at the back of your wardrobe with your Christmas jumpers and 'for-when-I'm-thin-again' jeans? (Recycle those by the way, they're bogus.) Miss Fury was KA-POW-POWing, BLAMming and WHAMing her way across comic panels long before Wonder Woman's golden lasso ever got flung. She wasn't simply the most stylish superhero in comic-land (*my kingdom for a Miss Fury costume!*), she was one of the earliest female action characters and the first to be conceived, written and illustrated by a woman – June Tarpé Mills.

June was raised in Brooklyn, New York and described herself as 'one of those imaginative kids who hangs around the house reading books instead of running around outside playing hopscotch'. (Hopscotch is overrated anyway.) June's house was a busy one but there was much heartbreak in the family. Her mum was a widow and raised her along with June's deceased sister's children. Ends didn't always meet and June had to find ways and work to help support her mum. She always had an eye for art, which would save her from an *under his eye* future and gained her a place at the prestigious Pratt Institute for art in New York, where June went off to study sculpture. To pay her way, she posed for her art friends as a model. Not, I imagine, in a 'draw me like one of your French girls' type scenario (but hats and pants off to her if that ever cropped up). There is little more documented about June before the Miss Fury fame (hence my smutty decline into Winslet/DiCaprio imaginings) but upon graduating, she soon realised there wasn't much work for a budding sculptor. Rather than spend her life making crumbs designing birdbaths, June discovered she could be bankrolled by her other passion, animated cartooning.

At first, June found ways in as a fashion illustrator before contributing to minor strips with action comic characters such as *Daredevil Barry Finn*, *The Purple Zombie* and *The Cat Man*. To conceal her gender, June signed her work 'Tarpé' and believed 'it would have been a major let down to the kids if they found out that the author of such virile and awesome characters was a gal'. (*Welp!*) There were some successful female cartoonists in June's day but it seemed that *action cartoons by women* were a step too far. Just look up the artists Caroline Sexton, who had to go by 'C. M. Sexton', Cecilia Paddock Munson, who became 'Pad', Ramona Patenaude, who went as 'Pat', or Mabel Burwick, who opted for 'Odin', and you'll see that pseudonyms were the only way they could work. Some modern-day fan sites *still* seem to think they were actually male and I had to take a pause from writing this sentence to go and lie face down on my bed for five minutes. The silver lining is that, without the pen-name, the world never would have known Miss Fury, June's most successful creation, who exploded into the national newspapers in 1941. June's readership reached the millions in no time at all and the fans wanted to know *everything* about it. At its height, Miss Fury was published in over 100 newspapers, and polls proved that it was a hit with men, women, boys and girls alike. June's anonymity would cease but only *after* it was established that Miss Fury was the best thing since tabbed browsing.

Reminiscent of film noir in style, Fury was originally known as *Black Fury* because the hero, socialite Marla Drake's alter ego, Miss Fury, gained her superpowers from a black panther skin suit. Marla looked just like June and it was the first time an illustrator had openly put themselves in a strip. June drew from her Manhattan apartment, which she rarely left, instead living vicariously through Fury's jet-setting escapades. June always wanted to go to Brazil, *so Miss Fury went to Brazil.* June had a white Persian cat, Perri-Purr, *so Perri-Purr got a role* (and not just any role, Purr was so momentous he even outlived all nine lives to escape assassination attempts by a bald, monocled, one-armed German general). If Marla Drake looked exactly like June to prove a point and make her mark, she certainly settled that she could handle herself and overcome adversity. Miss Fury had a penchant for clouting people over the head, kicking her high-heeled feet at criminals and saving the day. Over the years (ten to be exact), Miss Fury defeated baddies, spies, terrorists, Nazis and continuously fought off her arch-enemy, *the Countess Erica Von Kampf* (a platinum blonde antagonist with a swastika on her forehead. *Casual.*) Fury had some on/off romances but predominantly stayed single, leaving the men in the supporting roles. The 1940s' conventions might not have even considered women but in Miss Fury's world it didn't matter a dropkick, she was always the most intelligent, interesting, inspiring and important person in the room. Fury even adopted a son, a young boy she rescued from an evil scientist, and found time to raise him singlehandedly, alongside putting the world to rights. WHEN CAN WE HAVE THE FILM?

Miss Fury may have been hard as nails but it didn't mean she didn't know how to dress. Unlike the women in the average male comic in the 1940s (who were always depicted in tiny red dresses), Fury (Marla) had a proper wardrobe with proper detail and it was proper breath-taking.

The comic could be printed in a fashion history book on the era, readers were treated to such beautifully drawn, razzle-dazzle filled panels full of shoulder pads, satin slips, frilly lingerie and lace bodices. Fury was on the glam game and there were no apologies needed. Sometimes, the editors even believed her outfits to be *too racy* (there's a famous example of a sort of leaf bikini, à la *Sinitta*, which got the chop). The outfits were as in vogue as actual *Vogue* and there were even Fury paper dress-up dolls. Hours of fun. Slide into my DMs if you know how to get your hands on one of those Fury pages (asking for a friend). June wasn't interested in 'sexy' for the sake of 'sexy' as the male illustrators were – she was interested in realistic, iconic, high fashion and it only added to the mass appeal, which peaked during the Second World War. Fury's impeccably dressed image was painted on three American warplanes and Perri-Purr became the unofficial mascot for the Allied troops. There was a wartime paper shortage but it didn't stop eight issues of a Miss Fury comic book being published and printed, or stop June from flogging more than a million copies per book. The war was memorable for other reasons for female comic creators because when it ended, women in all industries were encouraged to leave their jobs and 'let the men back in'. Women had been drawing comics since 1901, but now they were expected to 'hand back' the adventure and action strips, which *never belonged to the men in the first place.* (Can someone commission a sitcom about this please?)

Towards the end of the 1940s, June's health had her missing deadlines and struggling to keep Fury alive. She hired a ghost artist but their drawings were lousy in comparison, nowhere near as magnetic as June's. There was no definitive ending to Fury's life adventures when the comic finished on 23 December 1951, but June couldn't quite put down the pencil. She started a graphic novel and wrote a short for Marvel called *Our Love Story* but her own love story with cartooning ended when she became homebound and then lost the battle she'd been fighting with emphysema. June never made it to Brazil. When her characters got mad, they swore through symbols. The thought of June only being able to live her dreams through a woman on paper and not in real life makes me *£@!%?*$!!! BUT she forever changed the role of women in the comic world. June may have faced more hardships as a female than Fury would ever know but simply by creating her, June refused to exist in the margins. June lived in every line, every ink mark, and across every single page.

SARASWATHI RAJAMANI
(1928–2018)

THE IRON-WILLED INDIAN FREEDOM FIGHTER
AND SPY

A crusty national flag flapping from your window does not a patriot make (© Anneka Harry 2020). If you love your country enough you are willing to die for it, you need to get off your sofa. The proof is in the pudding and Saraswathi gave us so much proof she may as well have been my mum's Hot Cross Bun & Bread and Butter pudding (the best pudding on this earth).

Saraswathi (born Rajamani) came from a family of freedom fighters in Burma (now known as Myanmar), where they had settled to escape the British authorities ruling India. Her dad owned a gold mine and as such the family were squarely sat on one. They were the richest Indians in the country but Saraswathi never wanted anything except JUSTICE AND FREEDOM FOR HER COUNTRY. The devotion to her homeland was certainly nourished by her family's stout support of the Indian independence movement (they campaigned and donated much to the cause) but Saraswathi also had her own ideas. When she was around ten years old, Gandhi came to visit her family home and he was shocked to see the young Saraswathi playing with guns in the garden. (Yes, the official, real-life Gandhi and yes, official, real-life guns.) He asked her why she was fooling around with firearms and she shot back (the answer, not bullet) 'To shoot down the Britishers, of course!' Saraswathi was determined to fight for her nation and she was ready to do so with weapons, but Gandhi helped her rein her neck in and consider a less violent approach. This ardour for India never ceased; saving her country was her mission and her calling.

Growing up, Saraswathi was crazy about the Indian National Army leader Netaji Subhas Chandra Bose. Her early teenage years were all *eat, sleep, learn more about Netaji Subhas Chandra Bose, repeat*, and her daydreams were full of imagined meetings with him. When she was sixteen, she lived those dreams when one day he came to her hometown of Rangoon to speak about the Free India fight. Saraswathi was front row with her eyes wide and head full of possibility. After the lecture, applause didn't feel like enough for Saraswathi. Instead, she donated all of her jewellery to the INA and all that sparkle party caught Netaji's attention. The next day, armed with the diamond and gold boodle, Netaji swung by Saraswathi's to return the goods. Because she was a young girl, Netaji thought Saraswathi had given the jewellery naively but she had been very much underestimated by her hero. Netaji tried to give the pieces back to her dad and she got narked, telling him: 'They are not my father's, they are MINE. I gave all of them to you, and I will not take them back.' He was thrown off for a second but soon saw into the spirited soul of our diamond, christening her Saraswathi there and then, telling her: 'You have the wisdom only Goddess Saraswathi has. Lakshmi [money] comes and goes but not Saraswathi. So, I name you Saraswathi.' Now that Saraswathi and the respected leader of India were bosom buddies, she stepped on the gas and twisted his arm to allow her into his army. Saraswathi's time had finally come.

Impatience was a virtue for Saraswathi and as such the very next day she was signed up to the Rani of Jhansi brigade (the Women's Regiment of the Indian National Army) on the military intelligence wing. At fifteen, she was probably India's youngest spy. The Rani Laxmi Bai was the world's first all-female army but not all of Saraswathi's allies would have been there to bring it home for India as she was. For some women, joining the army was a break from the poverty, sexual violence and social prejudice of their realities. Ironically, any woman who wanted to become a Rani needed the approval and signature of a father or husband to join. They had to have the permission of men and as covert agents, most had to *pretend to be men* to do their jobs. Saraswathi worked undercover and along enemy lines for two years. She was responsible for intercepting government orders and military intelligence from the British and she did so dressed as an errand boy she named Mani (apt). As a young 'boy', Saraswathi could gain access to the British military camps and even the officers' houses. There was nowhere she wasn't permitted to go as Mani and it meant that she was able to bring all sorts of golden nuggets of information back to the INA. Saraswathi knew how to read the room, switching up characters quicker than a Jim Carrey bloopers reel, and she used both to her advantage. On one occasion, she swapped her errand boy togs for those of a female dancer and infiltrated a British camp. Pretending she was there to entertain the troops, Saraswathi drugged the soldiers and rather than shake her hips for them, she rescued a captured friend. As they were boogie footing it out of the camp, Saraswathi was shot in her right leg but they still outran the guards: 'I ran with my leg bleeding. Both of us climbed on to a tree and sat there for three days. Only on the fourth day, we came down. Netaji was so happy with our bravery that he saluted us and congratulated us several times. I was given a medal by the Japanese emperor himself,' Saraswathi recounted. The bullet wound left her with a limp for life but she would smile if she was ever asked about it. For Saraswathi, it was a permanent reminder of the years of her life of which she was most proud.

After the Second World War was over, Saraswathi returned to India but she did not receive a hero's welcome. Her family had given everything they earned and owned to the freedom struggle, even the gold mine. She was isolated and in penury and did not live the life of a venerated veteran freedom fighter, as she deserved. Instead, Saraswathi's story was lost and her yet to be acknowledged accomplishments along with it. For nearly sixty years she lived in a dilapidated one-bedroom flat in Chennai, with few possessions apart from photographs of her precious Netaji Subhas Chandra Bose. After suffering numerous heart attacks, Saraswathi could go on alone no longer and asked the Tamil Nadu government for help. The then Chief Minister, Jayalalithaa, recognised her need and eminence immediately and gave her a sizable cheque and an upgraded, rent-free apartment. She also offered Saraswathi medical assistance but it was politely declined. Saraswathi had no time to be ill; she wanted to provide for her country in any way that she could, for as long as she could. She spent her final years collecting scraps of materials from tailors' shops and making clothes for orphanages and nursing homes. After the tsunami in 2004, she donated her skimpy monthly pension to the relief fund. She would gather with other freedom fighters in Madurai on Netaji's birthday to honour him every year, one year even leaving intensive care after a heart attack to ensure she didn't miss it. Saraswathi was a treasure and it took far too long for that to be unearthed.

In 2016, a Hindi channel called EPIC, which focuses on Indian history, featured Saraswathi's story in a series called *Adrishya* (meaning 'invisible'). It gave voice to a woman's story that could have been lost forever. Saraswathi believed that 'I CAN is more important than IQ'. Writers and historians may not have had the sense to sing her praises but we can all sing for our unsung hero of India now. Celebrate her with a salute and her favourite phrase, '*Jai Hind!*' (Long live India).

DAME STEPHANIE SHIRLEY
(BORN 1933)

THE CHILD REFUGEE TURNED COMPUTER SCIENCE MULTI-MILLIONAIRE AND PHILANTHROPIST

If Dame Stephanie's life had gone according to society's plan, she would have married a polite, professional man (who she'd probably have zilch crotch feelings for), been forced to slave away for him and their family for her whole life and never allowed a job. Thankfully, society's plan took a tumble. (Bathe in the relaxation of that huge, pent up breath for as long as you need to before reading on.)

Stephanie was born into a bourgeois family in Dortmund, Germany. Her mum was a casualty of the society booby trap but her dad was a high-flying high court judge (at least until the Nazis took his position from him for being Jewish). By the time Stephanie was five she had lived in seven different countries across Europe. The family stayed on the hop, trying to secure work and keep their financial autonomy. Eventually, money mattered no more because the Second World War would devastate them at every crossroads. In 1939, Stephanie (who was five at the time) and her nine-year-old sister, Renate, were sent to England, along with 10,000 other Jewish children, to escape the holocaust. Kindertransport saved those children's lives from Nazi Germany but tragically removed them from their families. Stephanie was sent to a country she did not know, a country that spoke a language she knew only a few words of, with no money and for reasons she only half understood. Most would never see their loved ones again but Stephanie and Renate were miraculously reunited with their parents after the war. However, they never bonded again. The break in the clouds lies in the fact that being a child refugee taught Stephanie a determination and conviction that left no minute frittered away; she vowed to 'break through, to do something new, to not be put off by the conventions of the day'. If you need any reassurance that she succeeded in packaging up that eureka and selling it to the masses, then just reread the chapter title.

Stephanie and Renate were adopted by Guy and Ruby Smith, a modest couple from Sutton Coldfield in the West Midlands, whom the sisters always called 'Auntie' and 'Uncle'. Stephanie went to the local village school until the Smiths became concerned she was picking up the Brummie accent (no comment) and sent her to a convent school instead. She loved maths and science, much to the horror of her teachers (they were *no subjects for girls!*), and so she had to go to a boys' school for these subjects, where she could pursue her interests. Stephanie had a straight-up love for learning but also recognised that to do well might be to escape the life of charity donations they had now found themselves surviving on. At the boys' school, Stephanie was the only girl among 'hundreds of drooling young men' and it was ick: 'I never reconciled myself to the daily gauntlet of leering and catcalls.' Turning her frown upside down once more, Stephanie stayed focused on her studies and it would turn out to be the best learning curve imaginable for the sexism she was to face in her professional life. The next step is usually perceived as a place at university but finances had that out of the question. Instead, Stephanie looked to the world of work, a world that would have been jammy to have her by now, her head for numbers and science was so sharp.

By 1951, she had officially become a British citizen and was living in London. Within a couple weeks of leaving school she had two interviews set up; the technology industries were flourishing and demand was high. Stephanie first got a job at the Post Office Research Station in Dollis Hill as an assistant. Her colleagues were mainly male and the money was low enough to mean that, on at least one occasion, she fainted from lack of food – but still she found inspiration in every nook and cranny. The mechanical calculator she was using was revered as the precursor to computers and despite being a bit bonk, Stephanie could see that with a bit of a brainpower bootleg, it could bowl over the technological industry. She started night classes in advanced maths and physics, studying on the side for a bachelor's degree and making friends with computer logic via Birkbeck College. All the while she was out there making the betterment of her knowledge and learning a priority, sexism in the workplace was pinching her on the bottom in boardrooms and throwing its arms around her, uninvited. After multiple run-ins with *#MeToo* moments, Stephanie found it easier to dress in suits and present as an 'honorary man'. She wasn't admitting defeat, rather finding ways to let it be known that she would not be seen as lesser. When male colleagues would persistently offer to carry her typewriter/calculator, she would hit back, 'I believe in equal pay, so I'll carry my own machine.' (And for responding with actions and words not wallops, I'd like to award Stephanie a Nobel Peace Prize.)

When Stephanie married one of her peers, physicist Derek Shirley, her company expected her to leave work (the done thing back then), but instead she accepted a promotion at a computer development firm. She learned a lot during her short time in this role but continued to get blocked by men, shut down in meetings and found herself fully acquainted with the glass ceiling by 1962. Stephanie was twenty-nine, she had '£6 of capital, a dining-room table, a telephone . . . and one other mad idea', to quit her job and start her own business. Her idea, a software house and the first of such start-ups in the UK, made her an instant laughing stock. Nobody was buying software then, it came free with the hardware and the idea of buying it from a woman at that was toppling the industry off a cliff. Stephanie wasn't only going to pioneer a change in the market, she set out to change the culture for women. Her company, Freelance Programmers (FP), was always intended to be an all-female staff. Women would be the professionals they had trained to be, rather than be seen as walking wombs or unemployable, and Stephanie wanted to allow all sorts of flexible work methods. Everyone would work from home, on their time, she would encourage job shares, profit-sharing, and, eventually, even co-ownership. To a freelancer, this is as celestial-sounding as an invoice paid early (or indeed on time) and to the industry then, it equally beggared belief. Stephanie had a small but sturdy team of intellectual women, ready to go, but nobody was biting to begin with. Gold star, a balloon and a lollipop to anyone who guesses what changed things . . . Yup, Stephanie traded her name to 'Steve' and suddenly everyone wanted a piece of FP. Stephanie has gone by 'Steve' ever since and loves the fact that the men who initially ignored her all had to congratulate 'Steve' when, later, her company was valued at over three billion dollars. Women weren't even allowed to open a bank account without the permission of a man in this nutcase era and yet here was Steve, mopping up (THE STOCK EXCHANGE!).

It didn't matter if Steve's employees were gay, straight, trans, single, mothers, married, divorced or consciously uncoupled, as long as they were the best for the job. The women knew they could handle the work in a heartbeat but the men couldn't believe it and so there were still some attempts to keep it under wraps that women were getting such adept work done from home. A year after Steve's business took off she gave birth to her own son, Giles, and used to have to play tape recordings of people typing underneath her phone calls, so the clients wouldn't hear baby cries and drop contracts. Freelance really meant *freelance* to Steve – we all feel the hardship of hump day but as long as the work got done, it didn't matter if anyone needed to take a day off. Nobody cooked kippers for lunch in a microwave, made you give over half your day rate to office sweepstakes and 'whip-rounds' for colleagues you didn't know existed or forced you to listen to them retelling their dreams. The women were the best computerheads and coders in the game and everyone knew it, despite newspapers still referring to them with derogatory terminology more akin to 'computerbirds'. Among their early customers, FP worked with companies such as Tate & Lyle, Mars, Rolls Royce, Castrol and British Rail; the projects, pay cheques and workforce were growing on a daily basis. Steve's team even worked on the programming for the black box flight recorder for Supersonic Concorde!

In 1975, thirteen years after its start-up, FP's pro-female policies were made illegal by equal opportunities legislation. Steve was forced to let the men in but they had to live up to the women, they had to be first-rate (and as FP was on track to reaching its multibillion-dollar world domination, it surely was a right convenient, opportune time for them to infiltrate!). The company was eventually owned by seventy-five per cent of its staff and when it was floated on the London Stock Exchange in 1996, it made seventy millionaires out of its workforce. Meanwhile and all the while, Steve was starting up other firms, serving as an independent non-executive director for companies such as Tandem Computers and the John Lewis Partnership and caring for her severely autistic son. Steve eventually retired in 1993 to concentrate on her philanthropic work. Her 'Shirley Foundation' has given away at least SIXTY-SEVEN MILLION POUNDS to over 100 projects, including computing and autism research in her late son's memory.

Steve has an OBE, DBE and made the honours list in the year 2000 for her services to information technology. She is an honorary member and fellow of every worthy board under the sun, and all the charities and foundations under the sky. Her global business empire has made and saved lives and given women influence in the computing industry, an industry that, let's be honest, rules our lives now. Steve reckons 'you can always tell ambitious women by the shape of our heads: they're flat on top for being patted patronisingly. And we have larger feet to stand away from the kitchen sink.' So, embrace your flat heads and big feet (not *another* unrealistic beauty standard for women!) and avoid anyone's plan for your life other than your own.

RENA 'RUSTY' KANOKOGI
(1935–2009)

THE STREET FIGHTIN', BLACK BELT WINNIN', JEWISH-AMERICAN JUDO LUMINARY

If I told you Rena spent the majority of her childhood at a theme park, she could go on all the rides for free and eat unlimited hotdogs, you might think it sounds as kid cloud nine as Richie Rich's pad. Although factual, her home in Coney Island, Brooklyn, minutes away from the amusements of the boardwalk, was in no way as idyllic as it sounds. When Rena wasn't being ignored by her parents, she was mistreated by them, forever becoming the 'unintentional' victim of objects being violently flung across the kitchen mid-argument. She ate hotdogs because that's all her opiate-addicted mother, who sold them on the street, could manage for her. Her dad tended a bar (when he showed up for his shifts) and blew anything he did make on the gee-gees. If Rena reached out to them, she would be told 'Go bang your head on the wall!' She learned to do it until it bled. Rena's was a street education, she didn't expect anything for nothing, and that tough lesson in survival would become her secret weapon – deadlier than the fake-blood-covered bayonet she used to strap to her leg for protection during those days.

By the time she was seven years old, Rena had already been sent out to wheel and deal around Coney Island. She peeled potatoes for French-fry vendors, assisted drivers at parking lots, sold confetti during Mardi Gras and ice water for five cents a cup at bus stops. When she wasn't giving it hutzpah on the hustle, she would socialise with anyone that gave her the time of day (namely the local 'freak show' performers such as 'Milo the Mule Face Boy', 'The Mermaid' or 'Albert Alberta, The Hermaphrodite'). The world might have viewed these people as abnormal then but to Rena, they were family. Their care and protection was *her* normal (and the best she'd known) but she still hankered after her mother's love. By the time Rena was a teenager, she was rolling deep with an all-girl street gang she had formed known as 'The Apaches'. They wore green-and-black satin jackets, bell-bottom pants and smeared their skin with Vaseline to avoid getting roughed up; they were the slipperiest gang on the block. Rena learned that if she came home with a serious wound, her mother would pay her attention but it was soon less about those cuddles, more about the tussles. Rena wanted to fight so badly she'd take on a candy-floss along the pier; she'd even break away from her girls when they didn't want to squad up and would take on rival gangs singlehandedly. Rena felt a 'churning, burning' rage inside her that was being misplaced, but she had no other outlet. She wanted to lift weights at the local YMCA but girls weren't allowed, so she got her fix in anything physical, aggressive, anything she could attack and win. Even if she was rollerblading she would imagine she was in a roller derby and plough down anyone who got in her way. Rena's hoodlum-ing was expert and always on point, there was nothing rusty about her street persona. (Apart from her nickname, 'Rusty', which she acquired after a local stray dog. There is no further information on this enticing titbit which is, as far as I'm concerned, a multisensory violation.)

In 1955, Rena was taught a judo move by a friend and instantly felt that lightbulb moment when the heavens throw open their golden gates and the angels croon sweetly. Unbeknown to Rena, she was about to enter into a battlefield that was a minefield of myths for women. Judo was a quiz-show-wrong-answer-buzzer-sound for girls as the world was certain all of that full-on contact would encourage them to be gay (because choking, arm locking and body slamming are well-known lesbian mating calls). There were also serious concerns that arduous exercise might displace a woman's uterus, their ovaries could fold up or their breasts spin off like Catherine wheels. Nobody seemed to be sweating about the male reproductive organs, which were jangling about *on the outside*. Rena was a girl (and a Jewish girl at that), so she was surmised as weak. (Try and explain that to the perv Rena practised her *Ōuchi gari* throw on when he exposed himself to her on the subway, or the trash collectors who'd switswooed her before their neat pile of garbage was scattered by her *De-ashi-harai* foot sweep!) In judo, Rena had found her focus, but her recently discovered discipline wasn't allowed outside of her neighbourhood classes.

By 1959, she was championship-ready but outlawed from competitions because of her risky female bits. She was the best in her team and it would be poppycock if she didn't compete and so she registered at the YMCA championships in New York as 'Rusty Stewart'. Her hair was already short but she cut it shorter, she taped down her gunpowder bosoms with bandages and put a T-shirt under her *gi* (judo uniform). Tactically, it would have been A-OK if 'Rusty' had drawn with her opponent in this particular match but she didn't know what it meant to tie – the second the players had bowed and touched, Rena threw her competitor. With the other club on the floor, Rena and her team were on the ceiling. Thanks to Rusty they'd all be heading home with medals but when it came time to award hers, the officials pulled Rena aside. They had espied the fact she was Adam's-apple-less and was told to give up her medal or forgo the entire team's. As she handed back her prize to the judges, she was calm but her insides were crying, *THIS CAN NEVER HAPPEN TO ANOTHER FEMALE AGAIN!* She didn't know how and she didn't know when, but she knew she had to spark that stick of dynamite.

Out of options in the US, in 1962 Rena moved to Tokyo, the spiritual home of judo, to train at the Kōdōkan School. Here, women had been welcomed in judo for over forty years but only ever separately from the men. Upon arrival and after 'pulverising' her teammates, who had been taught 'Women's Judo' (which natch meant nothing to Rena), she became the first woman to be invited by the masters to train in the main *dojo* with the men. Rena was respected by them and to her that didn't mean how they treated her but how they played her – like an *equal*. She practised for nine hours a day and was promoted to 2nd *dan* (a black-belt ranking). Later, she would become the first woman to be promoted to the rank of 7th. She sucked up the training, winning every match and even a husband, the Japanese black belt Ryohei Kanokogi (there was still some discrimination against interracial marriage at this time too; Rena was shoulder barging the stereotypes on all sides). When they returned to the States together, they set up the Kyushu Dojo Community Service Center for judo and devoted their energies to promoting the sport to the kids and the (still competition-deprived) women and girls. Rena was on the war path to shove that TNT up the backsides of the sports bosses but they threw in every obstacle they could to stop her. For nine months she was on the phone more than a telemarketing robot; she fundraised, lobbied officials, stormed offices and even remortgaged her house to pay for the first women's judo world championships, held at Madison Square Garden in 1980. Despite being a grand slam and bringing double the number of people to the sport, the judo governing body saw Rena rollin' and they were hatin'; they wanted her gone and even asked her husband to 'fulfill his duty and gag her'. But these male chauvinist piglets had messed with the wrong woman. Rena was just getting started.

In 1984, the International Olympics Committee decided that women's judo was not going to be allowed in the 1988 Olympics and in my favourite *#GenderRebels* quote, Rena said she 'almost began to hear the music to *Jaws* in my head. Da-da . . . da-da . . . DA-DA . . . DA-DA, DA-DA . . . What should I do? Take one of the IOC members and put him in an armlock? Go on a hunger strike? . . . For the first time in my life I was thinking terrorist thoughts. Then it hit me. . . . Sue the b*stards! Get 'em!' And funnily enough, a few days after a sex discrimination complaint was filed and Rena's shark bite filled the papers, the doors whooshed open to funding for women in judo. After fighting for more than two decades, twenty-four years after men's judo was recognised, Rena was the coach and now widely considered 'Mother of Judo' after bringing her women's team to the 1988 Summer Games. The awards and victories kept on coming; she rightly has a place in the International Women's Sports Hall of Fame, Japan's highest civilian honour (the order of the Rising Sun), which saw her made a *Kanokogi-sensei*, and in 2009, fifty years after it was taken away from her, Rusty got that gold medal back from the New York State YMCA. She fought like loco for her sport and for equal opportunities for women and girls. For Rena, judo gave her '. . .my purpose . . . direction . . . my family . . . my life'. Rena 'Rusty' Kanokogi gave *us* life and for that we should offer her the ultimate judo demonstration of respect and humility, *the deepest bow.*

BOBBI GIBB (BORN 1942)

THE MARATHON MOGUL AND WOMEN'S RIGHTS HERO

Suburban Boston in the 1950s was a sexist shambles (not that any of the other eras or places covered in this book haven't been). Women were expected to be passive, run around after their husbands, fix them martinis and attend to their male egos. (Anyone burdened with this task should know they need to be handled with care, require constant stroking, feeding on the hour, every hour and kept out of direct sunlight.) Bobbi was born to run but she didn't want to run after or for a man. For Bobbi, running wasn't only instinctive, it was her salvation.

Bobbi (Roberta) was the elder of two sisters; her dad was a chemistry professor, and her mum a frustrated housewife. Homemaking sat about as comfortably as the only token female on a comedy panel show might with her ma, but still she tried to force Bobbi to conform to the expected 'femininity' of the time (more concerned for the feelings of the apple cart than her daughters). During her years at high school in Winchester, Bobbi was the only one of her girlfriends not interested in prom gossip or the latest fashion and the only one still interested in sports post-puberty. Bobbi's hobbies™ were not seen as pastimes for girls – the thought of girls running through the woods with dogs or sleeping outside under the stars would have produced a collective sick-in-mouth from society. Her chosen subjects might have raised similar scrutiny because Bobbi loved maths and science, which she studied at Tufts University. She had hoped to go to medical school but she was told during the interview process that she was 'too pretty', which would upset her male classmates, so instead she had to take night classes. They reckoned she would leave early to 'get married and have babies' and refused her application. (I'm going to need a moment for this one. Please respect my privacy at this difficult time.) In the mid-1960s, she gained a place at the Boston Museum of Fine Arts, an eight-mile commute from Winchester and one she ran – *there and back* – in her Red Cross nurse's shoes. So out there were her actions, running shoes for women weren't even being manufactured at that time.

In 1964, Bobbi's dad took her to watch the Boston marathon and it was the first time she had seen other people running. She knew no other runners, she'd never even heard of the marathon, but she instantly felt at home. Bobbi had found her destiny; she describes it as: 'I ran as a way of reaffirming some semiconscious ancient bond between the Earth and myself as a human animal.' That summer, she travelled to California and back with her Malamute pup, Moot, in her VW bus. Her only plan was to run and keep running, pushing herself to go further each time. Unfortunately, she sustained an injury and had to miss the 1965 marathon but it wasn't the end for Bobbi (how many men have you heard say they could have been a pro footballer *if it wasn't for that injury . . .*). Instead, Bobbi simply trained harder and ran further. She once ran so far along the beach she got detained by the border control police for accidently crossing into Mexico! Bobbi knew she could run the twenty-six-mile marathon because she was already stomping forty-mile runs.

Two months before the 1966 race, Bobbi was twenty-three years old and she wrote to the Boston Athletic Association for an official marathon number. The race director replied to say that their regulations forbade women to compete in any race longer than 1.5 miles. Furthermore, 'women are physiologically incapable of running 26.2

miles'. Because she was a woman, Bobbi was seen as a medical liability. *Squint* Women competing in sports made no sense to them;
some people genuinely worried that if women exercised they might
die, become men, or worse – gay! Bobbi knew she needed to show the
world that these sorts of beliefs about females (athletes or otherwise)
were tosh. It had become a feminist statement – she had to be the first
woman to run the marathon. If she wasn't invited to the party, she was
going to be forced to crash it and so, in a three-and-a-half-day journey, Bobbi took a Greyhound bus across the country to Hopkinton,
where the race began. When her parents found out, they were petrified.
Bobbi's dad thought she was mentally ill but her mum came around to
the idea. A chord was struck when she recognised how empowering her
actions were about to be and they didn't only hug for the first time in
years but her mum drove her to the starting line. Hiding in the forsythia
bushes by the starter pen on the corner of Hayden Rowe Street, Bobbi
(wearing her brother's Bermuda shorts, black bathing suit, oversized
blue hoodie and a pair of men's size 6 Adidas sneakers) awaited the
starting pistol. When it fired she 'stumbled from the bushes into the
midst of the runners, wondering how many other women writers, artists, scientists, and soldiers had had to disguise their femininity; so well
that history has still not discovered'. (I'll send her a copy of the book.)
Bobbi herself was about to run into history.

Afraid she was going to get arrested, Bobbi kept her head down and
her hood up but it was scorchio and there was no way she could go the
distance in disguise. Before long, her fellow runners started to notice
she was a woman but rather than rugby tackle her off the course, they
encouraged her. It gave her the guts to strip a layer and when the crowds
realised too it caused a great commotion. Men and women delighted in
her involvement and their screams of enthusiasm propelled her every
step. Bobbi was slinging less than seven-minute miles, she had found
her happy pace and it was Speedy Gonzales. Just before the twelve-mile
mark she overtook Navy commander Charles Stalzer, who blinked hard

when a woman passed him. He couldn't catch up but that male ego kicked in and he said, 'No way a girl is going to beat me, so I stayed as close as I could.' (*Cool story, bro.*) By twenty miles, Bobbi was in searing pain, she wasn't used to running in sports shoes or on pavement, but she didn't want to set women's rights back any further. She could tell from the women's eyes in the crowd that things were never going to be the same again and they helped her to fly over the finishing line. Bobbi's time was three hours, twenty-one minutes and forty seconds! She finished ahead of two-thirds of her male competitors and the crowds and press went wild. Some tabloid twerps tried to get her to say that she was a man-hater but rather than sit and swig on male tears she simply said that she loved men and women. She was running for EQUALITY (and I hope she considers running for President). After all that running, all she had achieved and all the support she experienced, Bobbi still wasn't allowed to join the male runners in the post-marathon meal.

The papers the next day were farcical. Reporters, fluent in nincompoop, wrote articles such as 'A Game Girl in a Man's Game: Boston was unprepared for the shapely blonde housewife who came out of the bushes to crush male egos!' and 'A girl in the marathon! Egad, is nothing sacred?' Even the official who'd rejected her initial application crawled out of his pit to state that Bobbi *didn't* run the race, 'She merely covered the same route as the official race while it was in progress. No girl has ever run in the Boston Marathon.' (And then we woke up and it was all a dream . . . I. WISH.) But Bobbi's dream was realised. She inspired more women than we'll ever know. The year after Bobbi, Kathrine Switzer became the first numbered entry to run after she applied as 'K. V. Switzer'; mid-race, she was physically attacked for doing so by the director. Boston didn't allow women to run officially until 1972, by which point Bobbi had already joined the race successfully twice more. These days, tens of thousands of women run it every year. On the fiftieth anniversary race in 2016, Bobbi was too unwell to run but instead was made a grand marshal by the Boston Athletic

Association. That year's winner, Ethiopia's Atsede Baysa, gave her trophy to Bobbi. Without her, Atsede would never have been allowed to prove her running shenius.

After two decades of being a lawyer, Bobbi became an artist, motor neurone disease researcher and advocate for social change. The Bobbi Gibb Marathon Sculpture Project is her campaign to get a statue of a female runner in among all the male runner statues in Boston. You've allowed me to donate to the charities and causes mentioned in this book by buying it and supporting women. If Bobbi has taught us anything, it's that change can happen within our lifetime and we *can* make that happen. I hope her statue beats this book out into the world.

PILI HUSSEIN (BORN 1958)

THE GIN SWIGGIN', PRECIOUS GEM DIGGIN' FEMALE MINER

Pili grew up in a large family in Tanzania – her father had six wives and she is one of THIRTY-EIGHT children. Imagine trying to remember all of the names! My mum can't get my name right and I've only got one sibling (well, two if you count the cat she sometimes confuses me with). Pili's father kept livestock (as if his house didn't sound like enough of a zoo already) and she was forced to muck in and work long hours with the animals. Although Pili was well looked after, she was unhappy. Sadly for Pili, things got worse before they got better because she was married young and her husband was a wrong 'un as well. Pili stayed for as long as she was physically able to but her partner was abusive and she needed out. At the age of thirty-one, she found her inner riot girl and the courage to do a bunk. Pili was destined for and made of greater stuff.

As Pili had no education, her options were limited. She followed her nose to a small town called Mererani, in the foothills of Africa's highest mountain, Kilimanjaro. On the surface, Mererani might not look like the most happening place on the planet but scratch *below the surface* to find where the party's at. In a compact few square kilometres underneath Mererani, Third World meets First. It is the only place on Earth where mining exists for a rare violet-blue gemstone called tanzanite. If you thought the treasures in Aladdin's Cave of Wonders were shiny and mesmerising, get your eyes around a tanzanite stone. First discovered in 1967, it is now in extremely short supply and as such is one of the world's best-selling rare gems. These shimmering blue beauts are a thousand times rarer than diamonds and our Pili decided she wanted to get her hands on some. (Smart.) Now you're this far into a book exploring the vom-inducing superabundance of ways the women of this world have been held back, it will come as no great shock to you to learn that women weren't allowed in the mines. This was danger-ous and potentially exceedingly advantageous work; there should be no breasts anywhere near it, *ta very much!* But Pili let that stop her for all of a hot minute before she secretly followed some of the men into the mines to watch and learn how to do the job. Although back-breaking, Pili was more than used to and ready for a bit of hard work (and it was only digging and sieving, after all). That very same day she binned her skirt, cut some slacks into baggy shorts, chucked on a shirt and opted for a ski cap to hide her hair. 'Mjomba Hussein' (or 'Uncle Hussein') was born. It was 1978 and Uncle Hussein went on to work in the mines and keep his male mining colleagues fooled for over a decade . . .

My favourite part about Uncle Hussein (apart from the fact he's called Uncle Hussein) is that Pili also used her disguise to teach the men a thing or two about themselves. Uncy H became the don of the mines and the men really listened to his advice. So much so that Pili made sure she told them to STOP HARASSING THE VILLAGE WOMEN AND KEEP THEIR FILTHY HANDS TO THEMSELVES. Let's all just take a moment to appreciate Pili's fine work here. *Make a cup of tea (/something stronger) and cheers her, throw an Uncle Hussein themed party, design a felt-and-sequinned collage depicting that cher-ished moment . . . I'll leave it up to you how you celebrate her but make sure you do.* You see, all Pili needed to do to fit in with the blokes was apparently allow them to joke with Uncle about which girls he liked (LOL LOL LOLLIDGE), drink Konyagi (the local gin) and smoke marijuana with them. Pili said she 'acted like a gorilla . . . I could fight, my language was bad, I could carry a big knife like a Maasai [warrior]. Nobody knew I was a woman because everything I was doing I was doing like a man.' Uncle Hussein was a pot-smoking, gin-quaffing, gorilla-tempered mining ninja and she was about to strike gold. Well, tanzanite, the new *girl's best friend* . . .

Pili would be hundreds of metres underground for twelve hours a day; there were no shortcuts; she had to work like a trojan. Only a year after first heading down to the great depths of the mines, she found two massive clusters of tanzanite stones, 1,000 grams and 800 grams respectively. *Bling-a-ding-ding!* With more rocks than the inside of a rapper's jewellery box, Pili's life changed in an instant. She purchased brand spanking new tools, employed miners to work under her and bought farm land and property. By the early 1990s, Pili had built her own empire and it only continued to grow. She built new homes for her father, mother and twin sister, a shedload of houses in Mererani and back in her hometown. She applied for a mining licence and to her great surprise, the law *didn't* prohibit women from mining – men had simply decided somewhere along the line that they shouldn't and so they couldn't. That, my friends, is the patriarchy at its pits (loose mining pun intended). Pili went from strength to strength and nobody questioned Uncle Hussein. One day, however, when a local woman accused miners of raping her, the actual perpetrators framed Pili and she went on trial for the crime. She had no choice other than to reveal her secret but, by this point, she didn't care about being rumbled – she was raking it in and enjoying the good life.

Today, Pili has over seventy employees working for her, 150 acres of land, 100 cows, and a tractor (I love the fact she mentions the tractor – who wouldn't want to show off about that?). She has also sent thirty-two children from her family to school. Pili is currently working with younger women to teach them how to have successful businesses in the mining sector from her own mining camp named

Obama (inspiration overload!). Her outreach work and involvement in female empowerment in Tanzania and beyond is inspiring women and girls to strive for more: 'I never had anyone to guide me and had to live with a false identity as a man, just to access the mines. It doesn't have to be this way for the next generation.' Regrets, we've all had a few, but Pili says she has none. And why the flip should she? To this day, people still call her Uncle Hussein but it was Pili who busted out the big guns and bossed her life. Pili wasn't just as good as the men, she was a leader, the strongest and bravest. Pili Hussein is rarer than all the tanzanite in the land.

SISA ABU DAOOH (BORN 1950)

THE EGYPTIAN MUM WHO WENT TO WORK AS A DAD FOR FOUR DECADES

Sisa says that her story starts with a djellaba (a traditional Egyptian garment, native to the Nile Valley, which covers the entire body). As a Muslim, Sisa believes that dressing as the opposite sex is a sin but Islam also contemplates every action depending on its intention. Sisa chose to dress in the male robe and turban so as to care and provide for her family. She is certain her decision will not be opposed by her God. 'They know what I have done. And my djellaba is a symbol, a tool that has let me gain everything I have ever had.' (Forgive me if my self-control is non-existent in this chapter but I'm so proud of Sisa, I'm fizzing like a Berocca to tell you all about her.)

Sisa was born into poverty, in the small farming village of Al Aqaltah, on the west bank of the Nile, near Luxor. In her world, men are the breadwinners and the women stay home to bake it. Sisa never went to school or a kuttab (for Islamic studies); she was raised conventionally and married off young – so young she forgets exactly at what age but imagines it was around sixteen. In the early 1970s, when she was pregnant with her daughter, Houda, Sisa's husband died, leaving her penniless. Faced with a lifetime of begging on the streets, Sisa refused to walk the road to ruin and instead decided that she would do the unthinkable for women then – she would go out to work. Her family weren't having any of her cuckoo ideas; instead, her brothers presented her with a conveyor belt of potential new grooms, desperate for her to remarry and be done with it. But Sisa was unswayable, she refused to dishonour her husband, telling them, 'I'd rather eat dirt and feed my daughter stones than find myself another husband'. (A sentence that, I imagine, concluded that argument.) Any sort of manual labouring work was off limits to a woman but Sisa never learned to read or write, so (riddle me this) what was she to do? Before her siblings could protest any further, Sisa had shaved her head and made up her mind: 'To protect myself from men and the harshness of their looks and being targeted by them due to traditions, I decided to be a man . . . and dressed in their clothes and worked alongside them in other villages where no one knows me.' Sisa knew that, as a 'man', she could keep her child fed and go about her business without the threat of rampant sexual harassment (a tick for the positive in any prospective workplace checklist). She never doubted her ability or brawn, Sisa was as 'strong as ten men' by her own account and ready to prove it.

At first, Sisa would be out all day bob-a-jobbing while Houda was looked after by her grandmother. She started making and carrying bricks for a quarter of an Egyptian pound a day (a chihuahua-sized wage). From there, she went on to harvesting crops such as sugarcane and wheat and working the plough. She carried cement on building sites, set up her own shoe-shining business behind the temple on South Luxor's busy Mahatta Street, and built houses from the ground up with her own fair hands. Sisa even built her own home (and you've never seen anything so beautifully designed or genuinely shabby chic, without a *Live, Laugh, Love* triptych in sight). When Sisa couldn't find work, she survived on itsy bitsy bits of salted bread, tea and prayers, and when she could, she would share any food she did have with neighbours in need. Sisa never lied about being a female because most took her at face value and assumed she was a 'he'. Over the years she adopted more 'male' mannerisms and a deeper voice, perhaps as a result of the torment she experienced when her sex *was* discovered. In the early years, before she earned the complete respect of her peers, Sisa had to carry a club with her for self-defence. She was generally accepted as a man because she worked as hard as they did and interacted as one might expect a male to. However, there was always a handful of people who ran amuck and caused her great torment. Sisa often got spooked but she paid it no mind; the thought of her girl kept her immune to the physical and verbal blows. After sixteen years of creeping home at night, so as not to wake her sleeping daughter, she decided Houda should marry and arranged it to one of her cousins. In Sisa's world, this was still the best shot at independence she could offer her child. If she had had a son, she would not be worried, but a daughter meant she had to make sure Houda was protected by a man she knew. Over the next ten years, Sisa's daughter went on to have five sprouts of her own and (due to her husband developing a serious illness), Sisa now works to feed all of them too: 'I only want to provide for my family and buy them a good house. I'll give them everything I earn.'

Very gradually, Sisa's renown grew and after more than forty years of dressing in djellaba, the locals were no longer fazed to see her shooting the breeze with men in coffee shops or unwinding with them in the evenings (when all the women were indoors). Once the word was out further afield, however, fascination turned to hoopla. What had started as a way to escape rural poverty for Sisa had become a way of life for her and, to this day, she relishes the freedom it brings. All of the locals knew she was a woman but the rest of the world found out when, in 2015, the Egyptian president, Abdel Fattah el-Sisi, named her the city's most supportive mother. Her toil and half a lifetime of drudgery saw her gifted with money and described by el-Sisi as an 'exemplary working woman'. The few male stragglers who still hadn't accepted Sisa's way of life suddenly sat up and listened once the accolade brought Sisa a newfound celebrity status in Luxor. What's more, they'd tune-changed and now wanted to marry her! But Sisa would still rather feast on mud. Despite her cash prize, Sisa continues to live in abject poverty, but after giving an interview in Cairo in exchange for a snack kiosk and licence, she now runs her own small business selling from it, alongside shoe-shining. She says she will never stop living as a man: 'I have decided to die in these clothes. I've got used to it. It's my whole life and I can't leave it now.' She identifies as nothing other than a spiffing human being and her community thinks of her as a sheikh of the Arabs.

I watched a documentary about Sisa in which the production team take her to visit the Mortuary Temple of Hatshepsut (our homefry from the first chapter). She found it both hilarious and horrifying that, like her, Hatshepsut had to have a beard to get ahead (although hers was glued on, while Sisa spent her years at work pretending to have shaved hers off). It was quite emotional to see some of our *#GenderRebels* collide and a bittersweet reminder of how women are still having to live like this across the span of centuries. Of Hatshepsut, Sisa remarked, 'She was a woman but worth a hundred men! I'm proud of Hatshepsut. God rested her soul after death and so he will rest mine.' It will be a sad day for Egypt and the rest of the world when that day comes but I'm sure Sisa will be given the rest she deserves, Alhamdulillah (thanks be to God). More people need to know about Sisa than do now though. Vlog about her, tell your friends. I want to be able to ask Google or Alexa who Sisa Abu Daooh is and not have them pretend it's my accent they don't understand rather than the question.

TATIANA ALVAREZ
(D.O.B. UNKNOWN[13])

THE DANCE MUSIC DJ IN DISGUISE AT THE DECKS

Have a gander at the world's top 100 DJ list then call the press, write to the government and don't let any kids see it. Are we all going round the twist or does it seem that the editor missed out all the women? *Re-rewind!* More cats have scratched my furniture than women appear to have scratched records (and I've never even owned a cat). I wish I knew how to use Photoshop to change this picture but we can all get some shuteye later with the knowledge that people like Tatiana Alvarez are blazing their way to the top in this competitive, male-dominated industry.

DJ Tatiana (find *your* DJ name by putting 'DJ' in front of your own name!) has become top turntable talent in the EDM (electronic dance music) world and she is 15/10 quality (would recommend). Music has

---

13 Tatiana says 'My age is a secret' and I'm not mad about that (just disappointed). My chronological ordering is therefore guesswork and I can only hope it brings her 'profile photo' yay rather than 'the photo you've been tagged in' unyay.

motivated her every move in life and it all began in the small town of Agua Dulce, near LA, where she spent a childhood full of music reflective of her parents' Cuban and French-Canadian heritages. Her grandmother was a singer and she had uncles on both sides who were musicians and owned their own studios. Tatiana spent a lot of time rocking out with them and playing with her Mickey Mouse toy decks (WANT). Throughout her school years, Tatiana would make special mixtapes for friends, doing her own tape edits (playing a track on one deck and recording on the other, editing to make her own stutters and sounds). This memory is so #*ThrowbackThursday* for me it may as well be funded by Sunny D and the sound of floppy disks crunching as they were read. If you ever did it too, you'll remember how annoying it was if you were recording from the radio and the presenter talked over the track and ruined your life (especially if, like me, you were also filling in for them by recording your own links). When her addiction to sound and frequencies intensified, Tatiana almost began to see it as another language and her primitive DJ equipment was upgraded to vinyl and decks. By the time she was seventeen, she was underage raving, which most people do to get steaming on Smirnoff Ice but Tatiana was there for the DJs. She saw the award-winning Sandra Collins play one night and until then hadn't even realised DJing was a career that women could have. Tatiana's parents wanted her to become a lawyer but she knew she wanted to break the mould like Sandra: 'It was all guys and I thought, "I'm going to do that."' Tatiana was self-taught and practised throughout college, playing loads of free gigs and learning on the job. She started by playing funky house and house then moved on to techno and tech-house. These days, Tatiana often sidesteps genres and gets creative with whatever is inspiring her. Melodic trap, electronic with a bit of hip hop and dubstep thrown in, she has control of what she plays and how she plays it – *but she didn't always.*

Tatiana's sister Jennifer was a year younger than her and the pair were 'super close, like twins'. When Tatiana was eighteen, Jennifer was killed in a car accident and her world was thrown off its axis. Tatiana left home and, to keep her parents happy in all of their grief, went to college and studied English. Jennifer's death changed Tatiana's perspective on the world – 'I live life in a less conventional way, I live in the moment' – and she always knew it was DJing that would one day be her bread and butter. After graduating, she joined an agency who would send her out on commercial jobs, such as DJing for a car show called 'Hot Import Nights'. If the event title alone makes you feel the need to stage an intervention, your senses are correct. Tatiana wanted to play with likeminded DJs, with people who were on the same level as her, not be part of an all-female line-up for all-female sakes (with the added misery of being told to look *come-hither*). Tatiana got her personality back when her high heels came off (relatable) and the dumpster dive feel to these shows made her miserable. She was a skater girl at heart, she wanted to wear her baggy jeans, T-shirts and Vans, but the organisers and her management told her she couldn't, she was only booked to stand there and look pretty. (*Taps microphone* Hellooooo? Is this thing on? *GOOD BECAUSE I WANT TO SHOUT ABOUT THIS LUNACY!*) Tatiana wasn't interested in the clothes, she was only interested in the music and was far more versatile than the work she was given. She planned to go underground (i.e. avoid the mainstream scene rather than hide away in a bunker forever to escape the hysteria surrounding women wearing stilettos).

Tatiana gave a mixtape to a publicist producing underground techno music in New York to share among the bookers. The feedback was that everyone enjoyed it so much they assumed it had been mixed by a guy. When they were told otherwise, they all swiftly tracked back and were no longer interested, saying that DJ Tatiana was only ever booked for her looks, not the strength of her music. (Siri! Show me the epitome of insolence!) Tatiana naturally got the raging hump on hearing this (*Gets back on mic* ALL MY LADIES ALSO EXPERIENCING THIS RAGING HUMP MAKE SOME NOISE!). All she could think of to do was to reinvent herself to fool the fools. She considered using a male pseudonym but that wasn't going to be enough. Instead, she decided to make the most of her five-foot-ten stature and a make-up artist friend and transform herself into 'Matt Muset', aka DJ Musikillz! Tatiana realised, 'I need to be a guy, I need to look like a guy, I need to be the opposite of anything that's sexy' and her friend taught her how to create the appearance of an Adam's apple, how to widen her nose, apply extra hairs to her eyebrows and create a fake beard. To tank up, Tatiana padded her shoulders and her underwear, bandaged her breasts under a training bra that was too small and wore a wig. The plot thickened as she made up a management company and a fake female manager named Maya Feder, creating email accounts and Myspace pages to get those bookings sealed and locked. DJ Musikillz was immediately successful on the LA scene; she was working the venues and nights she wanted to and Tatiana found she could play in peace: 'When you're a female, there are always other people on stage watching what you're doing. They think you're stupid and say the most condescending things, but when you're a man they just leave you alone.' For the first time ever, everyone trusted that (s)he knew what (s)he was doing. (Never mind the decks, my head's rotating with all the hypocrisy.)

'Maya' would take the booking over the phone but Tatiana would worry her 'feminine' voice would give her away on the job, so she always took along a friend to pretend to be Muset's partner and do the talking for her. It was never questioned (because everyone knows women *love a chinwag!*) but the more it went on, the harder it was to always find someone to cover. Tatiana studied Eminem and tried to be as unapproachable as he was, so nobody questioned her too much, but truly, she just wanted to concentrate on the records and lose herself in the music. DJ Musikillz was blowing up in the EDM circles and Tatiana had never experienced so much respect from her peers, so she couldn't collapse her cover – but sometimes she needed the toilet so badly she couldn't even fade straight, and using the men's bathroom was a risk too far. Tatiana played as Musikillz for a year before she got run down with hiding her true self. It even lost her a relationship because her boyfriend at the time got too freaked out seeing her as a man (no doubt he has since either kicked himself or come out). It was time for her to really prove her point by dropping the disguise and showing all the dingbats that she was just as capable, if not better, than her male counterparts.

These days, DJ Tatiana is firmly established in the international EDM world; she produces alongside playing sets worldwide, has residencies in Las Vegas and LA and regularly fronts headliners to crowds craving summer bangers at festivals like Coachella, Electronic Daisy Carnival and Burning Man. Despite all her efforts, Tatiana still sees the industry as a man's game and one in which the women should be making much more money and having much more success: 'So many people still think women are not as solid as men . . . Many people think because I am an attractive woman, that I'm a diva. I carry my own bags. I stay up later and go harder than most guys. Throw down the same and have the same knowledge of the music.' But something she can make a scene about is that Warner Brothers have purchased the life rights to her story! Tatiana would like Jennifer Lawrence to play her and so would we all because, like Tatiana, she is probably-reverses-her-car-with-her-arm-around-the-passenger-seat cool. As far as her future is concerned, Tatiana simply wants to 'make people happy, dance and feel good. I am for the people.' And we are for DJ Tatiana.

MARIA TOORPAKAI WAZIR
(BORN 1990)

THE TALIBAN TRICKING, WEIGHTLIFTING,
PAKISTANI SQUASH PRO

Maria may be from the twenty-first century but she was born in a place then still so much in the Stone Age it would have stoned every woman in this book, including Maria, to death if given half a chance. South Waziristan, Pakistan, commonly referred to over the years as 'the most dangerous place on Earth', was, during Maria's childhood, a remote tribal area with unforgiving terrain and a paralysing Taliban presence. Girls and women rarely left the home. If they did it was forbidden ('haram') for them not to be completely covered. The birth of a girl in the Pashtun tribe was mourned. Each household is headed by a man who rules supreme and ensures the women don't get *ideas above their station*, including an education, job, the freedom to socialise or play sport. Change is snailing its way forward but it takes an extraordinary soul with unimaginable intrepidity to break free. Meet Maria . . .

Maria's parents, Yasrab and Shams Qayyum Wazir, had an arranged marriage but the tribal elders didn't anticipate the power-couple mind-meeting they had constructed. Shams is an absolute fireworks show of a human being and was a renegade among the Pashtun men – he allowed

Yasrab to live burqa-free and study degrees. The whole family (Maria, her parents, brother Taimur, sister Ayesha and younger twin brothers) all lived in a mud-brick home and were treated as equals. They adhere to the Muslim faith but were encouraged to be freethinkers. Ayesha was permitted to participate in debating competitions all over the region; Maria was allowed to run free; their mother set up a school for girls, which was such a dangerous idea she had to take it underground. Their home was routinely attacked and shot at with AK47s but Maria's parents persisted in trying to teach the younger generation literature, grammar, arithmetic and, above all, *ambition*. Shams was imprisoned by the elders many times and had to keep moving the family, relocating around the tribal province, eventually settling in Peshawar. In the end, Shams was thrown out of the tribe and they attempted to murder him, but you can't keep an outstanding man down.

Maria hated being a girl. She wanted to leap across the village rooftops, ride a bike, throw a ball, fire slingshots and shoot marbles. Her clothes were boulder heavy, as though they were suffocating her; dresses shrouded her as if she were 'confined head to toe like a coffin'. For a while, she tried to ignore the feeling, but doing so felt like a death sentence. Just before her fifth birthday, Maria's cork popped with such ferocity it might have imploded the system. She tore off her dress and went on a rampage around her house, ripping up all of her dresses like a human shredder, before pouring kerosene over the lot and striking a match. Maria found her brother's shalwar kameez (trousers and tunic) and put them on before taking scissors to her hair and lopping off great chunks, throwing them into the fire. In spectacular scenes that may sound Hollywood, her dad stood by and watched, silently – for this wasn't the movies but their reality. He had lost his sister, Maria's aunt, to suicide because she could not live as the strong, androgynous woman she was. The unsparing and hardboiled culture took the lives of so many more – women poisoned, starved and set fire to themselves to escape it. Shams couldn't allow the same fate for his daughter. He ran his fingers through her new haircut and told her: 'My new son must have a name befitting a great warrior and the battle just won without blood. We will call you Genghis Khan.' (Be still my beating heart.)

School was a myth for Maria. I hated my own dump brown, itch fiesta, acrylic knit school jumper that made my teeth squeak when my desk mate chewed their sleeve, but it didn't kill me to wear it. Maria simply couldn't be in a classroom because her uniform (a dress) brought her fresh hell. She was taken out and instead ran errands for the family (jobs her dad invented to keep her up, out and at 'em) but trouble soon found her. A mysterious, unknown 'boy' out on the streets was piece of cake prey for the Peshawar street posses, who laid hands on her in every corner and alleyway. Before her cuts had time to scab over, Maria was leading a ten-strong street gang of boys she had proven herself to by thrashing (well, that escalated quickly). Save one trip to the hospital for a scalp-load of stitches, Maria was untouchable and dauntless. She would say more than boo to a goose and probably clonk it one while she was at it. To save her from getting killed, her dad needed to find Maria a hobby. He chose to send the young, ripped, enraged, sucker-punching muscle-buster to weightlifting training and it suited her to the ticket (can't think why). As a girl, she would never have been allowed to compete. Female athletes didn't exist but she was 'Genghis Khan of Peshawar'! and Genghis sauntered through 'his' first competition, despite being the youngest, taking home the trophy and wiping the mats with all the male competitors. At the sports complex where she practised, Maria saw men playing squash for the first time. Next to cricket, it's the most popular sport in Pakistan but she knew nothing about it. She *had to* know EVERYTHING.

Shams took Maria to a squash academy run by the Pakistani air force. Her first coach, who she called The Wing Commander, not only allowed her to play but gave her her first racket. It had world number-one squash player Jonathan Power's signature embossed on the handle and felt more potent in Maria's hand than any street weapon. She was silly good from the beginning, walloping balls until they split like she was exorcising her demons. She played with the boys and although her sex was never mentioned, at the end of one practice The Wing Commander told her, 'You'll break the racket before long, Maria.' The cat was out of the sports bag. Squash had become Maria's addiction but the boys made it a lifemare for her. She understood 'their male pride was too raw . . . the truth was, they feared me.' They harassed Maria constantly, calling her a 'slut', a 'shame on her father', and telling her she played like a girl. Too hot-tempered and quick to fight, Maria had to leave the academy. Instead, she spent her days (and nights) playing squash against imaginary opponents in the kitchen, hitting until the balls went kaput, her hands and knees were bleeding and the kitchen was wrecked. By now, the Taliban reign of terror was more devastating than ever. Not an hour passed without a suicide bomb, gunfire – death was all around. Maria couldn't sit back and wait to die, she had to *squash* the terrorists.

When her registration to play competitively against the boys was refused, Maria entered the under 13s girls' tournament in Wah Cantonment. Her parents sacrificed everything for her to be there but she more than paid them back, returning home with the 1400-rupee prize! In 2006, Maria went professional and represented her country around the world. When she became national champion (praise be), she was photographed receiving an award from President Musharraf and the exposure made her the Taliban's number one target. The Pakistani squash federation provided Maria with security because the death threats stopped at nothing. She couldn't play without snipers surrounding her court or step out without spies on her tail. Maria tried to throw them off with erratic training schedules but decided things had gone too far when a fake bomb was left on centre court as a final warning. She couldn't put anyone else's life at risk and so three gruelling years ensued in which she was confined to her room, practising for ten hours a day. She still managed to make some tournaments by stowing away, registering unannounced, purchasing tickets last minute, borrowing cars, changing the number plates and travelling at the dead of night in hoodies. She may have tricked the Taliban but the threats to her life never ceased. By the time she was eighteen, Maria had sent thousands of emails to squash academies in the Western world, in pursuit of a career and a life. Three years of emailing in, Maria heard back from somebody (and not just anybody) – her hero, *Jonathan Power*. In 2011, she went to Canada to train at his National Squash Academy and only ten months later, Maria WON the Liberty Bell Open (and I am spun because I've never rooted for anyone so hard in my life).

Maria fled the Taliban with nothing more than a duffel bag and a squash racket. She now has her own charity and wants the world to know 'I am determined to bring positive change to the world through education, sports and healthcare. I am raising my voice on behalf of the millions of "Marias" I left behind, who remain the hostages of regimes and ideologies that have stripped them of their most basic human rights.' Preach, sis. I implore you to check out her website for more information. Donate. Let's save another Maria.

SAHAR KHODAYARI (1990–2019)

THE FOOTBALL FANATIC, STADIUM SMUGGLER AND 'DAUGHTER OF IRAN'

Originally known only as 'Blue Girl' on social media (the colour of her favourite Persian Gulf pro team, Esteghlal FC), Sahar was someone I longed to connect with during my research for this book. I never imagined that I'd be writing this following her death in Tehran, soon after her release from prison for the audacious act of attending a football match. The stories of women dressing as men to watch football in Iran are widespread, but few of them were able to talk openly about their experiences, fearing for their liberty and lives. As such, this final chapter won't include as much personal information as some, but it is dedicated most lovingly, ardently and honourably to her memory.

Born in Salm, Kiar County, in the Chaharmahal and Bakhtiari Province in southwest Iran, Sahar lived alongside her seven siblings in a strict, traditional and religious household. She had her sights set on a career as a police officer from an early age, but her father excelled in his self-appointed 'Bad Cop' role; cuffing her dreams, he told Sahar she would never achieve them because she was 'a girl and weak'. She might not have gone on to fight crime as she originally wanted, but she found a new path for herself, ignoring all the headassery and fighting stereotypical expectations instead, graduating from university with a degree in Computer Sciences. All we know from here is that Sahar dedicated any other spare time entirely to her beloved Esteghlal FC. Football in Iran has an immense female fandom, but thanks to unwritten laws and systemic discrimination, women are not allowed to attend stadiums to watch the male teams, and women's professional sport is not tolerated. The country's rules about women and football have been this way since the 1979 Islamic Revolution brought an end to the freedom Iranian women had only recently got a taste of.

Football officials argue that not having women at matches protects them – the head of security at the Azadi Stadium in Tehran (*Azadi* absurdly meaning 'freedom') explained that the ban is 'to save their honour, because the stadium's atmosphere, mess, and crowds are [*and believe me, I quote*] no place for women'. In response, a female fan (who I will keep anonymous) told of her similarly maddening experiences: 'In my country, everyone says that women have nothing to do with football. They want women to stay at home and cook food and take care of the children. They want us to just listen, and not speak. Here women cannot become presidents. Here women cannot travel to other countries without the approval of their husbands.' For over two decades, an ever-increasing number of women have been fighting back and celebrating their love of the great game to prove to society at large that their opinions are way offside. In the mid-1990s, for example, reports began to surface of women painting their faces, disguising themselves as male fans and conceding to being frisked by security to get into games. This is still happening today, and of those I got in contact with, very few could offer their names or reveal anything about themselves because it is simply too hazardous. It's not only football stadiums that women are banned from: in 2014, for example, Ghoncheh Ghavami, an Iranian-British activist, was imprisoned for more than five months for attending a volleyball match. Over the years, the lobbying and pressure on Iran's government to cease with the stupidity has multiplied, but women are *still* having to find ways in. And they're not simply risking it for a chocolate biscuit, as Sahar's story grievously shows; these women are risking *everything* in order to enjoy the everyday free rein that men in Iran take as their due.

Sahar's parents never stopped her from watching football at home but (Bad Cop particularly) spoke a lot of stank about the practice of women smuggling themselves into the grounds as men, believing 'it is not appropriate for women to go to stadiums. It is a crime.' On 12 March 2019, Sahar rejected the blue funk and headed for her blue bliss. The women of Iran's incalculable years of hurt never stopped her dreaming. There was an AFC Champions League match between Esteghlal and Al-Ain FC at the Azadi and she could wait no longer to support her boys in blue. Dressed in a long blue overcoat and hiding behind a blue wig, Sahar attempted to blend her way into the grounds among the men, pretending to be one in order to watch the game. We can only guess at how she felt that day. Speaking to another Iranian woman gives us a clue, though. She explains that on the day she managed successfully to get into the stadium, disguised as a man, it was an unimaginably emotional moment: 'I wanted to scream in excitement but I couldn't. I cried, quietly and softly, out of happiness but also sadness of having had this right taken away from me for so long.' Sadly, Sahar never made it this far: she was noticed by security personnel, promptly arrested and detained in Shahr-e Rey prison (also known as Gharchak). After her release, the Islamic Revolutionary Court went on to sentence Sahar to six months' imprisonment for the crimes of 'openly committing a sinful act by . . . appearing in public without a hijab' and 'insulting officials'.

On 2 September 2019, as Sahar left the courthouse, in an act of distress and premeditated protest she poured gasoline over her head and body and set fire to herself outside the court. Suffering 90 per cent burns, Sahar spent the next few days in the ICU at the Motahari Accident and Burn Hospital, in the care of its head, Dr Mustafa Deh Mardaei, before her death was announced on 9 September. Sahar had been silenced; she died in fear of her future, but still battling for her human rights. Her sister has since told the media that her mental health deteriorated while in the dangerous and dire conditions of Shahr-e Rey. In the end, self-immolation was her only *azadi*. Sahar was buried in the holy Shi'ite city of Qom but the details were kept under wraps by the government. They tried to do the same to her legacy (some programmes on Iranian state television even denied Sahar's story altogether) but it was undeniable that hearts bled blue for her worldwide. Candlelight vigils were held in the capital and her adored Esteghlal boys even held a one-minute silence in tribute to Sahar ahead of a training session.

Despite outcry and accelerated activism from many prominent Iranians and celebrities worldwide, FIFA and the IFA are still feuding with the country to make certain they move the goalposts. At the time of writing (and as a direct result of the mounting pressure following Sahar's death) the ban had been lifted to allow women in to the stadium for the 2020 World Cup qualifier against Cambodia on 10 October 2019. Those lucky enough to bag a ticket had to watch from segregated sections, alongside a heavy police presence. For this historic match, only 3,500 tickets were made available to women in the 90,000-seater venue, but they sold out in minutes. There is much speculation as to whether this will simply turn out to be a publicity stunt, especially as this was all less than a month after Iran's prosecutor-general, Mohammad Jafar Montazeri, told the world 'it is a sin for a woman to go to a stadium and face half-naked men. We will not be silent in the face of those who break the taboos.' To counteract these fossilised opinions, let us all worship at the churches of anyone believing anything but. People like Parvaneh Salahshouri, a reformist lawmaker who named Sahar 'the daughter of Iran' and took to Twitter to remind us that we can all do more to ensure this does not continue: 'We are all responsible for the imprisonment and burning of [all] Sahars of this land.' And Masoud Shojaei, an Iranian football captain, who apologised to the women of the country after Iran beat Hong Kong two days after Sahar's death, saying, 'Condolences, girls of Iran. Today, Team Melli lost because Sahar wasn't with us.'

Today the world loses because Sahar is no longer with us. After travelling centuries of #GenderRebels to reach the modern day, I'm heartbroken that we have had to end on a story so beyond belief it feels as though it should be ancient history. But Sahar and the women who fought before her did so for our futures. In my mind, tomorrow's world always starts yesterday. Sahar's fight made the need for change an international emergency and has brought hope to all of our tomorrows. Rest in Power, Sahar Khodayari.

CONCLUSION

Firstly, may I take this opportunity to say thank you for reading *#GenderRebels* (if indeed you still are). From pitch to the page you see before you, my sun has risen and set with these women and it's been an absolute privilege to share their stories with the world. I'm only sad that now it's over I'm going to have to leave the house and put a bra back on (for personal liability not 'female aesthetic' reasons).

I defy anyone to disagree that bringing these women's names back into our minds and mouths is as overdue as a cull of CEOs called 'John'. We should no longer have to feast on a few sentences or the scraps of information about the women who have changed our worlds; we need to be gorging on the well-versed, informed rump (replace with the latest vegan/clean eating/fad equivalent as required). By waking their memories, understanding the battles, the hardships, the hurt, the sacrifices, the deaths, we can commemorate the significance and impact on our lives today. As we unearth the women who strived for happy endings, we recognise how they helped us towards ours and remember that nobody who died for the cause, died in vain. There's certainly room on this pedestal for plenty more than the fifty shared here, but I must reiterate that those you met are solely the examples I was able to find easily or *not so easily* (excavated only via official records, documentation, court manuscripts, newspaper snippings or indeed their infamy). Our history and present day is ram-a-jam with formidable females, the nameless and voiceless who will never get a mention, and although that turns my head into the spinning rainbow beach ball of doom, it similarly stirs up much hope.

As I was writing this book, Saudi Arabia repealed its ban on female drivers (which was very on-brand of them) but by my second draft, it was revealed that at least a dozen Saudi women's rights activists had been arrested, simply for their involvement in the campaigns to lift the prohibition. The deeply entrenched discrimination and guardianship systems still remain, haunting and hunting the country's women. I found countless examples of modern women hiding in plain sight in male clothing across the Middle East but we are unable to know anything more about them as they live in fear of their lives. There are also women fleeing war-torn countries in disguise, whole villages of Afghani girls being raised as boys to stay alive, 'sworn virgins' in Albania, living as men to escape their patriarchal society, and gay women wearing male clothing to appear to conform in over seventy countries where homosexuality is still illegal. Although we may automatically think of the countries very much renowned for their inequality, the same was true of stories uncovered from right across the globe. The never-ending lists such as 'Worst Places to Be Born a Girl / a Woman / a Mother / LGBTQ+ / anything other than a white, cisgendered, non-disabled, neurotypical, straight male' catalogue more countries than I could point to on the world map. For the nth time it has to be said, *O, I am out of breath in this fond chase for equality!*

I don't doubt you will know of cloak or guise examples on your doorstep or have at least considered, at some point, how much more lemon squeezy life and times are for most men. The more we are ignored, the more cases I clock of women getting creative with their masquerading to prove a point. It's impossible not to notice everyday examples that testify we are marked whatever we do. Let's call *Game Over* on female gamers having to change their avatars to boys to negotiate gamergate, women needing to post anonymously or under pseudonyms to share their opinions on social media without the threat of rape, and women still throwing up hoods and changing their gait to walk home safely after dark. There are women in workplaces in the US and UK who are blogging about their experiences of applying for jobs under male names instead of their own, starting up companies as 'male' execs, changing their email signatures to be shown more respect and power at their desks, even keeping their sex only *slightly* secret squirrel so as to 'appeal' to everyone. Although 200 years have passed since the Mary Ann Evans and Brontë wonders of this world, my mind can't help but rove on over to thinking about modern-day examples such as J. K. Rowling. There may have been a plan behind her *Slytherin* on to the shelves as something other than 'Joanne' but now Joanne is RICHER THAN THE QUEEN OF ENGLAND, I think we can all do well to remember that she forever possessed that genius, she was just told to find a way to get boys and men to recognise it. Surely the time to bulldoze open this gargantuan can of worms is NOW? In fact, it was years ago, *centuries* ago, but we really can't wait any longer.

In my life to date, the best time to be female is a distant childhood memory. It's December 1997 – my teeth are stuck together with popcorn kernels and classic cola Chupa Chups and my brain is exploding with ideas about the infinite meanings of 'Zig-a-zig-ah'. My cousin and I are hunched up in my Wendy house dissecting every precious moment of *Spice World: The Movie* in between creating a band called 'Chaos' and planning to take over the world that very same day (after tea). We felt like we could do anything – if Baby Spice could spit out her dummy in the face of adversity, Ginger could stick out her tongue to the cynics and Mel C could somersault across a table in a crop top, then we could have it all! We didn't know about gender pay gaps and inequality, the patriarchy or that we'd spend half of our lives avoiding being told to smile by men. We didn't know about *#NotAllMen* or that we'd wish we never did when we did. We only knew that we had super brains and we wanted to dive right in and use them. I knew that being a girl meant I was all sorts of magic; I knew that we were strong and unwavering (even in seven-inch Spice Girls shoes); and I knew that I always wanted it to feel that way. 1997 me was naive. She needed some sort of pre-warning that simply being a girl would hold her back from getting all the stuff done she was dreaming and capable of. We cannot keep calm and carry on any longer (and if you're not fuming about all of this by now, you've not been paying attention).

We live in a ballsed-up world but we can mend it. If you see unexpected misogyny in the bagging area, demand to see the manager. Call it out and get *mangry* when they tell us to 'calm down'. Shout it from the rooftops – or a balcony perhaps (health and safety). Hold any pillocks you come across up to scrutiny (and if you ever meet anyone who will never see the light, it's probably best you have them put down). Don't give up. Don't give over. Don't give in. Don't give anything less than everything you've got. If I didn't keep trying, I'd probably just go home and sad eat Flumps every night and (as beguiling as it sounds) I didn't sign up to a marshmallow-related departure.

I never saw my nan cry but I witnessed the flash of over ninety years of stringent tear dams in practice when I spoke to her about the lack of change since the feminist and liberation movements of her day. Nobody can believe we STILL have to protest this sh*t but the women who did so as men helped us to be out and proud. Millions of us may be galvanised around the world to fight old injustices and fresh sexism but this new wave is a long way from its crest. The time is now, the world is unable and unwilling to wait. We are trudging through an age of rage and (as I'm sure you've seen on more than one occasion over the course of these pages) I myself can be guilty of expending my energy on seething. We have to trade our outrage to outcome and spend it instead on *change*.

These #*GenderRebels* paved the way for us to be soldiers, saints, spies, kings, queens, firefighters, doctors, writers, pilots, sport stars, musicians, politicians, bosses and a Swiss Army knife's-worth more. We must never take for granted what they did to allow some of us to honour our true selves, do as we please, love who we choose to and live freely. Let's hope that one day this can be true for everyone and that the rest is feministory.

And so, to all those up in arms, under arms, to those whose arms have been tied or need the supportive arms of the sisterhood – *HAI-SI-JA!* HOLD TIGHT.

BIBLIOGRAPHY

GENERAL

Girls Will Be Boys: Cross-Dressed Women, Lesbians, and American Cinema, Laura Horak (Rutgers University Press, 2016)

'In Disguise: Cross Dressing and Gender Identity', Jennifer Levonian (Heritage Philadelphia Program and The Library Company, 2010)

'Shakespeare and Gender: The 'Woman's Part', Clare McManus (British Library Essay, 2016). https://www.bl.uk/shakespeare/articles/shakespeare-and-gender-the-womans-part

Transgender History & Geography: Crossdressing in Context, G. G. Bolich (Psyche's Press, 2007)

Women in Men's Guise, Oscar Paul Gilbert (John Lane, The Bodley Head, 1932)

HATSHEPSUT

Hatshepsut: From Queen to Pharaoh, Catharine H. Roehrig, Renée Dreyfus and Cathleen A. Keller (The Metropolitan Museum of Art / Yale University Press, 2005)

Tan Men/Pale Women: Color and Gender in Archaic Greece and Egypt, a Comparative Approach, Mary Ann Eaverly (University of Michigan Press, 2013)

The Finest Pharaoh of All!, Stewart Ross (Evans Brothers Ltd., 1999)

HUA MULAN

Mulan's Legend and Legacy in China and the United States, Lan Dong (Temple University Press, 2010)

'The Ballad of Mulan' (source), Asia for Educators – Columbia University http://afe.easia.columbia.edu/ps/china/mulan.pdf

Women Warriors and Wartime Spies of China, Louise P. Edwards (Cambridge University Press, 2016)

SAINT MARINA

'Being Gay and Coptic', http://gaycopt.blogspot.co.uk/2010/11/cross-dressing-saints.html

'Saint Marina the Monk: Part I', Guita G. Hourani, http://www.maronite-institute.org/MARI/JMS/january00/Saint_Marina_the_Monk.htm

Selective Narratives of Holy Women, Agnes Smith Lewis (C. J. Clay and Sons, 1900)

The Legends of the Holy Harlots, Andrew M. Beresford (Boydell & Brewer Ltd., 2007)

JOANNA OF FLANDERS

Barzaz Breiz, Théodore Hersart de la Villemarqué – translation (Éditions Delloye, 1867)

Essays on Sex Equality, Harriet Taylor Mill and John Stuart Mill (University of Chicago Press, 1970)

The Creation of Brittany, Michael Jones (The Hambledon Press, 1988)

The True Chronicles of Jean le Bel: 1290–1360, Jean le Bel, translated by Nigel Bryant (Boydell Press, 2015)

World Clothing and Fashion: An Encyclopedia of History, Culture, and Social Influence, Mary Ellen Snodgrass (Routledge, 2013)

ONORATA RODIANI

An Annotated Index of Medieval Women, Anne Echols (Markus Wiener Publishers, 1992)

Life Stories of Women Artists 1550–1800: An Anthology, Julia Kathleen Dabbs (Routledge, 2009)

The Obstacle Race: The Fortunes of Women Painters and Their Work, Germaine Greer (Tauris Parke Paperbacks, 2001)

JOAN OF ARC

Amazons to Fighter Pilots: A Biographical Dictionary of Military Women, Reina Pennington (Greenwood Press, 2003)

God's Unusual Saints, Edward J. Hahnenberg (AuthorHouse, 2006)

Joan of Arc: A History, Helen Castor (Faber & Faber, 2015)

Joan of Arc: The Image of Female Heroism, Marina Warner (University of California Press, 2001)

Joan of Arc: The Warrior Saint, Stephen W. Richey (Praeger, 2003)

ELENO DE CÉSPEDES

Inquisitorial Inquires, Richard L. Kagan and Abigail Dyer (The Johns Hopkins University Press, 2011)

Queer Iberia: Sexualities, Cultures, and Crossings from the Middle Ages to the Renaissance, Josiah Blackmore and Gregory S. Hutcheson (Duke University Press, 1999)

The Lives of Women: A New History of Inquisitorial Spain, Lisa Vollendorf (Vanderbilt University Press, 2005)

MARY FRITH

Counterfeit Ladies: The Life and Death of Mary Frith, Janet Todd and Elizabeth Spearing (New York University Press, 1994)

Medieval and Renaissance Drama in England v. 21 (Medieval & Renaissance Drama in England), S. P. Cerasano (Fairleigh Dickinson University Press, 2008)

Rogues and Early Modern English Culture, Craig Dionne and Steve Mentz (University of Michigan Press, 2006)

The Book of Days: A Miscellany of Popular Antiquities in Connection with the Calendar, Including Anecdote, Biography, & History, Curiosities of Literature and Oddities of Human Life and Character, Volume 2, Robert Chambers (W. & R. Chambers Limited, 1832)

The Life and Death of Mrs Mary Frith, Randall S. Nakayama (Garland Publishing, 1993)

The Life and Death of Mrs Mary Frith, commonly called Mal Cutpurse, Mary Frith (1662)

CATALINA DE ERAUSO

In Search of Catalina de Erauso: The National and Sexual Identity of a Lieutenant Nun, Eva Mendieta (Center for Basque Studies, 2009)

The Lieutenant Nun: Transgenderism, Lesbian Desire & Catalina de Erauso, Sherry Velasco (University of Texas Press, 2000)

The Life of Catalina de Erauso: The Lieutenant Nun, Sonia Pérez-Villanueva (Fairleigh Dickinson University Press, 2014)

Who's Who in Gay and Lesbian History: From Antiquity to World War II, Robert Aldrich and Garry Wotherspoon (Routledge, 2001)

QUEEN CHRISTINA OF SWEDEN

A Relation of the Life of Christina Queen of Svveden: with her resignation of the crown, voyage to Bruxels, and journey to Rome. Whereunto is added, her Genius, translated by I. H. (1656)

Christina Queen of Sweden, Veronica Buckley (HarperCollins, 2004)

Queen Christina of Sweden and Her Circle, Susanna Akerman (E. J. Brill, 1991)

Women in Men's Guise, Oscar Paul Gilbert (John Lane, The Bodley Head, 1932)

CHRISTIAN 'KIT' CAVANAGH

Mother Ross: An Irish Amazon, G. R. Lloyd (AuthorHouse UK, 2012)

The Life and Adventures of Mrs Christian Davies: Commonly Call'd Mother Ross, Daniel Defoe (London, 1743)

JULIE D'AUBIGNY

Between Genders: Narrating Difference in Early French Modernism, Nathaniel Wing (Rosemont Publishing, 2004)

Goddess, Kelly Gardiner (HarperCollins, 2014)

Women in Men's Guise, Oscar Paul Gilbert (John Lane, The Bodley Head, 1932)

ULRIKA ELEONORA STÅLHAMMAR

Encyclopedia of Lesbian and Gay Histories and Cultures, Bonnie Zimmerman and George Haggerty (Routledge, 2000)

'It's a Man's World', Anna Belfrage (2015) https://annabelfrage.wordpress.com/tag/cross-dresser/

Swedish Biographical Dictionary, Gunlög Fur (2009) https://sok.riksarkivet.se/sbl/Presentation.aspx?id=34664

MARY READ

A Brief History of Pirates and Buccaneers, Tom Bowling (Robinson, 2010)

A General History of the Pyrates, Daniel Defoe (Dover Publications Inc., 1999)

She Captains: Heroines and Hellions Of the Sea, Joan Druett (Simon & Schuster, 2001)

The Pirates' Who's Who, Philip Gosse (BiblioLife, 2008)

Under the Black Flag: The Romance and the Reality of Life Among the Pirates, David Cordingly (Random House Trade, 2006)

ANNE BONNY

A Brief History of Pirates and Buccaneers, Tom Bowling (Robinson, 2010)

A General History of the Pyrates, Daniel Defoe (Dover Publications Inc., 1999)

Sea Star: Private Life of Anne Bonny, Pamela Jekel (Random House Value Publishing, 1983)

The Pirates' Who's Who, Philip Gosse (BiblioLife, 2008)

Under the Black Flag: The Romance and the Reality of Life Among the Pirates, David Cordingly (Random House Trade, 2006)

MARY EAST

Kirby's Wonderful and Eccentric Museum; Or, Magazine of Remarkable Characters, R. S. Kirby (Kirby, 1803)

'Mary East, the Female Husband', in *Homosexuality in Eighteenth-Century England: A Sourcebook*, Rictor Norton, 2003, http://rictornorton.co.uk/eighteen/1766east.htm

'Mary East AKA James How and Mrs How of The White Horse, Poplar' (East End Women Museum) https://eastendwomensmuseum.org/blog/2017/6/23/mary-east-aka-james-how-and-mrs-how-of-the-white-horse-poplar

'The Story of Mary East by Bram Stoker' (Isle of Dogs Life) https://isleofdogslife.wordpress.com/2014/11/25/the-story-of-mary-east-by-bram-stoker/

CATHARINE VIZZANI

'Butch Heroes', Ria Brodell, https://www.riabrodell.com/catterina-vizzani-aka-giovanni-bordoni/

'When Giovanni Becomes Catherine: Lauding the Female Virginity of the Male Libertine', Katie Gunn (Literary Undergraduate Research University of West Georgia) https://www.westga.edu/academics/coah/english/assets/docs/LURe.pdf

Who's Who in Gay and Lesbian History: From Antiquity to World War II, Robert Aldrich (Routledge, 2000)

The True History and Adventures of Catharine Vizzani, Giovanni Bianchi (First edition, 1755)

MARGARET 'PEG' WOFFINGTON

Lovely Peggy: The Life and Times of Margaret Woffington, Janet Camden Lucey (Hurst and Blackett, 1952)

Peg Woffington and Her World, Janet Dunbar (Heinemann, 1968)

Stage Favourites of the Eighteenth Century, Lewis Melville (Doubleday, Doran & Co, 1929)

MARY HAMILTON

'Butch Heroes', Ria Brodell, https://www.riabrodell.com/charles-aka-mary-hamilton/

The Female Husband, Henry Fielding (first edition, published anonymously, 1746)

The Female Thermometer: Eighteenth-Century Culture and the Invention of the Uncanny (Ideologies of Desire), Terry Castle (Oxford University Press, 1995)

The New Newgate Calendar; Being Interesting Memoirs of Notorious Characters, Who Have Been Convicted of Outrages on the Laws of England, Andrew Knapp (Gale, 2012)

HANNAH SNELL

Hannah Snell: The Secret Life of a Female Marine 1723–1792, Matthew Stephens (Ship Street Press, 2014)

Iron Men, Wooden Women: Gender and Seafaring in the Atlantic World, Margaret S. Creighton and Lisa Norling (The John Hopkins University Press, 1996)

Women Adventurers, M. M. Dowie (Adam Matthews Publications, 1893)

MARGARET ANN BULKLEY

Dr James Barry: A Woman Ahead of Her Time, Michael du Preez and Jeremy Dronfield (Oneworld, 2016)

'James Barry', University of Edinburgh (College of Medicine and Veterinary Medicine), https://www.ed.ac.uk/medicine-vet-medicine/about/history/women/james-barry

The Perfect Gentleman, June Rose (Hutchinson, 1977)

The Secret Life of Dr James Barry, Rachel Holmes (Tempus, 2007)

QUQUNOK PATKE

Kauxama Nupika or also known as Gone to The Spirits, Robert Clark (HarperCollins, 1995)

'Nineteenth-Century Indigenous Women Warriors' (Women's History Matters, 2014) http://montanawomenshistory.org/nineteenth-century-indigenous-women-warriors/#more-1381

Oregon and the Collapse of Illahee: U.S. Empire and the Transformation of an Indigenous World, 1792–1859, Gray H. Whaley (University North Carolina, 2010)

Transgender History & Geography: Crossdressing in Context, G. G. Bolich (Psyche's Press, 2007)

AMANDINE-AURORE-LUCILE DUPIN

George Sand: A Brave Man, The Most Womanly Woman, Donna Dickenson (Berg Publishers, 1989)

Story of My Life: The Autobiography of George Sand, George Sand (1854)

The Double Life of George Sand, Renee Winegarten (Basic Books, 1978)

CHARLOTTE DARKEY PARKHURST

'A Driver in Disguise: The Story of Charley Parkhurst', Hushed Up History (2016) http://husheduphistory.com/post/144458529593/a-driver -in-disguise-the-story-of-charley

'The Fearless Character of One Eyed Charley, Challenging Gender Boundaries: A Trans Biography Project', Bryan Kennedy, http:// outhistory.org/exhibits/show/tgi-bios/charley-parkhurst

The Whip, Karen Kondazian (Hansen Publishing Group, 2011)

Via Western Express and Stagecoach: California's Transportation Links with the Nation, 1848–1869, Oscar Osburn Winther (University of Nebraska Press, 1979)

THE BRONTË SISTERS

Life and works of Charlotte Brontë and her sisters: in seven volumes, Charlotte Brontë (J. Murray, 1872)

The Four Brontës: The Lives and Works of Charlotte, Branwell, Emily, and Anne Brontë, Lawrence Hanson and E. M. Hanson (Oxford University Press, 1950)

The World of the Brontës, Jane O'Neill (Carlton Books Ltd, 1997)

MARY ANN EVANS

George Eliot: An Intellectual Life, Valerie A. Dodd (Palgrave Macmillan, 1990)

George Eliot: Gender and Sexuality, Laura Green. From *A Companion to George Eliot*, Amanda Anderson and Harry E. Shaw, eds (Wiley-Blackwell, 2013)

The Transferred Life of George Eliot, Philip Davis (OUP Oxford, 2017)

Women Reviewing Women in Nineteenth-Century Britain: The Critical Reception of Jane Austen, Charlotte Brontë and George Eliot, Joanne Wilkes (Routledge, 2010)

ELLEN CRAFT

Love, Liberation, and Escaping Slavery: William and Ellen Craft in Cultural Memory, Barbara McCaskill (University of Georgia Press, 2015)

Rethinking the Slave Narrative: Slave Marriage and the Narratives of Henry Bibb and William and Ellen Craft, Charles J. Heglar (Greenwood Press, 2001)

Running a Thousand Miles for Freedom: Or, the Escape of William and Ellen Craft, Ellen and William Craft (SMK Books, 2012)

LORETA JANETA VELÁZQUEZ

Inventing Loreta Velasquez: Confederate Soldier Impersonator, Media Celebrity, and Con Artist, William C. Davies (Southern Illinois University Press, 2016)

She Went to the Field: Women Soldiers of the Civil War, Bonnie Tsui (Falcon Guides, 2006)

The Woman in Battle: The Civil War Narrative of Loreta Janeta Velazquez, Cuban Woman and Confederate Soldier, Loreta Janeta Velázquez (Leonaur Ltd., 2010)

LILLIE HITCHCOCK-COIT

'Heroes, Heroines and History', (Nancy J. Farrier 2017) https://www.hhhistory.com/2017/04/lillie-hitchcock-coit-woman-of-adventure.html

'Lillie Hitchcock Coit, a San Francisco lady', Carl Nolte (*The San Francisco Chronicle*, 2012) https://www.sfchronicle.com/news/article/Lillie-Hitchcock-Coit-a-San-Francisco-lady-3188302.php

'Mrs. Lillie Hitchcock-Coit', (The Virtual Museum of the City of San Francisco,) http://www.sfmuseum.net/hist1/h-coit2.html

Some Personal Recollections of Lillie Hitchcock Coit, Floride Green (The Grabhorn Press, 1935)

CATHAY WILLIAMS

Amazons to Fighter Pilots: A Biographical Dictionary of Military Women, Reina Pennington (Greenwood Press, 2003)

Cathy Williams: From Slave to Female Buffalo Soldier, Phillip Thomas Tucker (Stackpole Books, 2009)

'National Park Service report and archive', https://www.nps.gov/goga/learn/education/upload/BS_PrimarySources_2008-01-18_med.pdf

JEANNE BONNET

Frog Music, Emma Donoghue (Picador, 2014)

'Jennie A Bonnet Memorial', Find a Grave, https://www.findagrave.com/memorial/133023607/jennie-a-bonnet

News and Sexuality: Media Portraits of Diversity, Laura Castañeda and Shannon B. Campbell (SAGE Publications, 2005)

'The Little Frog Catcher', Paul Drexler (*San Francisco Chronicle*, 2018) http://www.sfexaminer.com/little-frog-catcher/

'The San Miguel Mystery: The Documents', Emma Donoghue, http://www.emmadonoghue.com/images/pdf/the-san-miguel-mystery-the-documents.pdf

VIOLET PAGET

Vernon Lee: A Literary Biography, Vineta Colby (University of Virginia Press, 2003)

'Vernon Lee: Aesthetics, History and the Female Subject in the Nineteenth Century', Christa Zorne Belde (University of Florida dissertation, 1994) https://archive.org/stream/vernonleeaesthet-00zorn/vernonleeaesthet00zorn_djvu.txt

Vernon Lee: Violet Paget 1856–1935, Peter Gunn (Oxford University Press, 1964)

MARY ANDERSON

Cross Dressing, Sex, and Gender, Vern L. Bullough and Bonnie Bullough (University of Pennsylvania Press, 1993)

Gay American History: Lesbians and Gay Men in the U.S.A, Jonathan Ned Katz (Crowell, 1976)

Studies in the Psychology of Sex, Volume 2 Sexual Inversion, Havelock Ellis (Random House, 1937)

'The Mystery of Murray Hall', Karen Abbot (*Smithsonian*, 2011) https://www.smithsonianmag.com/history/the-mystery-of-murray-hall-35612997/

CLARA MARY LAMBERT

'Catherine Wilson: a dangerous woman in UK Parliament', Dangerous Women Project (Dr Mari Takayanagi 2016) http://dangerouswomenproject.org/2016/03/19/suffragette-dressed-as-man/

'Clara Lambert – A Militant Catford Suffragette', Running Past: South East London History on Foot https://runner500.wordpress.com/2018/06/13/clara-lambert-a-militant-catford-suffragette/

Goldaming Museum, 2015 http://www.godalmingmuseum.org.uk/index.php?page=clara-mary-lambert

Rise Up Women!: The Remarkable Lives of the Suffragettes, Diane Atkinson (Bloomsbury Publishing, 2018)

QIU JIN

Chinese Women in a Century of Revolution: 1850–1950, Kazuko Ono (Stanford University Press, 1988)

Encyclopedia of Lesbian and Gay Histories and Cultures, George Haggerty and Bonnie Zimmerman (Routledge, 2000)

Late Imperial China volume 25 (John Hopkins University Press, 2004)

Women's Literary Feminism in Twentieth-Century China, Amy D. Dooling (AIAA, 2005)

ISABELLE WILHELMINE MARIE EBERHARDT

Feminism and Documentary, Diane Waldman and Janet Walker (University of Minnesota Press, 1999)

Isabelle: The Life of Isabelle Eberhardt, Annette Kobak (Virago, 2006)

Isabelle Eberhardt and North Africa: Nomadism as a Carnivalesque Mirage, Lynda Chouiten (Lexington Books, 2014)

The Destiny of Isabelle Eberhardt, Cecily Mackworth (Avon Books, 1985)

DOROTHY LAWRENCE

'Sapper Dorothy Lawrence', Dorothy Lawrence (online copy) https://archive.org/stream/sapperdorothyla00lawrgoog/sapperdorothyla00lawrgoog_djvu.txt

'Sapper' Dorothy Lawrence: A forgotten Wiltshire Heroine, Wiltshire at War (Community Stories) http://www.wiltshireatwar.org.uk/story/sapper-dorothy-lawrence-a-forgotten-wiltshire-heroine/

UMM KULTHUM

Making Music in the Arab World: The Culture and Artistry of Tarab, A. J. Racy (Cambridge University Press, 2004)

The Voice of Egypt: Umm Kulthum, Arabic Song, and Egyptian Society in the Twentieth Century, Virginia Danielson (University of Chicago Press, 1998)

Umm Kulthūm: Artistic Agency and the Shaping of an Arab Legend, 1967–2007, Laura Lohman (Wesleyan, 2010)

FLORENCE 'PANCHO' BARNES

High-Flying Women: A World History of Female Pilots, Alain Pelletier (Haynes, 2012)

The Lady Who Tamed Pegasus: The Story of Pancho Barnes, Grover Ted Tate (Maverick, 1984)

'The Legend of Pancho Barnes and the Happy Bottom Riding Club', 2016 documentary film, Nick Spark

Women Aviators (Women of Action), Karen Bush Gibson (Chicago Review Press, 2013)

DOROTHY TIPTON

In a Queer Time and Place: Transgender Bodies, Subcultural Lives (Sexual Cultures), Judith Halberstam (NYU Press, 2005)

'One False Note in a Musician's Life; Billy Tipton Is Remembered With Love, Even by Those Who Were Deceived', Dinitia Smith (*New York Times*, 1998) https://www.nytimes.com/1998/06/02/arts/one-false-note-musician-s-life-billy-tipton-remembered-with-love-even-those-who.html

Suits Me: The Double Life of Billy Tipton, Diane Middlebrook (Virago, 1999)

JUNE TARPÉ MILLS

A Century of Women Cartoonists, Trina Robbins (Kitchen Sink Pr; Second Printing edition, 1993)

Pretty in Ink: North American Women Cartoonists 1896–2010, Trina Robbins (Fantagraphics, 2013)

Tarpe Mills online, http://www.tarpemills.com/june-mills.html

Third Person: Authoring and Exploring Vast Narratives, Pat Harrigan and Noah Wardrip-Fruin (MIT Press, 2009)

SARASWATHI RAJAMANI

'The Forgotten Spy', Rediff, http://www.rediff.com/news/2005/aug/26spec2.htm

'The Young Female Spy Who Assisted India To Achieve Independence', War History Online https://www.warhistoryonline.com/war-articles/young-female-spy-assisted-india-achieve-independence.html

'Voice of an Independent Indian', Kaushik Sridhar, https://www.youtube.com/watch?v=m6kRPNk5C_A

DAME STEPHANIE 'STEVE' SHIRLEY

Let It Go, Dame Stephanie Shirley and Richard Askwith (AUK Authors; 3rd edition, 2012)

Official 'Steve' Shirley website http://www.steveshirley.com

'Why do ambitious women have flat heads?' (TED Talks, 2015) https://www.ted.com/talks/dame_stephanie_shirley_why_do_ambitious_women_have_flat_heads/discussion?quote=1757

Woman's Hour (BBC Radio 4, 2014) https://www.bbc.co.uk/programmes/b0375xv4#play

RENA 'RUSTY' KANOKOGI

Game Changers: The Unsung Heroines of Sports History, Molly Schiot (Simon & Schuster, 2016)

'Rumbling with Rusty', *Vault*, 1986 https://www.si.com/vault/2016/06/13/rumbling-rusty

'Rusty Kanokogi: The Mother of Women's Judo', Brooklyn Museum talk, 2011 https://www.youtube.com/watch?v=YUJAzLgsPtI

'Rusty Kanokogi, Fiery Advocate for Women's Judo, Dies at 74', Joshua Robinson (*New York Times*, 2009) https://www.nytimes.com/2009/11/23/sports/olympics/23kanokogi.html

BOBBI GIBB

Bobbi Gibb official site http://www.bobbigibbart.net

'Finally honoring Bobbi Gibb, the first woman to run the Boston Marathon', Jen. A Miller (ESPN, 2017) http://www.espn.com/espnw/culture/feature/article/15190954/50-years-later-paying-tribute-bobbi-gibb-first-woman-run-boston-marathon

'First Lady of Boston', Amby Burfoot, 2016 (*Runners World*) https://www.runnersworld.com/races-places/a20791759/first-lady-of-boston/

'The Incredible Story of Bobbi Gibb', Brigit Katz (Women in the World, 2015) https://womenintheworld.com/2015/04/20/the-incredible-story-of-bobbi-gibb-the-first-woman-to-run-the-boston-marathon/

To Boston With Love, Bobbi Gibb (CreateSpace Independent Publishing Platform, 2016)

PILI HUSSEIN

'From where I stand: "I became a man just to access the mines"', Pili Hussein (UN Women Mapping Study on Gender and Extractive Industries in Mainland Tanzania, 2017) http://www.unwomen.org/en/news/stories/2017/2/from-where-i-stand-pili-hussein

'I acted as a man to get work – until I was accused of rape', Sarah McDermott (BBC World Service, 2017) http://www.bbc.co.uk/news/magazine-39705424

'I Dressed As a Man to Work in a Mine' (BBC World Service, Outlook podcast, 2017) http://www.bbc.co.uk/programmes/p050jckm

SISA ABU DAOOH

'Egypt's "Best Mother" wears men's clothes', Amanda Figueras (*The Islamic Monthly*, 2015) https://www.theislamicmonthly.com/egypts-best-mother-wears-mens-clothes/

'Egyptian Woman Reveals 42-Year Secret of Survival: Pretending to Be a Man', Jared Malsin (*New York Times*, 2015) https://www.nytimes.com/2015/03/26/world/middleeast/egyptian-woman-reveals-42-year-secret-of-survival-pretending-to-be-a-man.html

'Egyptian woman who has lived as man for 40 years voted "best mum"', Patrick Kingsley (*Guardian*, 2015) https://www.theguardian.com/world/2015/mar/22/egyptian-woman-award-lived-as-man

'The Untamed Shrew', Natalia Karachkova (RTA Documentary Channel) https://rtd.rt.com/films/the-untamed-shrew/

TATIANA ALVAREZ

'DJ Tatiana Alvarez: Why I had to dress as a man to get ahead', Joyce Lim (*Telegraph*, 2015) https://www.telegraph.co.uk/

women/womens-life/11350294/Why-I-had-to-dress-up-as-a-man-to-get-ahead-DJ-Tatiana-Alvarez.html

'The DJs – DJ Tatiana Alvarez and Lea Barrett' (BBC World Service, *The Conversation*, 2016) https://www.bbc.co.uk/programmes/p041svv9

MARIA TOORPAKAI WAZIR

A Different Kind of Daughter: The Girl Who Hid from the Taliban in Plain Sight, Maria Toorpakai and Katherine Holstein (Twelve, 2016)

Maria Toorpakai official website, http://mariatoorpakai.org

'Maria Toorpakai: The Pakistani squash star who had to pretend to be a boy', Bethan Jinkinson (BBC News, 2013) https://www.bbc.co.uk/news/magazine-21799703

'Squashing Extremism: Maria Toorpakai Wazir at TEDxTeen', 2013 https://www.youtube.com/watch?v=fe9DfC8mt14

SAHAR KHODAYARI

https://www.theguardian.com/world/2019/sep/10/iranian-female-football-fan-who-self-immolated-outside-court-dies

https://www.ft.com/content/2e379f74-d499-11e9-8367-807ebd53ab77

https://sputniknews.com/viral/201804301064038369-iran-women-football-ban-viralra

https://www.amnesty.org/en/latest/news/2019/09/iran-shocking-death-of-football-fan-who-set-herself-on-fire-exposes-impact-of-contempt-for-womens-rights/

https://www.nytimes.com/2019/09/10/world/middleeast/iran-women-sports-sahar-khodayari.html

https://www.amnesty.org/en/latest/news/2019/10/iran-limited-allocation-of-football-tickets-for-women-a-cynical-publicity-stunt/

https://www.theguardian.com/football/2019/oct/09/iranian-women-allowed-to-watch-football-at-stadium-for-first-time-in-decades

ACKNOWLEDGMENTS

Thank you to my agent, Laura Macdougall at United Agents. Laura, let me count the ways in which I love thee! You took a chance on a mucky pup and scrubbed me up good enough for Crufts. I'm so chuffed to be in your gang.

All the merci beaucoups in the cosmos to my editor, Victoria Pepe, to Jenni Davis, Jill Sawyer, Emily Arbis and everyone on the team at Amazon Publishing. You're all excellent feminists and book brains and I'll forever boast about working with you. Thank you, Alex Carr, for opening the door.

To my illustrator, Tegan Price, seeing your work for the first time put me on Cloud Ten and I'm excited all over again to be sharing it with the world. And to Lisa Horton, for the cover of dreams.

Thank you, Bethan James and the Ed PR team, you've been on the same page as me right from the jump and it's been joyous.

To my family, especially Mum, thank you for always backing my every waking idea (I'm aware that's on average forty-five per nanosecond). My superlative sister and I are *surely* living proof of your boundless love and support!

Mad props to Kirk Grant for the iMac (you're never getting it back) and Sandra Grant for my ergonomic chair. Big love to Anita Rani, who I'll always remember when I think of my career progression – I'm forever thankful to you for getting me over that first hurdle. 'Good job!' Bryna Turner, my National Theatre green room sent Americanglish translation saviour. Thanks to Nicola Han for her assistance and friendship from afar, Golnaz Rouhi and Arash Sedighi for their Persian translation and wisdom, Laura Dockrill for always being my book hype girl (and all round HEY GIRL) and the staff at the British Library who are only ever holy shiza helpful.

And, *of course*, Sabrina, who may have been in a relationship with my back at the desk for the last six months but is the reason I keep going. I'm so proud of this but I'm most proud of us.

Finally, thank you to the fifty women, particularly the football fans of Iran (some of whom I had the pleasure of getting to know personally). They all make me feel so blessed to be a woman, I'd doff my cap to them until I got RSI.

ABOUT THE AUTHOR

Photo © 2017 Richard Davenport

Anneka Harry hates bios because 1) it's awkweird talking about yourself in the third person and, 2) pinning down a job title for herself is like exiting a swimming pool without a wedgie (impossible). She wants to do it ALL.

If Anneka was pushed to describe herself in a nutshell she would say she's a 'Comedy Hustler (Performer, Producer, Writer, Etc.)'. The 'etc.' leaves it open so that she can pursue whatever she decides to do tomorrow. Her writer/performer work consists of series, episodes and features for the BBC, Channel 4, ITV2, Radio 4, MTV and various online platforms including Stylist and Grazia magazines.

When Anneka isn't parading around waving rainbow flags or trying to win feminism, she likes to be a thoroughly decent human being, drink alcohol (all types) and obsess over her sausage dog. The amount of work there is to do in the fight for equality gives Anneka regular stress migraines. She hopes this book (her first) will at least momentarily soothe anyone feeling equally overwhelmed.